Asian Religions

Praise for *Asian Religions: A Cultural Perspective*

"This book is a unique introduction to Asian religions, in that it combines the scholarly rigor of an established historian of Asian religions with the willingness to engage empathetically with the traditions and to suggest that readers do the same. Its focus is on the traditions in the modern world and their spiritual and experiential dimensions. It takes seriously the possibility that Asian religions, understood in their own contexts (not as mere screens on which to project Western needs and desires), can offer viable options to those in other cultures who may be seeking for meaning beyond the traditions into which they were born."
Joseph A. Adler, Kenyon College

"Randall L. Nadeau has accomplished what only a few have tried, but which has been much needed in the study of religions. He has written a genuinely novel approach to the religions of Asia. The goal of the book is not primarily historical or phenomenological – the volume is designed to stimulate self-reflection and personal engagement to the "wired generation" reader, who wants to find out what kinds of spiritual resources are meaningful for them. The approach is more cultural than theological; practical than abstract; behavioral than conceptual; embedded than distinctive. This is a work that should find its way into Asian humanities, history, religion, and civilization courses."
Ronnie Littlejohn, Belmont University

Asian Religions

A Cultural Perspective

Randall L. Nadeau

WILEY Blackwell

Library of Congress Cataloging-in-Publication Data is available for this title.
Hardback ISBN: 9781118471975
Paperback ISBN: 9781118471968

A catalogue record for this book is available from the British Library.

Cover image: Heian Jingu shrine, Kyoto, Japan. © PhotoAlto/Corbis
Cover designer: Simon Levy

Set in 10/12.5 pt Minion by Toppan Best-set Premedia Limited
Printed in Malaysia by Ho Printing (M) Sdn Bhd

1   2014

Contents

List of Figures

Preface

I am sitting in a second-story coffee shop, one franchise of thousands around the world. The shop overlooks a busy intersection in central Taipei, a steady stream of busses, private cars and taxis, motorcycles and bicycles passing beneath me, skirting the construction of a new trunk line of Taipei's ultra-modern rapid transit system. Customers around me are scanning the internet via Wi-Fi, and I see open social network pages in both Chinese and English. Students chat excitedly about their school friends, young men and women relax at the end of a hectic day, and small groups engage in earnest debate about the recent elections.

I have just come from a study session of the Whole Earth Society, one of hundreds of syncretistic groups dedicated to the "dual cultivation" of body and spirit. These groups promote a holistic conception of physical and spiritual well-being that integrates traditional religious teachings with new expressions of human flourishing. Taipei, like many Asian cities, faces challenges to traditional values and lifestyles alongside new opportunities for self-expression and personal growth. In East Asia, education levels are expanding (college enrollments are approaching 90 percent of students of college age), young people are delaying marriage to age 30 and beyond (and the ratio of women choosing not to marry at all is at its highest level in history), and childbirth rates are far below the level of sustainability (Japan's population is expected to fall by two thirds in the next 20–30 years). These changes have brought about a new focus on self-actualization and personal enrichment, as traditional values of marriage and family are replaced by a search for purpose and meaning that is often at odds with conventional expectations. This is true of every modernizing Asian city – from Seoul and Tokyo to Beijing, Shanghai, and Hong Kong and on to Bangkok, Delhi, and Colombo. The thirst for spiritual self-cultivation, satisfied by groups like the Whole Earth Society, is a pan-Asian phenomenon.

The Whole Earth Society sponsors lectures on world religions, teaches techniques of meditation and physical exercise (massage, yoga, and deep breathing), and offers courses on healthy eating and traditional arts and crafts. At the same time these traditional pursuits are adapted to modern needs and interests, responding directly to the hectic lifestyles of modern urbanites, the single status of most of its members, and modern technologies of communication and entertainment. Today's syncretistic religious organizations succeed only to the extent that they are able to marry traditional principles and practices with the individualist values of working young people in the modern world.

The aim of this book is not to describe the Whole Earth Society and similar groups across Asia, but rather to follow their lead in recognizing both the lasting viability and the remarkable adaptability of Asian religions in the modern world. The Whole Earth Society is in some ways representative of a much wider phenomenon: a newly enlivened, global thirst for meaning and purpose. The integration of nature, self, and cosmos has been the goal of Asian religious traditions for centuries, and their practices and insights are rapidly becoming universal in themselves, as cultural globalization has come to include Europeans and Americans (not to mention educated urbanites in other parts of the world) among adherents of Hinduism, Buddhism, and East Asian religious traditions. What is inspiring about the Whole Earth Society (as one representative example) is its ability to respond directly to the interests and aspirations of increasingly cosmopolitan populations, whose members see themselves not just as citizens of Taipei, or Taiwan, or China, or Asia, but as citizens of the world. In this respect they are no different from their Euro-American analogues (the young urban professionals of the "wired generation"), forming a generational cohort that shares an increasingly overlapping set of needs and aspirations. What are these common needs and aspirations? And how are they shared across cultures? Perhaps they are best expressed by a set of common questions:

- No longer satisfied by the unselfconscious religious practices of my parents and grandparents, what kind of spiritual resources are most meaningful to me?
- As I am less interested (for the time being at least) in the traditional religious focus on family responsibilities and domestic life, how can my religious practice inspire me as an individual?
- Busy as I am with my education and career, I do not want to "live to work" but rather to "work to live," inspired by new experiences and new perspectives – but what kind of life do I want to lead?
- Unwilling to limit myself to a single defining identity (son, student, investor, mother, laborer, engineer, artist, citizen), I seek to develop a multifaceted, protean self – but how can I guide this process in an integrative way, and how can spiritual insight aid me in this process of self-defining and self-becoming?

- Pulled in multiple directions by school, work, family, and society, how can I maintain a coherent sense of self, where the various dimensions of my identity can inspire and complete one another?
- What is my role as an individual vis-à-vis a wider community – a role not limited to my family or country but extending to the world as a whole? What does my spiritual understanding of myself and my spiritual work, both mental and physical, contribute to my sense of global citizenship? Though my interests are intensely personal, I recognize that they are shared with my cohort, which includes not just the citizens of Taipei (or London or New York), but the citizens of every country and the adherents of every religion.

In reading through these questions, you may have picked up on their individualistic emphasis. While "individualism" is a modern Western phenomenon (with its own history and cultural contingency), it is increasingly the driving motivation and self-conception of educated persons around the world. It is no longer accurate to describe individualism as *exclusively* Western or to generalize an individualist West in contrast to a collectivist East. Indeed the thesis of Western individualism in contrast to Eastern collectivism is an overstated generalization, even when applied to traditional culture. And this is all the more true today, when the individualist tendency is as pronounced in Asia as it is in the West. This is partly a function of globalization and Western "influence," but even more of the modern development of societies around the world, as they become more diverse and decentralized, and of economic trends that favor creativity, mobility, and adaptability. More and more, the scope of cultural self-expression (including spiritual self-cultivation) is focused on the individual, interacting with natural, social, and global environments.

So this book is directed primarily to *individuals*. Its goal is to stimulate self-reflection and personal engagement. It is my hope and expectation, as author, that the reader will ask, and ask repeatedly: "What does this mean to me? How does this resonate with my own experience and understanding? How might I be able to apply this insight or practice to my own life?" In teaching courses on Asian religions to students in Texas, USA, I urge my students to think of their education as an exercise ("exercise" means application and action, not just passive learning) in what I call "sympathetic imagination" – imagining oneself sympathetically or empathically as "believing" and "doing" what "other people" in "other religions" believe and do. Only in this way can they begin to understand others (the practicality of which should be obvious in today's interpenetrating world) and only in this way can they begin to appreciate the power and potential of Asian religions in their own lives. Sympathetic imagination often leads to creative adaptation – going far beyond passive understanding.

I have taught a course on Asian Religions for 20 years at Trinity University, a liberal arts college with selected pre-professional programs in San Antonio, Texas. I have emphasized both humanistic and more "practical" benefits of the study of religion – including self-reflection, appreciation of human diversity, and cultural understanding, as well as in the service of international trade, government diplomacy, and global citizenry. This orientation – with head in the clouds and feet on the ground – is one that I have learned to embrace, and it has forced me to examine the role of religion in culture more deeply than a purely humanistic approach alone would permit. Religion is embedded in the economic, political, and social dimensions of human cultures. It shapes and is shaped by worldly pursuits. This is the basic orientation of this book.

I am indebted to Trinity University for granting me an administrative leave in spring 2012, after seven years as chair of the Department of Religion, affording me the time to devote to this project. During that semester I was in residence in the Department of History at National Chengkung University in Tainan, Taiwan, Republic of China, and I am indebted to the former and current chairs, Professors Cheng Wing-sheung and Chen Heng-an, for their hospitality. I also benefitted from conversations with Professor Tsai Yen-zen of the Institute of Comparative Religions at Chengchi University in Taipei on the category of "religion" as a means of comparative cultural analysis and understanding. Finally, I wish to express my special appreciation to Tang Ming-jer, president of Tunghai University, for his commitment to holistic education and interdisciplinary research in the humanities and in natural and social sciences. I am grateful to Mackenzie Brown, Bradley Kayser, Fernando Triana, and to friends new and old for inspiring me to write a book that would be interesting not only to scholars or students, but to a general audience of interested readers: I have tried to address you as my conversation partners in writing this book. I am indebted to my anonymous readers and to Rebecca Harkin, General Editor of Religion at Wiley Blackwell, for helping me to sharpen the language and to address errors and infelicitous phrasing in early drafts; whatever errors or misleading generalizations might remain are my responsibility. And I am forever grateful to my wife and my children for their understanding and support through the transition rites, both painful and immensely satisfying, of high school and college graduations, and bold steps forward in life. Thank you, Ruth, Miranda, and Adrian. You have all inspired me to take risks, to find joy in others, and to find self in family. It is to you that I dedicate this book.

Part I
Introductory Material

1

Religion

There are plenty of books on the market which describe Asian religions for the introductory college course or the casual reader. They define Hinduism, Buddhism, Confucianism, Taoism, and Shintō as distinct beliefs and practices. More recent textbooks are conscientious about presenting Asian religious traditions in multiple aspects – not just as scriptural traditions or "systems of thought," but as living religions, especially in their behavioral and ritual dimensions. Many are illustrated, or contain photographs of an ethnographic nature. Most are accurate, making use of both academic scholarship and insider experiences. I recommend these books for seeing how important religion has been and continues to be in Asian cultures.

This book may differ from others of its kind in recognizing that the study of religion has intrinsic value (it is humanistic) but at the same time supports the practical objective of intercultural exchange. One goal of this book is to further social and cultural *commerce* – a word that is related not only to trade, but also to communication, understanding, even appreciation. I do not subscribe to the prejudice that humanism and practical work are mutually opposed. In fact they inform one another.

The impact of religious tradition is felt in virtually every dimension of cultural life: politics, economics, medicine, ethics and law, marriage and family, human rights, media and communications, science and technology. The role of religion in shaping these institutions may no longer be obvious or apparent, but it runs so deep that, had religion been absent, the shape and contour of these cultural traits would have evolved in utterly different ways or would never have come into existence at all. In this sense, the study of religion also involves description of cultural practices, as well as personal understandings of social purpose and value. I often tell my students that my courses deal less with "religion" in a narrow sense than they do with "culture" as a whole: Whom do

Asian Religions: A Cultural Perspective, First Edition. Randall L. Nadeau.
© 2014 John Wiley & Sons, Ltd. Published 2014 by John Wiley & Sons, Ltd.

people marry, and why? How do people order themselves – who is higher in status, who lower? Who has the right to rule, and why should we follow them? How are families organized, how do they stay together? What accounts for economic progress or collapse? What do people like to eat? How do they prevent and treat illness? What kinds of artistic expression are funded, supported, encouraged or reviled?

These are, indirectly, "religious" questions, because so much of cultural and social history has been shaped by the impact of religious practices and conceptions on economics, politics, sexuality, ethnicity, and aesthetic expression. In the nineteenth century the German sociologist Max Weber wrote, in *The Protestant Ethic and the Spirit of Capitalism*, that the most dominant economic system in the world – capitalism – would not have emerged if not for the Protestant Reformation.[1] Similarly, we can better understand East Asian economics in relation to Confucian values, Southeast Asian practices surrounding death and dying in relation to Buddhist cosmology, Japanese trade and immigration policies in relation to Shintō conceptions of purity and pollution, Indian marriage and sexuality in relation to the conflict between freedom and duty in Hindu practice, and so on. In this sense, "studying religion" involves the description of institutions and practices across a wide spectrum of social structures and individual experiences.

Some of these may not seem explicitly religious at all, in that their modern social expressions may be have become completely "secularized," their followers having lost sight of the religious conceptions, priestly commands, or behavioral norms that first inspired them. Most Chinese are "family-oriented," make regular offerings to their ancestors, and enjoy delicious combinations of vegetables, spices, meats, and grains without thinking of themselves as "Confucian" or "Taoist" – but these norms and practices certainly had their roots in religion. Most Japanese would never dream of burying or cremating the dead without the sponsorship of a local Buddhist temple, and yet they describe themselves (in sociological surveys) as "non-religious." Most Indians try to balance individual identity and achievement with a sense of duty and responsibility, and yet they may not see this goal as especially "Hindu." And so on. This is to say, the impact of religion on daily life is far more subtle and more pervasive than the declaration of "beliefs," the citation of scriptures, or the "great thoughts" of religious leaders. It is this cultural dimension – inclusive of a great range of personal and social beliefs, norms, and practices – that we will examine here.

This book represents a different approach from others in the university library in that it assumes an understanding of religion that is more cultural than theological, more practical than abstract, more behavioral than conceptual, more embedded than distinct. At the same time it recognizes that religions, in all their various forms, respond to basic, universal needs, hopes, and fears.

The comparative study of religion affirms "otherness," and a second purpose of this book is to highlight differences in the values, worldviews, and psychological and spiritual assumptions that people of Western and Asian cultures make about their everyday lives. I will point out contrasts, not in an effort to defend superiority or inferiority, but in an effort to affirm what should be a very simple, obvious fact: the fact of religious pluralism. At the same time, by showing how others view the religious problems of meaning, of value, of "reality," it is hoped that this book will provide the Western reader with a lens, a new perspective through which to view – and to understand, even to critique – his or her own religious experience.

While acknowledging cultural contrasts, we should recognize that people are much alike: there are no cultures that "lack" religion, and there is a profound sense in which people are religious by nature, whether one defines this as a religious "mind" or predisposition, or even as a "religion gene." Some patterns of thought and practice are universal; they are religious patterns that individuals-in-community share across cultures. Another way of saying this is that all religions meet basic human needs: the need for hope in the face of death or despair, for order in the midst of chaos, for unity in the midst of division and strife. In this sense, the basic materials of Asian religions are no different from those of Judaism, Christianity, and Islam. They respond to the same concerns, address the same questions, provide behavioral and conceptual solutions to the same problems; that is, they speak to us on a human level. Perhaps this is why Asian religions have become so popular in the West: because they answer universal questions and address universal wants and needs in a way that is new and fresh. Who has not lost a loved one, or faced her own mortality? Who has not confronted illness or disappointment, or sought a way out of trouble? Who has not fallen in love, or yearned to satisfy emotional and sexual needs that would otherwise remain unfulfilled? Who has not found meaning and belonging in family, friendship, calling or career, cooperative effort, ethnic or national pride, and religious identity? Asian religious traditions are grounded in the same ideals and the same anxieties. To understand them is to understand human life – and this is why the study of religion is, at heart, a humanistic enterprise.

How is this orientation reflected here? I ask the reader to relate his or her own experience – at this basic human level – to the values and practices of South and East Asian religious traditions. Through surveys and questions for discussion or consideration, I encourage the reader to reflect upon questions of life and death, nature and spirit, the "existence" or role of gods and spirits, gender and sexuality, physical and mental well-being, ethnicity and nationalism, and social identity. The surveys can be found online, and, as readers react to them, a database of responses will be generated that will be accessible to anyone who participates in them. The goal of these surveys is both to promote a sympathetic appreciation for Asian religious beliefs and practices and to serve as an instrument for sociological analysis.

"Religion" and the Religions

One of the effects of globalization – and in particular of new technologies of communication such as the internet – is the weakening of boundaries. These ever more porous boundaries – between nations, cultures, languages, religions – make people less inclined to define themselves in narrow terms, as "simply" an American, an English speaker, a heterosexual male, a Caucasian (as I once would have defined myself), but rather as "hybrid" or "protean" individuals. Travel, education, internet access, consumption – all have become both more global and more universal. More and more young people regard themselves as "citizens of the world" who can see and experience, and buy from, every country and culture. They are no longer constrained by resources, race, or religion – at least at the level of *exposure* to the alternative modes of living that they can see every day on a television set or computer screen.

Social and cultural interconnectedness also extends to religion and the religions. In the commercially and technologically networked world in which we live in the twenty-first century, religions increasingly come into contact with and mutually influence one another. Buddhists and Christians promote inter-religious dialogue (there is a society dedicated to this work, as well as a journal published by the society),[2] and the effect is in many cases a level of sharing and participation that is truly hybrid: I am no longer a "Christian" encountering a "Buddhist," but a "Buddhist Christian" or a "Christian Buddhist." Such dialogues are taking place between other traditions as well, and, in some sense, they are replicating a pattern of religious hybridization or syncretism that is a central part of the history of most of the great religious traditions of the world. Christianity, for example, arose from both Jewish and local "pagan" roots, while developing its own vision and practice, and thus was itself a product of such "dialogue." Shintō, the indigenous religious tradition of Japan – a religion that we tend to think of as closed and self-contained – is also a product of hybridity, influenced especially by Japanese forms of Buddhism such as Shin'gon. Buddhism in Sri Lanka today borrows institutional structures and patterns of congregational identity from European and American Christianity and has been described as "Protestant Buddhism."[3] Modern Hinduism is a product not only of ancient Vedic religion, but also of the European Enlightenment and of cultural encounters with the West. And we could cite innumerable other examples, all demonstrating that virtually every religion in the world, including those that would seem to be the most "closed" and "exclusive," were products of several others. What is different now, however, is that this process is occurring at an accelerated pace, stimulated by communication technologies and higher levels of education worldwide. More and more, people yearn to formulate a syncretistic or eclectic religious identity, drawing upon many traditions.

Not only are the "religions" porous, but so is the concept of "religion." Traditionally, scholars defined "religion" as "supernaturalism" or the belief in gods (or God). While this traditional definition serves the West adequately (the belief in God is arguably the central and defining characteristic of the Abrahamic traditions: Judaism, Christianity, and Islam), it raises two fundamental problems when we look at religion from a more global or comparative point of view.

First, the definition of religion as the belief in God or gods overemphasizes "belief" – a kind of "mental" affirmation or activity. But even a cursory understanding of religion shows that religion is hardly limited to "belief"; indeed most religions put greater store on practices, whether behavioral (the realm of ethics and morality) or liturgical (the realm of religious ritual). Some traditions are so focused on practice that belief becomes virtually irrelevant: this is certainly true of Confucianism, which most scholars of religion identify as "religious" even in the absence of religious "beliefs," and, arguably, can even apply to Judaism – where religious leaders, especially in the Reform tradition, will often counsel their followers not to worry about "beliefs or doubts" but to keep the tradition intact through practice. On the whole, the emphasis on belief shows a Christian bias, derived from its Greek philosophical roots, professing the *credo* (Latin meaning "I believe") of intellectual affirmation. The emphasis on belief as a defining characteristic of religion is parochial and Christocentric. (It should be noted, however, that, even among Christians, "belief" is empty if not accompanied by liturgical and ethical practice.)

Second, the definition of religion as "supernaturalism" is proven unhelpful when we look deeply at the immense variety of "gods" and conceptions of "divinity" that we find in the world's religions. It is not only the case that some religions deny the existence of gods altogether (this is true of Confucianism, and also of more intellectual forms of Buddhism and Hinduism), but also that some religions, while recognizing the *existence* of gods, still deny their *importance*: the Buddha readily admitted that gods "exist," but he minimized their importance – he denied that gods had the power to heal the spiritual ills of his followers. To give another example, Taoist priests acknowledge that gods and spirits "exist" (and liturgically interact with them), but they claim their own powers to be far greater than those of the gods. If gods are "irrelevant" or "inferior," then it would seem to be unhelpful to define religion in purely supernaturalistic terms.

If religion is not "supernaturalism," then what is it? Scholars of comparative religion began to discuss the general concept of "religion" in the late nineteenth century, and the history of the discipline is fascinating in itself. I will not repeat that discussion here, but draw upon two or three definitions that strike me as especially useful; indeed my own definition (and the operational definition for this book) is syncretic, and I am grateful to these scholars for shaping my own identity as a student of religion through their inclusive and insightful analysis. We will see that all of the traditions covered in this book can be understood with the help of an overarching definition:

> Humans are religious by nature. They seek patterns of meaning and action that are ultimately transformative. As such, religion is a model of and a model for reality, as experienced by individuals in the context of social, natural, and cosmic existence.

Let's look briefly at the three statements contained in this definition:

1   "Humans are religious by nature."   What does it mean to say that people are religious by nature? Religion is fundamental, and it is universal. No society has existed without religion, that is, without some conception of super-mundane reality (however we might describe it) and ritual and behavioral norms directed toward personal and social transformation. Recently neurobiologists have even tried to identify a "religious gene," and some have claimed to have found it. My own appreciation for this point follows Mircea Eliade (1907–1986), who, in his book *The Sacred and the Profane*, describes the human being as *homo religiosus* – "religious man" – not based on any particular beliefs or practices (and certainly not on the basis of "the belief in God or gods"), but rather based on a sense of reality having two dimensions, the sacred and the profane.[4] These dimensions are profoundly distinct from each other, but they interact and interpenetrate in what Eliade calls "irruptions" of the sacred, moments in time and points in space where the sacred is experienced within the world of everyday life. By "sacred reality" or the experiential "sense of the sacred," Eliade understands all of the dimensions of religious experience that we would expect (encounters with divine beings, practices of prayer or meditation, places of gathering and worship), but also other kinds of extraordinary consciousness – occasions when our normal sense of space and time are suspended, such as when we are seeing a movie or reading a book, recalling a first kiss, being moved by nature, and so on. These too are "religious" experiences. From this point of view, it is difficult to imagine any human being who lacks a religious sensitivity.

2   "They seek patterns of meaning and action that are ultimately transformative."   This part of our definition is derived from the work of another important scholar of the comparative study of religion, Frederick Streng (1933–1993). Streng was a student of Buddhism, especially the "doctrine

of emptiness" of the Madhyamaka (Middle Way) School. His translation of Nāgārjuna's *Mūlamadhyamakakārikā* (*Fundamental Verses of the Middle Way*) was a path-breaking study of this concept, further developed in his book *Emptiness: A Study in Religious Meaning.*[5] Partly on the basis of his studies of Buddhism and of his personal engagement as a devout Lutheran Christian, Streng formulated a general definition of religion as "ultimate transformation."[6] For Streng, religion is fundamentally "active"; it promises change, and it delivers on that promise. Religious change (personal, social/political, and cosmic transformation) goes to our very core – it is "ultimate."

3   "As such, religion is a model of and a model for reality, as experienced by individuals in the context of social, natural, and cosmic existence." The elaboration on "ultimate transformation" expressed in this part of the definition is borrowed from Clifford Geertz (1926–2006), an anthropologist whose work on culture and symbolism brings together theories of meaning (symbol systems and semiotics), aesthetics and literary theory, political expression, economics, and social organization. It was Geertz who defined religion as "a model of and a model for reality." As a *model of* reality, religion gives meaning and structure to the world of experience, taking what is inchoate (indescribable and confused) and making it meaningful and manageable. That is to say, religion gives people an accurate understanding of what reality "really is." As a *model for* reality, religion gives people a blueprint or set of instructions and norms to create a "new" reality, to achieve Streng's "ultimate transformation." Taken together, as "model of" and "model for," religion is both *descriptive* (telling us the true nature of the world) and *prescriptive* (instructing us on how to transform it).[7]

We might reframe Geertz's definition in terms of Eliade's categories of the sacred and the profane. To describe religion as a "model of" reality suggests that, *prior to* religion or *without* it, our ordinary or "profane" understanding of reality is fundamentally mistaken. We are blind to reality as it really is, and we are lost in ignorance (in fact many religious traditions – including Christianity, Hinduism, and Buddhism, to name only three – describe the basic problem of humankind as ignorance); only religion can transform ignorance into knowledge. Then religion also gives us the tools to move from ignorance to knowledge – it provides a "model for" thought and action that is *ultimately transformative.*

Dimensions of religion that fit into the "model of"/descriptive category would include belief systems and creedal commitments, myth, cosmology (theories of the structure of the universe – the existence of the afterlife, of places equivalent to our Western "heaven" and "hell," and so on), cosmogony (theories of the origins of the cosmos, creation stories), hagiography (stories of religious heroes), and theories about human nature as well as about the nature of supernatural realities (gods and spirits, ghosts and demons, souls and spirits of the dead).

Dimensions of religion that fit into the "model for"/prescriptive category would include behavioral norms (morality and ethics), liturgical norms (ritual, worship, meditation, prayer), and practical ways of living (renunciation; mendicancy; ordination as a priest, rabbi, imam, monk, or nun; and other religious lifestyles or avocations) – all directed toward the "ultimate transformation" that envisions a perfected self, society, and cosmos.

Although we cannot explore every aspect of every tradition studied in this book, we can use this definition as a template for what to include when studying the religious dimensions of Asian cultures. No doubt, the definition seems broad – this is intentional: religion permeates culture and is, in many profound ways, the basis for a wide variety of cultural systems, from government and politics to family structures, medicine, labor, even sports and entertainment. For the entire history of humankind, religion has functioned to inspire and sustain virtually every dimension of human social existence. Religion is not simply "belief," nor is it simply "ritual" – it is the cultural spring and foundation of the needs, motivations, thoughts, and behaviors that make up the totality of human experience.

Notes

1 Max Weber, *The Protestant Ethic and the "Spirit" of Capitalism and Other Writings*, trans. Peter R. Baehr and Gordon C. Wells (New York: Penguin Books, 2002).

2 *Buddhist-Christian Studies* was founded in 1981 and published its thirty-second volume in 2012.

3 Richard Gombrich and Gananath Obeyesekere, *Buddhism Transformed: Religious Change in Sri Lanka* (Princeton: Princeton University Press, 1988).

4 Mircea Eliade, *The Sacred and the Profane: The Nature of Religion* (New York: Harcourt, Brace, Jovanovich, 1987).

5 Frederick Streng, *Emptiness: A Study in Religious Meaning* (Nashville, TN: Abingdon Press, 1967).

6 Some years ago, shortly after Streng died, I published an article on the influence of Buddhism on his general theory of religion: "Frederick Streng, Mādhyamika, and the Comparative Study of Religion," *Buddhist-Christian Studies*, 16 (1996), pp. 65–76. His own theory is most completely developed in his book *Ways of Being Religious* (New York: Prentice-Hall, 1973).

7 Geertz developed this definition in two essays. They can be found in *The Interpretation of Cultures* (New York: Basic Books, 1973): "Religion as a Cultural System" (pp. 87–125) and "Ethos, World View, and the Analysis of Sacred Symbols" (pp. 126–141).

2

Language

There is one other preliminary step we should take before we begin our investigation of Asian religions, and that is a discussion of language. In this book we will examine, in their respective languages – Sanskrit, Chinese, and Japanese – a number of terms relating to both belief and practice. Why do I favor using these terms rather than their English translations (or approximations)? And why is language so important to begin with?

Clifford Geertz, one of the authors of our definition of religion in Chapter 1, defined "culture" as a "system of symbols." This definition highlights how closely culture is related to language – after all, what is "language" if not also a "system of symbols"? Languages employ words (nouns) to refer to things, by symbolizing those objects in letter or sound, or evoke descriptors (adjectives and verbs) to describe their shape, movement, appearance, form, orientation, attitude, and so on. By virtue of language we communicate with one another, and thus we set our culture (our language) apart from those of others. If you have traveled abroad, you know that one of the first and most significant obstacles to cross-cultural understanding is simply the language barrier. *They* are different from *me*: they speak a different language, one that *I* cannot understand. And any professor of modern languages will tell you that the first and only way to truly understand another culture is by mastering its language. It is important, even crucial, that our educational system encourages fluency in numerous languages, for all of our citizens; only then can we be citizens of the world and not just a narrow slice of it.

But language is not merely a tool for understanding a culture. In a very real sense, a language *is* a culture. Or, to put it another way, the highest form and expression of culture is language. In Chinese the earliest character (word/

Asian Religions: A Cultural Perspective, First Edition. Randall L. Nadeau.
© 2014 John Wiley & Sons, Ltd. Published 2014 by John Wiley & Sons, Ltd.

symbol) for "culture" was *wen* (文) – a character that also means "language" or "writing." The mythical inventor of writing, Cang Jie (倉頡), "culture minister" to the legendary Yellow Emperor, did not "invent" writing so much as he discovered it – in the prints of birds and the striations of jade. Chinese language and culture are thus inextricably tied to the very landscape of the Middle Kingdom, *Zhongguo* (中國) – the Chinese name for China. Indeed the phrase meaning "Chinese language" is exactly this: *Zhongwen* (中文), the culture of the Middle Kingdom. And what is true of China is true of all people: our language is our mother tongue, related to birth, childhood, and home. It is what I talk with and think with, and it forms the very basis of my self-identity. It is as deep as my soul (to use a religious term), and thus language is not only culture, but religion as well.

We will examine the religious dimensions of language throughout this book, but let's begin by comparing the impact of oral and written languages on the cultures of India, China, and Japan in terms of these countries' social and political histories. In many ways, language has been determinative of culture in each one, with widely divergent results.

We can start from the obvious fact that people in India, China, and Japan speak different languages. In fact the languages spoken in these countries belong to completely different language groups. The languages of India belong to the Indo-European (or, more narrowly, Indo-Aryan) language group; the languages of China belong to the Sino-Tibetan language group; and the languages of Japan belong to the Japonic language group. Such classifications indicate that these peoples speak languages that are radically "foreign," with strikingly different linguistic and phonetic patterns. This is why it is extraordinarily difficult for the Japanese, for example, to learn Chinese: Chinese is as linguistically foreign to native Japanese speakers as it is to native English speakers.

Why is this important? Because India, China, and Japan have such long histories of cultural interaction, especially in terms of religion. From India, Buddhism spread to Tibet and to China, and eventually to Korea and to Japan. Translation teams consisting of monks from India, China, and Central Asia met in the first centuries of the Common Era to render Sanskrit Buddhist texts into Chinese, a task that proved extraordinarily difficult because of linguistic barriers. Even today, when Chinese people practice the liturgical recitation of sacred Buddhist texts (*sūtras*), one can hear the curious (that is, foreign-sounding) admixture of Sanskrit phonemes, which are ritually powerful but make "no sense" to most Chinese. Similarly, when the Japanese adopted Chinese characters in the fourth century CE, they were making use of a writing system that had no linguistic connection to their own indigenous language. The result was a writing system in which the same "word" (Japanese *kanji* or "Chinese character") could be read in either of two different ways: the native *kun* or "Japanese" reading; and the foreign *on* or "Chinese" reading. The long history of cultural interaction among these three countries has certainly been complicated by their vastly different language systems.

An accurate census of languages and dialects is difficult to substantiate, but, according to *Ethnologue: Languages of the World*, the number of mutually unintelligible languages spoken within each of these three countries differs enormously between them:

- India: 461 languages;
- China: 299 languages, with 14 major dialects of Chinese;
- Japan: 15 languages.

Examples of the 461 languages spoken in India include Hindi, Bengali, Gujarati, Marathi, Telugu, Tamil, Urdu, and Punjabi (all spoken by at least 50 million native speakers). *Ethnologue* categorizes Chinese as a "macrolanguage" with 14 major dialects. These dialects are so different that they are mutually unintelligible. Among the most widely spoken are Mandarin, Hakka, Cantonese, and Taiwanese (a variant of the Southern Min language). The most widely spoken languages of Japan are Japanese and Ryukyuan (a language confined to a tiny population on the island of Ryukyu).[1]

Ethnologue's "diversity index" is even more telling; this index shows the likelihood that any two individuals within a country will speak a different language:

- India: 0.916;
- China: 0.510;
- Japan: 0.027.

That is, in India there is a 92 percent likelihood that any two individuals, surveyed at random, will speak different languages; in China, a 51 percent likelihood; in Japan, only a 2.7 percent likelihood. Among the 10 countries in the world with populations over 100 million, India has the highest diversity index, Japan the lowest. *Ethnologue* reports that 21 percent of the population of India are fluent speakers of its official language (Hindi); 70 percent of Chinese are fluent speakers of Mandarin; while over 98 percent of Japanese are fluent speakers of Japanese.

One can easily imagine the immense social and political impact of these differences. How easy it must be to imagine oneself as part of a single cultural whole when nearly everyone in the country (in the case of Japan) speaks the same language! And how difficult it must be to unify or govern a nation when only a small number of people (as in the case of India) speak the official language (or they speak it only as an acquired or second language). Chinese governments are intensely concerned with this problem, which is why they have imposed Mandarin as the "common" language (普通話, *putonghua*) in China (the People's Republic of China), Taiwan (the Republic of China), and Singapore.[2] For more than half of Chinese, however, Mandarin is an acquired language. The sensitivity of this issue is one reason why Chinese linguists refuse to categorize the languages of China *as* "languages" (語言, *yuyan*), labeling them as "dialects" (放言, *fangyan*) instead. But, no matter how they are labeled, the fact is that Cantonese (the language or dialect spoken in the southern Chinese provinces of Guangdong/Canton and Hong Kong) and Mandarin (originally a northern language or dialect native to central China, including the capital of Beijing) are mutually unintelligible. Cantonese speakers and Mandarin speakers simply cannot understand one another, unless they happen to have acquired the other language as a second language. The same could be said of any other Chinese language.

Language preservation is a political issue going to the heart of cultural unity and diversity. In Hong Kong most people have adopted Mandarin since the Handover (from British to Chinese sovereignty) in 1997, but some stubbornly resist the change and will insist on speaking Cantonese – or feign ignorance of Mandarin – when confronting Chinese visitors. Similarly, a major platform of the Independence Movement as supported by the Democratic Progressive Party (民進黨, *minjindang*) on the island of Taiwan is the preservation of the Southern Min or Taiwanese language – though Mandarin has been the language of instruction in Taiwan public schools since the late 1940s.

Turning to written forms of these languages, the cultural contrasts between East Asia (China and Japan) and South Asia (the Indian subcontinent) are sharpened. Chinese characters – employed in China and Japan – are pictographic; they have the same meaning regardless of what language or dialect is used to read or pronounce them. Chinese characters appeal to the eyes; they are visual, and aesthetic in form. One of the most recognized of the visual arts is calligraphy, and virtually any two-dimensional art (for instance landscape painting or woodblock printing, such as the one seen in Figure 2.1) contains written characters and owners' seals, which represent a central aspect of the completed work.

Recall that the Chinese word for "language," 文 *wen*, refers specifically to writing, the heart of Chinese culture. Until the end of the Qing Dynasty (the last of the imperial dynasties), paper containing writing could not be disposed of idly – to trample on written words was a punishable offense.

Chinese written characters are a cultural unifier. Because they are pictographic rather than phonetic, they mean the same however they might be pronounced.[3] Using our earlier example, even if two businessmen from Hong Kong and Beijing are unable to communicate orally, they can simply write a letter or email in Chinese and be readily understood. They will "sound out"

Figure 2.1 "Travelers among mountains and streams" by Fan Kuan 范寬 (fl. 990–1020). National Palace Museum, Taipei. © Corbis.

their communication in their own languages (or dialects), but the meaning will be the same regardless of what the characters sound like in the mind's ear. Throughout Chinese history, written communication has made linguistic diversity irrelevant to social cohesion and political rule. The common written language has allowed China to remain unified for more than two millennia; because of its written language, China is the oldest extant culture in the world.

Sanskrit is the classical language of India. While not strictly a "dead" language (like Latin), it is a spoken language for only a tiny few communities in India; principally it is the priestly language of religious scriptures. The written script of Sanskrit has been adopted in almost all of the Indo-Aryan languages, including Hindi, the official language of India. Like the Roman alphabet (and, obviously, in contrast to Chinese), this system is phonetic: each symbol represents a sound. The script is called, in Sanskrit, *devanāgarī*, "the script of the gods." A Sanskrit dictionary is organized in a way that emphasizes the symbols' sounds: 11 vowels followed by 33 consonants. The sound corresponding to the first letter – equivalent to the English *a* but pronounced more like *a-u* or the *ou-* in the word "out" – is formed at the back of the throat and comes from deep within one's vocal range. Similarly, the first of the consonants, an unaspirated *k* (it is not breathed but vocalized, and resembles the English sound of a hard *g*), also begins at the back of the throat. The last letter of the Sanskrit alphabet is like an *m* – it is the last because it is formed at the front of the mouth, that is, with the lips. So, by representing all the sounds that can be made by the human voice, beginning at the back of the throat and ending with the lips, Sanskrit represents the oral basis of language – and of culture.

When a Hindu yogin (that is, a practitioner of yoga) meditates on the sound *om* (or, more accurately, *aum*), as represented in Figure 2.2, he or she is beginning at the back of the throat and ending at the front of the mouth – vocalizing, in abbreviated form, all of the sounds that the voice can produce. This is believed to replicate the sounds of the gods, the sounds of the cosmos.

This oral basis of Indian languages, and especially of their root language, Sanskrit, illustrates that India is primarily an oral and aural culture. For centuries, the scriptures of Hinduism were not even written down at all, but passed on from teacher to student, generation after generation. To be a student requires being in the presence of a teacher, and to be a devotee or a worshipper requires invoking and being in the presence of a god. In Sanskrit this is called *darśan*. It means "being present" or "being in direct contact" – Hindus talk about "giving" or "receiving" *darśan*. In Buddhism, a disciple is an *upāsaka* (male, a monk) or an *upāsikā* (female, a nun), one who "sits at the feet" of one's teacher. Both Hinduism and Buddhism emphasize this immediate and intimate relationship between teacher and student.

Figure 2.2 The Sanskrit word *om*, composed of the first and last letters of the Sanskrit alphabet, and thus representing "all of the sounds of the universe."

Just as China is primarily a visual culture, based on its pictographic written system, India is primarily an oral/aural culture, based on its phonetic written system. So much follows from this. Whereas Chinese education emphasizes reading and writing, classical Indian education emphasizes hearing and reciting. Whereas Chinese arts are primarily two-dimensional (painting and calligraphy), Indian arts are primarily three-dimensional (sculpture and architecture – as well as music, which moves three-dimensionally through space). Whereas Chinese culture is vertically oriented (moving through time, with a conception of history that is linear), Indian culture is spatially oriented (moving through space, with a conception of history that is circular). For India, the universe has no beginning or end, but "vibrates" and "hums" like a spinning wheel. The idea of "creation" in Hinduism (an idea we will explore later in this book) entails an originating sound, the thrumming of a drum.[4] In short, China is a culture of the eyes, of what can be seen; India is a culture of the ears, of what can be heard.

To be sure, Indian influence on China has been significant, but always exotic and foreign. China did not develop sculptural arts until it imported Buddhism, and the most accomplished forms of Chinese sculpture are Buddhist statuary. Moreover, the tradition of recitation of scripture, which is now very common in China and Japan, came from India. Indeed, the emphasis on sound is so important in Buddhism that the chanting of scripture is more religiously important than its meaning. Recitation alone has spiritual efficacy, regardless of whether or not the devotee knows the meaning of what he or she is reciting. Recall our discussion in the last chapter about belief: belief, which requires understanding the meaning of words, is relatively unimportant when it comes to Buddhist practice, even though it is religious texts – scriptures – that are being recited.

Throughout this book we will examine terms in Chinese, Sanskrit, and Japanese, and we will often have to leave them untranslated – as they entail a cluster of meanings that can be used to explain them. Here too, knowing the etymology of terms (their origins and structure) will be beneficial to understanding their religious significance. While I have reproduced in this book the terms as they are actually written, we will also see and discuss them in Romanized or transcribed form, in order to help with pronunciation. But bear in mind that, from a Chinese, Indian, or Japanese point of view, our Roman alphabet also looks foreign and exotic. In fact English words are often used because they are "eye-catching" and "modern," sometimes without concern for their meaning. I have a marvellous collection of t-shirts that I have purchased over the years with all kinds of strange English words and phrases, some unintentionally humorous. One of my goals in this book is to take the "strangeness" out of the religious language of Asia and to penetrate religious teachings and practices through the terms that they themselves employ.

Notes

1   For these and other data, see http://www.ethnologue.com/web.asp (accessed August 29, 2013).

2   Why is the official language called "Mandarin"? In English, "mandarin" was the old name for a Chinese official – it was a term coined in the British colonial period. It is a direct translation of the Chinese word *guan* (官), which designates an official of the imperial court. Indeed, the old name in Chinese for this dialect was *guan-hua* (官話), "the language of the officials." They needed a common dialect to be able to communicate with one another, since they had come to court from different parts of the country and thus had different native tongues. Today Chinese people simply refer to Mandarin as the "common" language.

3   A small number of Chinese characters have a phonetic element. However, these "phonetic lexigraphs" represent fewer than 5% of all Chinese characters.

4   Contrast this with the Abrahamic traditions (Christianity is especially "visual" in orientation), which conceive of creation as an originating light.

Part II
The Confucian Tradition

3

Defining "Religion"
The Confucian Response

The first test of our definition of religion is Confucianism. Ask any ordinary Chinese, Japanese, or Korean (residents of the East Asian cultural area), and they are likely first to deny that they are "Confucian" and second to deny that "Confucianism" is a religion! There is an historical reason for this: the very idea of religion as a general category, which could be applied to a multiplicity of diverse cultural traditions, is relatively new in East Asia and was imported from the West. In fact the English word "religion" is one of the few foreign words that were first translated into Japanese and only then into Chinese. This is unusual, because most of the major religious concepts of East Asia first arose in India or China, and then were transmitted to Korea and Japan. In seeking a translation of the English word *religion*, Japanese scholars of the nineteenth century coined the word *shūkyō* (宗教); it was adopted by Chinese scholars only later, with the same characters, and pronounced *zongjiao* in Mandarin.[1]

Why would the Chinese be reluctant to define Confucianism as a religion? And why would most Japanese, even today, describe themselves as *mushūkyō* (無宗教), "non-religious"? It is not because they are not religious in our understanding of the word "religion," but rather because they understand religion as *shūkyō* (宗教), a term that literally means "institutional teaching" or "school of instruction" and connotes a religious "sect," institution, or organization (such as a Buddhist monastery or a Protestant seminary). Since Confucianism is pervasive and diffused – it is the air that Chinese and Japanese breathe, as opposed to a "church" that one joins – Chinese and Japanese do not see Confucianism as a religious entity.

This discussion is further complicated by the fact that not only Chinese and Japanese deny the "religious status" of Confucianism, but so do many Western scholars of religion! Here are some reasons why:

Asian Religions: A Cultural Perspective, First Edition. Randall L. Nadeau.
© 2014 John Wiley & Sons, Ltd. Published 2014 by John Wiley & Sons, Ltd.

- Confucianism *does not have a specific founder or date of founding*, even though it appears to be named after a single individual (Confucius).
- Confucianism *does not profess belief in God*. In fact a major stream of Confucianism denies the existence of gods altogether.
- Confucians *venerate or respect ancestral spirits without "worshipping" them*. It is a common misdescription of Chinese religion to refer to it as "ancestor worship."
- Confucians generally see *belief* as having less importance than *practice*. Confucianism *emphasizes orthopraxy* (right action) *over orthodoxy* (right belief).
- Confucianism *does not have a closed canon*. Confucian texts continue to be written and to be incorporated into the historical tradition.
- Confucianism *has no specific institutional identity*. There is no Confucian "pope" and no religious headquarters or governing body.
- Confucianism *has no fixed religious services* and can be practiced anywhere, from shrines and temples to private studies and mountain peaks.

Rather than saying that these are "criteria" for what a religion is – and concluding that Confucianism is not a religion – it may make more sense to conclude that they are unserviceable criteria, in other words that our understanding of "religion" needs to be broadened so as to include the Confucian tradition. By our definition of religion from Chapter 1, we can say confidently that Confucianism aims toward the ultimate transformation of self and society and provides the means for achieving perfection in Confucian terms. Confucian norms and values permeate East Asian cultures to the core – even in Communist China, which explicitly repudiated Confucianism during its revolutionary period but has now embraced Confucianism as the highest expression of Chinese cultural identity.

Confucian Cultures in East Asia

The English word "Confucianism" is a relatively late invention (one scholar has found no occurrence of the term before 1687), and Confucius himself was not known in Europe until Jesuit missionaries visited China in the 1600s. The Christian missionaries saw a strong link between the cultural values that they observed among Chinese officials and the classical texts attributed to Confucius and his followers, so they named this tradition Confucianism.[2]

Interestingly, the word Confucianism does not exist in the Chinese language. Of course, there is the name "Confucius" – pronounced in Chinese *Kongfuzi* (孔夫子), "the Grand Master or Great Teacher surnamed Kong" (our word "Confucius" is a Latinized, imperfect representation of "Kongfuzi"). But there is no "religion of Kong," no 孔教, *Kong-jiao* in Chinese, and in a very real sense the tradition we are discussing in this chapter has *no name*. This is partly because Confucian values and behaviors pre-date Confucius himself. Confucius' contribution was to collect, organize, and highlight the beliefs and practices that had been definitive of his culture for several centuries. He is recorded as saying: "I transmit but do not create. I place my trust in the teachings of antiquity."[3] As a transmitter or systematizer of values, Confucius was certainly important, but the values and behaviors of Confucianism were central to Chinese culture even before the beginning of recorded history, some one thousand years before Confucius. Neither Confucius nor his followers considered the First Sage to be a religious founder.

The terms that are more specifically related to Confucianism in Chinese are *Ru jia* (儒家), *Ru jiao* (儒教), or *Ru xue* (儒學) – the Ru school, the Ru tradition, or Ru studies. In Confucius' time, the Ru (儒) were "scholars," but at a much earlier date, 1000 BCE or before, the Chinese character Ru referred to religious priests or shamans who were ritual experts – masters of religious music and dance – especially skilled in summoning good spirits, exorcising evil spirits, and bringing rain and other blessings. By the time of Confucius, the Ru were also historians, because the shamanic rituals of the past had fallen into disuse and were known only from the historical records. Confucius was an exemplary Ru scholar, as he was especially interested in cultural history (the history of music, dance, and other arts) and in ritual. One of his major contributions was to codify and advance the ritual traditions of the early Zhou Dynasty. Consequently "Confucianism" refers to all of the values and practices of the Ru tradition; it does not refer simply to the "religion of Confucius."

For Chinese, then, Confucianism is the general term for the religious and ethical ideals, values, and behaviors that have shaped Chinese culture for the past three to four thousand years. These include:

- the veneration of ancestors;
- education in history and culture (poetry, music, painting, and calligraphy);
- the cultivation of harmonious, hierarchical relations in one's family and social life; and
- the grounding of moral teachings and ethical principles in a religious or cosmic reality.

These are Confucian behaviors and values in the sense that Confucians value them, and not because Confucius "invented" them. In fact they are so much part of the "cultural DNA" of East Asians (a phrase coined by Bill Moyers in a PBS interview with Tu Weiming)[4] that most people would not recognize them as "Confucian" – they are simply "our" values, practices, and commitments, which have been with us for centuries.

Originating in China, the Confucian cultural sphere extends throughout East Asia. Figure 3.1 shows four waves of Chinese cultural influence: a first wave to Southeast Asia (especially Vietnam), in the first centuries of the Common Era; a second wave to Korea and Japan, beginning in the fourth century but having its greatest impact from the eighth century onward; a third wave to Hong Kong (here singled out because of its admixture of Western cultural influences during the 150 years of British colonial rule); and a fourth wave to Taiwan, one of the provinces of China but now functioning autonomously: because of the disruption of tradition brought about by China's revolutionary period after the "Liberation" of 1949, Taiwan is often regarded as a repository of traditional Confucian values. The history of this cultural migration is fascinating in itself, but it is beyond the scope of this book. What the map indicates is that today "Confucianism" is not in any way limited to China but is the underlying religious system of the East Asian cultural region as a whole. China, Taiwan, Hong Kong, Korea, Japan, and Vietnam (not to mention Singapore, Malaysia, and the Philippines, all of which have large Chinese communities that have brought Confucian values with them) – all can be described as Confucian cultures.

The Confucian Program

There are many adequate biographies of Confucius in English, and I will not repeat one here. Moreover, as we have seen, Confucianism is not limited to the teachings of Confucius. The troubles that the Confucian tradition was facing and responding to were not unique to his time or that of his immediate followers (the sixth and fifth century BCE), but may simply be basic to the human condition:

- warfare and strife, driven by selfish, greedy, and acquisitive impulses;
- disharmony in families and communities, caused by interpersonal conflict and social inequalities;
- religious and moral decline (has there ever been a time in history when prophetic voices, like those of Moses, Socrates, or Confucius, did not warn that things were getting progressively worse – and haven't they usually been right?);
- the manipulation of religious beliefs and values for political gain;
- a fracturing of the world while religion is trying to hold things together (*legere*, the Latin verb that *religio* derives from, means "to bind together").

These problems, certainly with their specific forms at the time of Confucius and the early Confucian tradition, are with us in the present day. So the Confucian *solution*, the Confucian prescription for an ultimate transformation,

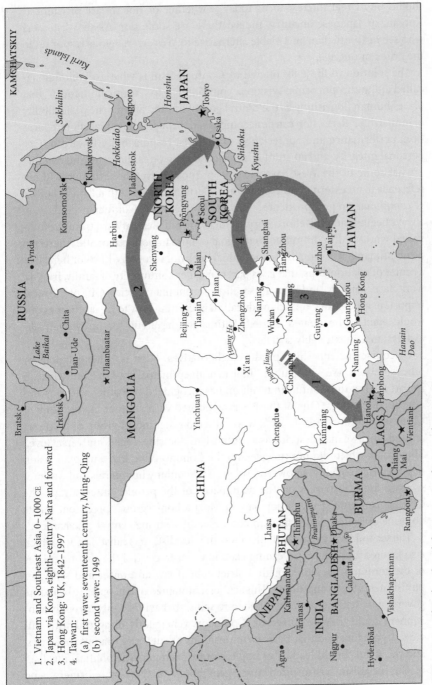

Figure 3.1 China's cultural diaspora: Confucian cultures in East Asia.

1. Vietnam and Southeast Asia, 0–1000 CE
2. Japan via Korea, eighth-century Nara and forward
3. Hong Kong: UK, 1842–1997
4. Taiwan:
   (a) first wave: seventeenth century, Ming-Qing
   (b) second wave: 1949

should be of real interest to us today – whether or not we are of Chinese, Korean, or Japanese ancestry. Indeed there are some non-Asian Westerners who see in Confucianism a viable alternative to Western religious responses to the crises of our age.

The solution to these ills offered by Confucianism is what Tu Weiming has called an "anthropocosmic" vision: a commitment to "cosmic humanism" that places human flourishing as the central goal of life and affirms the perfectibility of human life.[5] Perfection can be accomplished through individual effort: educa-tion, performance and appreciation of the arts, responsibility toward others, personal integrity, and an attitude of seriousness in one's character and conduct – what some in the West have called a "purpose-driven life," though without reference to an external director or force. Certainly the idea that Confucianism is *communal* or group-oriented is partially true, but Confucian cultivation always begins with self-effort. Purposeful living radiates outward from the indi-vidual who is fully committed to the goal of human perfection. Still, there can be no human flourishing if the individual does not recognize him- or herself as a center of relationships, that is, as part of a wider community of family, friends, workplace, country, and human as well as non-human species. One of the most important aspects of Confucian education is learning how to treat others as one would want to be treated oneself. Ultimately the arena for individual self-expression is inextricably social.

Of course ancient China produced alternatives – that is, other religions or other solutions. We will examine Taoism as the principal rival to Confucianism in Part III, but the Confucian tradition has recognized two other religious and ethical competitors. One of these was associated with another major figure of Chinese antiquity: Mozi (墨子), who gathered a significant group of followers around what we may describe as a "utilitarian" doctrine, called "universal love." This group, which did not survive into the Common Era, had a utopian vision of proletarian equality, a powerful ruler, and "economy in funerals and warfare" so as to focus resources on the daily needs of the people.[6] Interestingly, the Chinese communist revolution saw in Mozi a home-grown precedent for its doctrine of radical egalitarianism controlled by a strong central government.

The second rival to Confucianism was the "legalist" or "realist" school, which also favored a powerful governing class in order to control the chaotic desires of the common people through a strict rule of law and order and stringent punishments for wrong-doing. This school maintained that people are by nature governed by self-interest and inclined to selfish behaviors. Only through pun-ishment could they be corrected. Confucius vehemently disagreed with this view, arguing instead that persons in positions of authority (parents, teachers, and the state) should lead by example, not by coercion. The political idealism of Confucianism has inspired many generations of Chinese reformers, who have frequently raised a prophetic voice against the autocratic tendencies of the state (whether the imperial state of traditional times or the communist state of the present). That is to say, Confucianism – despite attempts by the Chinese government, past and present, to claim it as their own – has never supported any concentration of power in the state.

Over against Mo-ism and legalism, the Confucian vision emphasizes differentiated relationships (the cultivation of family and friendship ties) and morality or righteousness that comes from within rather than being imposed from without. We will explore these themes more fully in the chapters that follow.

Notes

1   Technically speaking, the term *zongjiao* (宗教) did exist in very early Chinese books, and it is possible that modern Japanese scholars found their inspiration there. But it certainly did not mean "religion" in the general, comparative sense in which we use it today. See Anthony Yu, *State and Religion in China: Historical and Textual Perspectives* (Peru, IL: Open Court Publishing Company, 2005).

2   See Lionel M. Jensen, *Manufacturing Confucianism: Chinese Traditions and Universal Civilization* (Raleigh, NC: Duke University Press, 1998).

3   Here and in subsequent chapters, all the quotations from Confucius' *Analects* (論語, *Lunyu*) are translated by the author. The Chinese text can be found at http://ctext.org/analects, an online resource of the Chinese Text Project. For a complete English translation of *The Analects*, see D. C. Lau, trans., *Confucius: The Analects* (New York: Penguin Classics, 1979).

4   The interview can be found at http://www.youtube.com/watch?v=xxBJUc4wVms (accessed July 21, 2012). Tu Weiming (杜維明) is dean of the Institute for the Advancement of Humanistic Studies at Peking University and formerly Professor of Religion at Harvard University. He has published extensively on Confucian thought in both English and Chinese.

5   Tu Weiming, "A Confucian Perspective on Learning to be Human," in his *Confucian Thought: Selfhood as Creative Transformation* (Albany: SUNY Press, 1985), pp. 51–66.

6   Burton Watson, trans., *Mozi: Basic Writings* (New York: Columbia University Press, 2003), pp. 53–64, 69–80.

4

The Religious Dimensions of Confucianism

In Chapter 1 we explored some definitions of religion and found the traditional definition – religion as the belief in supernatural beings – to be problematic for a number of reasons. First, it overemphasizes "belief" against practice; and, second, it focuses on an idea of "supernaturalism" that is understood very differently in different traditions. In the case of Confucianism, there is no *super*natural world per se, though gods and spirits (especially the spirits of ancestors) have been venerated in China from the time of Confucius to the present day. Rather than being supernatural, these spirits are present, or immanent, in the world of everyday experience: they are not "pure spirit" over against matter, not "heavenly" over against "earthly," not "wholly other" (to use a phrase coined by Christian theologians to describe God) or "beyond" or "outside" the world.

Confucian spirits are spirits of the dead, that is, spirits of those who have once lived – ghosts and ancestors. The Confucian cultures of East Asia practice "ancestor veneration": families make offerings to their deceased parents and grandparents on a daily basis, and again on the Pure Brightness Festival (清明節, *Qingming jie*) in early spring. The early Confucian tradition described the rites that should be extended to the ancestors, including funerals, mourning rites (traditionally the mourning period lasted for three years), and death-day anniversaries. While today these rites are not as elaborate as they once were, the spirit of Confucian ancestor veneration remains strong.

The Chinese term for "ritual" is *li* (禮; see Figure 4.1). The graphic components of this character show a stand supporting an incense container, which recalls an even earlier time when "burnt offerings" of animal meat were provided to the gods. In the later dynasties sacrifices were made once a year at the imperial palace. Today, however, the primary ritual of offering to ancestors consists in burning incense and imitation paper money. Prior to Confucius,

Asian Religions: A Cultural Perspective, First Edition. Randall L. Nadeau.
© 2014 John Wiley & Sons, Ltd. Published 2014 by John Wiley & Sons, Ltd.

Figure 4.1 *Li*: ceremony, ritual; ceremonial living, propriety, conscientiousness, personal comportment.

the *li* also included grand ceremonies at the imperial palace, seasonal celebrations associated with the movement of planets and stars, and great offerings for success in warfare, hunting, planting, and harvest.

By the time of Confucius the *li* had fallen into disuse. There was so much political and social strife then that the subsequent era was named the Warring States period. It was a time of social unrest, mass migrations, want, and starvation. Religious practices were viewed cynically. They were deemed useless, a waste of resources, a distraction from the "real world" of military preparation, management of labor, and the suppression of rampant lawlessness. But, rather than seeing *li* as a distraction, Confucius felt that its restoration would actually alleviate these problems – not so much because the gods or spirits would intervene or save the world (as we might think of the purpose of prayer), but because *li* had an intrinsic, transformative value. Confucius and his followers felt that, if people could be taught how to practice *li*, then they would become more appreciative of order, harmony, community, and cooperation.

Since the *li* had largely disappeared from daily practice, their restoration required education in history, reading and interpretation of ritual manuals, moral preparation, and the arts. Confucius took his inspiration from ritual performances that had been held centuries before. These were elaborate rites, featuring performances by large orchestras with wind and percussion instruments and by dancers wearing beautiful clothes and arrayed in perfect rows and columns. In other words, religion for Confucians was highly aesthetic – it was *performative* in every sense of the word. Confucius loved this performative aspect even if the actual rituals could no longer be conducted, and he trained his followers in music and dance.

Confucians believe that, if people are trained in the arts, history, and literature, if they come together to celebrate significant events or to ritually express concern for social problems, if they model their daily lives on ritual patterns, then it does not matter if gods and ancestors can "hear" them – indeed it does not even matter if they actually exist! The early Confucian thinker Xunzi (荀子) said this explicitly. He was philosophically skeptical about the existence of gods and spirits, but still advocated that people perform *li* and lead a *li*-patterned life. This point is difficult for Westerners to understand: most atheists would see no point in worship or prayer. If you do not believe in God, why would you still make offerings to God? Wouldn't these acts seem empty, pointless, even hypocritical? The answer is "yes" only if "belief" is the central definition of religion. For Confucians, the performance of ritual is much more important than what we would call religious belief.

Why? It is worth exploring this idea further.

One of Confucius' great innovations was a reinterpretation of *li*. As we have seen, the traditional definition of *li* was something like "worship," "offering," or "rite." Confucius was enamored of the ancient rites and hoped to restore them. But his reason for doing so – to change the world radically, to harmonize human relationships, and to bring order to a chaotic situation – led him to a deeper understanding of *li*. His understanding can be expressed in this way: "*Li* are the proper patterns of human action in a living, social context." That is, the model of *li* should be applied to every situation, whether religious or not. "The Master said, 'Do not look at what is contrary to *li*, do not listen to what is contrary to *li*, do not speak what is contrary to *li*.'"[1] Confucius encouraged his students to make every gesture, every look, every word in accordance with *li*. Just as we can use the word "ceremony" as a synonym for "ritual," I describe the Confucian ideal of human existence as "ceremonial living." This means that we live each moment of our lives as if we were participating in a ceremony. "Greet others as you would a great guest," Confucius said in the *Analects* ("Yan Yuan," chapter 2); the most frequently seen image or statue of Confucius shows him holding his hands together, in the traditional gesture of greeting (see Figure 4.2).

How often do you do each of the following? How important do you think these actions are?

- looking others in the eyes when speaking with them;
- identifying yourself when making a phone call;
- greeting the people you meet;
- introducing people who do not know one another;
- avoiding gossip;
- saying "May I help you?" to lost strangers;
- saying "How are you?" on the street/sidewalk/halls;
- helping little old ladies to cross the street;
- saying "Excuse me" when appropriate;

Figure 4.2   Statue of Confucius at the Confucian Temple in Shanghai, China. © Philip Lange / iStockphoto.

- following through on promises;
- addressing elders respectfully;
- inviting acquaintances to social events;
- helping friends in need;
- maintaining a respectful appearance;
- dressing neatly;
- getting up early in the morning;
- making your bed;
- sitting up straight;
- waiting patiently in line;
- serving others at the dinner table;
- helping in the kitchen.

You might agree that they are important, but for Confucians they are of ulti-mate importance – they are religious, both in the sense that they were derived from religious ritual in antiquity and in the sense that they can transform individuals and societies in an ultimate sense. Confucians believe in the per-fectibility of persons and societies; they are quite optimistic about human nature, at least with respect to its potential.

For Confucians, these behaviors are indicative of good character. But, more significantly, they also "come naturally." Of course, we don't just "know" these behaviors from birth – they have to be taught to us – but our desire to perform them, to be part of a family or a community, to see ourselves as "social animals" is something we possess naturally and desire from a very early age. In other words, anyone can practice them, and in fact most people are inclined to do so. This is because from birth we are living with others: we are raised by our parents, and we learn reciprocity (the spirit of give and take) from our family experience. Confucians would even say that becoming a good person – becoming fully human – is a natural process that does not require any outside force apart from the guidance of our parents and teachers. It is when these social patterns are disrupted that "evil" or socially aberrant behaviors appear.

Li (禮) can then be translated as both "ritual" and "ceremonial living." Some scholars have understood the second sense of *li* to be "propriety" or "decorum," but I think that these words suggest a certain stiffness or elitism that we do not find in Confucianism. Confucius thought that *anyone* could master *li*, because everyone has a natural inclination to live harmoniously with others. This idea is expressed through another term, *ren* (仁), meaning "love," "kindness," "benevolence," or, as I prefer to translate it, "co-humanity." "Co-humanity" works well for this character, because graphically the character is made up of two parts (see Figure 4.3), the left side referring to something "human" and the right side to the number two. So we exist as humans in co-human contexts, in pairs, or, by extension, in relation to others (indeed the number two here should not be taken literally: it means "more than one"). One of the important early Confucians, named Mengzi (孟子, Latinized as Mencius), put it very simply: "To be human means being co-human" (人仁也).[2]

Ren is a feeling or emotion – what it expresses is not just the "fact" that we live in community, but that we are *inclined* to do so, that we *want* to live with others, to belong. So, to translate Mengzi's simple sentence again, "I am human insofar as I want to be part of a family and community." That is to say, belonging comes naturally. This sense is very close to our hearts. Confucius said in the *Analects*: "As soon as I want *ren*, I have it" ("Shu Er," chapter 30): as long as I want to be part of a group, I am part of a group. And, since being a "good

Figure 4.3   *Ren*: kindness, benevolence; human-heartedness, "co-humanity."

person" means living harmoniously and responsibly with others, Confucians would say that we have a natural inclination to be good. Though what makes up *li* has to be learned (I don't know how to hold chopsticks properly unless someone teaches me), the sense of *ren* does not: it is innate.

Mengzi taught that this natural inclination was present in people from the start. He said that we have four "sprouts" of virtue:

1 Humans all have the sprout of compassion, 惻隱之心.
2 Humans all have the sprout of disdain for evil (sometimes translated as a "sense of shame"), 羞心.
3 Humans all have the sprout of respect for others (sometimes translated as "deference"), 恭敬心.
4 Humans all have the sprout of approval and disapproval (the ability to distinguish between right and wrong), 是非之心.

Allowed to develop naturally (under guidance, not by coercion), these sprouts develop into the virtues promoted by the Confucian tradition:

1 Compassion gives rise to *ren* (co-humanity, 仁).
2 Disdain for evil gives rise to *yi* (righteousness, 義).
3 Yielding gives rise to *li* (propriety, 禮).
4 Judgment gives rise to *zhi* (wisdom, 智).[3]

There is a famous story about Mengzi that illustrates his point. Interestingly, the story did not appear until several centuries after Mengzi actually lived, but it became very well known and is widely repeated. Every young person knows it. The story is called "Meng's Mother Moved Three Times" (孟母三遷, *Meng-mu san-qian*):

Mengzi's father died when he was very young. His mother, surnamed Zhang, raised her son alone. At the beginning they lived near a burial ground. Mengzi picked up the habit of crying and wailing, and he and his friends together mimicked the anguish and pain of the mourners. His mother said: "I can't let my son live here."

So they moved next to a marketplace. Mengzi learned how to haggle and cajole. His mother said: "This is not a good place to live either."

So they moved next to a meat market, and Mengzi learned how to butcher animals and how to earn a living on their suffering. Again his mother said: "Nor is this the place to raise my son."

Finally they settled down near a school, and on the first day of every month Mengzi witnessed the ritual performances and the gestures of respectful greeting. Seeing this, he learned things one by one, and took them to heart. His mother said: "This is the place where my son should live." And they stayed there.[4]

As long as there is a proper environment for us to grow up, our "sprouts" will naturally grow into full-fledged virtues. In fact Confucians place great emphasis on one's social environment: one's community, school, workplace, and country. As long as these are places that encourage what is best in us – to be responsible, caring, and involved – we will be good people. Any time someone does something anti-social (theft, drugs, prostitution, and so on), it is assumed that his or her environment was deficient. There is a strong tendency to blame the parents for the wrong-doings of children, and in fact parents of social outcasts usually experience shame and self-recrimination. This also places a great deal of pressure on children: behaving badly is bad enough, but the pressure not to disappoint our parents extends even to the best of us. If I'm not successful (doing well in school, playing a musical instrument, or achieving recognition in my career, as reflected in my status and salary), what will my parents think? Anything less than "perfection" will make my parents feel they did not raise me right! This pressure to succeed is a powerful social force in Confucian societies.[5]

In this chapter we have examined the Confucian conception of "ritual" and "ceremonial living" (*li*). We have found it to be a religious concept, not only because the idea developed from religious practices in ancient times, but because a life governed by ceremonial attitudes of decorum and propriety is ultimately transformative, at both a social and a personal level. We also discovered that, for Confucians, the harmonizing tendencies of *li* are found within ourselves, in the idea of *ren* (co-humanity). *Ren* is the inward disposition that leads to the performance of *li* in everyday acts. From this point of view, the ultimate transformation of self and society is deeply humanistic – an unfolding of natural inclinations rather than a fundamental alteration of our character as human beings. This is the anthropocosmic vision of Confucian learning.

Notes

1 *The Analects of Confucius*, "Yan Yuan," ch. 1. Chinese Text Project. At http://ctext.org/analects (accessed July 17, 2013). All translations are by the author; for a complete English translation of *The Analects*, see D. C. Lau, trans., *Confucius: The Analects* (New York: Penguin Classics, 1979).

2 *The Book of Mencius*, ch. 22. Chinese Text Project. At http://ctext.org/mengzi (accessed July 17, 2013). All translations here and in subsequent chapters are by the author; for a complete English translation of *Mengzi*, see D. C. Lau, trans., *Mencius* (London: Penguin Books, 1970).

3 *The Book of Mencius*, ch. 2A.

4 Liu Xiang, *Lienuzhuan* (孟母三遷. 西漢·劉向《烈女傳·卷一·母儀, *Tales of Exemplary Women*), ch. 1, "Mothers." Chinese Text Project. At http://ctext.org/lie-nv-zhuan/zh (accessed July 16, 2013). Translated by the author.

5   In early 2012 a pop star of Taiwanese and Japanese parentage named Makiyo got
    caught up in a brawl that resulted in severe injuries to a taxi driver. The pop star
    not only apologized to her fans for her bad behavior, but also bowed abjectly before
    her mother, in front of a bevy of television cameras. In acting irresponsibly, Makiyo
    had shamed her mother.

5

The Self as a Center of Relationships

Confucius said in his *Analects* ("Yong Ye," chapter 30):

> A man of *ren* helps others to establish what he wishes to establish for himself, helps others to attain what he wishes to attain for himself. To be able to take what is near to oneself and make it an analogy for the treatment of others – that is the way of *ren*.

What did Confucius mean by "taking what is near to oneself and making it an analogy for the treatment of others"? He meant that the deepest feelings I have – hopes for a prosperous future, for good health and a healthy family, for being treated with respect and consideration, for being a good father or mother, son or daughter – are most certainly shared by others. People are fundamentally alike; all of us have the same basic hopes, fears, desires, and expectations. By taking those innermost feelings and "making of myself an analogy for others" – that is, by recognizing that what I hope for is analogous to what other persons hope for – I am recognizing our "co-humanity." This is *ren*.

When Confucius was asked to define *ren* directly, he said: "*Ren shu ye* [仁恕也]: *Ren* is *shu* [恕]" (*Analects*, "Wei Ling Gong," chapter 24). The graphic components of *shu* are "mind/heart" on the bottom part (心) and a character meaning "like, similar to, as" (如) at the top: so, literally, "like-mindedness" or "like-heartedness." In being co-human (kind, good, benevolent), I am recognizing what I have in common with others.

This simple, elegant definition of goodness goes to the heart of the Confucian project. By recognizing, developing, and cultivating human relationships, I am not only creating a better world, but I am also realizing my own potential as a human being. To the extent that I can carry this forward deliberately and conscientiously, I am *practicing Confucianism*.

Asian Religions: A Cultural Perspective, First Edition. Randall L. Nadeau.
© 2014 John Wiley & Sons, Ltd. Published 2014 by John Wiley & Sons, Ltd.

Figure 5.1 Though traditional family courtyards, around which three generations lived "under one roof," are now being replaced by urban high-rise apartments, the sense of family remains central: three of the five lasting relationships are within the family. © Keren Su / Getty Images.

Later on the Confucian tradition developed the idea of *ren* by spelling out the entire range of human relationships in a proper order. The resulting series they called the "five lasting relationships" (五常, *wu chang* or 五倫, *wu lun*). Three of the five lasting relationships are within the family: even in the urbanized setting of modern Chinese life, the family remains central (see Figure 5.1). Here is one version of the five relationships:

1 parent ↔ child
2 husband ↔ wife
3 sibling ↔ sibling
or
friend ↔ friend
4 teacher ↔ student
5 ruler ↔ subject

Lasting Relationships

What does it mean to say that these relationships should be *lasting*? These are relationships that should be entered into with seriousness and sincerity. They are not short-term relationships; in fact, one could almost say that they are "eternal," to the extent that they continue beyond death. Let's look at some illustrations of how deeply East Asians cherish and hold on to their interpersonal relationships:

1 *The parent–child relationship*   We have already discussed Chinese ancestor veneration: isn't this simply an extension of the gratitude and affection that one feels for one's parents even after they have died? Traditionally, families maintained these genealogical ties for many generations, by constructing ancestral halls and placing within them dozens, even hundreds of commemorative tablets bearing the names of deceased relatives. This is rarely practiced today, but daily offerings to parents and grandparents continue in most households, the spirit tablet being placed in an alcove within the home. The offerings consist of food that is consumed by the family, so the ancestors are symbolically gathering with the family as they did in life, by sharing a meal together.

2 *The husband–wife relationship*   This relationship, too, is meant to be lasting. While the divorce rate is rising rapidly in East Asian cultures (due to a number of economic and cultural factors), it still does not approach its counterpart in Western cultures. East Asian marriages are remarkably stable and have remained so even after evolving from "arranged marriage" to "marriage by choice" over a century ago. In imperial times, a woman was expected to remain "faithful" to her husband even after her husband's death, by avoiding remarriage. In Chinese this is called "protecting one's chastity" (守節, *shoujie*). This attitude does reflect the traditional view that men were given higher status than women, as men who became widowed were expected to remarry, especially if they had not yet acquired sons to continue the family line. I observed a remarkable example of marital fidelity about twenty years ago, while I was living in northern China. One day, while waiting to cross a busy intersection, I was witness to a terrible accident: a 20-year-old woman was struck by a truck while riding her bicycle and was killed instantly. Several days later I attended the girl's funeral rite, and (no doubt because of my foreigner status) I was treated as an honored guest at the funeral banquet. A number of months later, a friend remarked to me: "Do you remember the girl who was killed in the traffic accident? She's getting married tomorrow." Sure enough, she had been engaged to be married, and her fiancé followed through, by arranging for her ashes and spirit tablet to be carried in the traditional way (by a palanquin or sedan chair) to his home, to be cared for there. Of course, the expectation was that he would eventually "remarry," but her spirit will always be honored by his descendants.

3 *The sibling relationship* Sibling relationships are certainly lasting, but so is friendship. Friendship is taken seriously in East Asian cultures. In Japanese, the word *tomodachi* (友達; ともだち) is reserved for only the closest of friends, whereas in English we use the word "friend" quite loosely – there are many people I once may have called "friends" whose names I can no longer recall, and I have students whose "friends" lists on Facebook number in the hundreds or thousands. This point is significant, because some Americans and Europeans, when living in Asia for a period of time, experience their hosts to be reticent, even aloof; Westerners feel that Asians do not make friends easily, and they feel discouraged and lonely as a consequence. But this is a misperception. Friendship is highly esteemed in Confucian cultures, and it is cultivated over many years. Once friendships are made, they are never broken.

4 *The teacher–student relationship* I observed a wonderful example of the lasting quality of the teacher–student relationship a few years ago, while living in Japan. One Friday afternoon, a friend about 30 years of age picked me up in his car to drive out to the countryside for an evening of snacks and sake at a rural eatery. Before leaving town, we stopped briefly so that he could call on an elderly woman, who came briefly to the door. Presenting her with a small gift, my friend addressed his elder as *sensei* (先生), a word we know as "master" and associate with martial arts instructors and Zen abbots. When I asked my friend who the lady was, he replied: "Oh, she was my third grade teacher. I stop by now and then to make sure she's doing all right." In this instance the teacher–student relationship had persisted for some 25 years – that is, for most of my friend's life. Indeed, having taught several semesters in China, Taiwan, and Hong Kong over a number of years, I am still addressed by my former students as *laoshi* (老師), teacher.

5 *Ruler–subject relationships* The lasting quality of the ruler–subject relationship is socially and politically significant because it reinforces stability, often over centuries. The great dynasties of the Confucian countries – the Han, Tang, Ming, and Qing in China; the Heian, Kamakura, Muromachi, and Edo periods of Japan; the Goryeo and Joseon Dynasties of Korea (not to mention the Three Kingdoms – Goguryeo, Baekje, and Silla – of Korean antiquity) – all lasted for at least two centuries, and in some cases many more. Of course, this is related to power structures that go well beyond Confucian teachings, but there is no doubt that the Confucian emphasis on maintaining relationships "eternally" has contributed to political stability. Even today, these are politically hierarchical societies, and democracy, with its much more fluid dynamic, has been adopted with markedly Confucian characteristics.

Another characteristic of the five lasting relationships is also significant: they are not only permanent or long-lasting, they are also hierarchical. The five relationships are hierarchical to the point that one can say that there is no such thing as a relationship of "complete equals" in Confucian cultures. All relationships are characterized by differentiation – differentiation of roles, duties, and responsibilities. Recall that the early Confucians contrasted their own teachings with those of Mozi and his followers, who advocated "universal love," *jian'ai* (兼愛) – a phrase in Chinese that is perhaps better translated as "undifferentiated care." For Confucians, differentiation (hierarchy) is indispensable in a well-ordered society.

The five relationships are hierarchical on two axes: from top to bottom and from left to right:

↓ parent → child
↓ husband → wife
sibling → sibling
↓ or
friend → friend
↓ teacher → student
↓ ruler → subject

The five relationships are hierarchical from top to bottom

In contrast to the Mo-ist philosophy of "universal love," Confucians maintain that relationships should be differentiated. In his repudiation of Mozi, Mengzi expressed the belief that it was absurd to think that one could love a stranger as much as one loved one's own father or mother. He found Mozi's idealism "unnatural," and even "inhuman." We are embedded in a wide range of relationships, but they are arrayed hierarchically or concentrically, with the parent–child relationship closest to the center and the ruler–subject relationship most distant and abstract. Moreover, since the parent–child relationship is the most important one, it should serve as a model for the others; that is, the teacher–student or ruler–subject relationships should be modeled upon the parent–child relationship – the teacher or ruler should act like a parent toward the students or the citizens – but in an attenuated way: such a figure should be a reflection of, not a substitution for one's real parents.

In a conversation recorded in the *Analects* ("Zi Lu," chapter 18), Confucius illustrated this point through the example of an especially authoritarian ruler of a small state. Borrowing from Legalist philosophy, the ruler boasted to Confucius that in his state, if a father stole a sheep, the son would turn him in. "This is not my idea of righteousness," said Confucius. "A father should protect his son, a son should protect his father."

Notice that three of the five relationships are familial, and that these take precedence over the non-familial relationships. One's social existence, one's "co-humanity," begins in the home and is only extended peripherally to others.

The five relationships are hierarchical from left to right

In traditional terms, the parent is superior in status to the child, the husband to the wife, and so on. You might be able to guess how the sibling–sibling or friend–friend relationship can be hierarchical: the older is higher in status than the younger. In terms of address, there are four words for "brother" and "sister" in Chinese: *gege* (哥哥, older brother), *didi* (弟弟, younger brother), *jiejie* (姐姐, older sister), *meimei* (妹妹, younger sister). Even twins have a birth order, and one is addressed as *gege* or *jiejie*, the other as *didi* or *meimei*.

The hierarchical nature of Confucian relationships is troubling to the modern, democratic West and, at its worst, can be oppressive. Certainly the emphasis on hierarchy has had immense social consequences. Confucian societies are stable and close-knit; people have a sense of responsibility for their elders and they are mindful of their conduct. But there have been "unintended consequences" as well: oppressive tendencies have led to two major revolutions in the past century in China and to what some young people in Japan and Korea have experienced as a generation gap with their parents. The negative aspects of this generational hierarchy have contributed to Japan, Korea, and Taiwan now experiencing the lowest birth rates in the world, though economic factors are also significant.

The hierarchical nature of relationships also means that one's duties and responsibilities are dependent upon one's social position. Traditionally, the duties and responsibilities of the "lower" party in a dyadic relationship were considered to be more pressing that those of the "higher" party. These traditional values can be represented as follows:

Child's duty toward the parent: filial piety *xiao* 孝	Parent's duty toward the child: kindness *en* 恩
Wife's duty toward the husband: fidelity *cheng* 誠	Husband's duty toward the wife: affection *qing* 情
Younger friend's duty toward the older: reliability *xin* 信	Older friend's duty toward the younger: concern *guanxin* 關心
Student's duty toward the teacher: respect *jing* 敬	Teacher's duty toward the student: guidance *jiaodao* 教導
Subject's duty toward the ruler: loyalty *zhong* 忠	Ruler's duty toward the subject: benevolence *ren* 仁

In this list of 10 moral values, certainly "filial piety" (孝, *xiao*) stands at the top. *Xiao* means love and respect for one's parents and gratitude for their guidance. It can be said that *xiao* is the highest virtue in the Confucian tradition; Confucius described it as the defining characteristic of co-humanity (仁, *ren*).

Does this hierarchy demand strict obedience? This is a misconception. Confucius said in the *Analects* ("Li Ren," chapter 18):

> When serving your parents, you may criticize them gently; if they do not follow your advice, you may press further, but you should be even more respectful. Never let your efforts lead to anger.

One may disagree with one's parents, as long as one's disagreement is expressed respectfully; there is no expectation of abject obedience toward one's superiors. Another example comes from Mengzi: when his students complained to him about an inhumane, oppressive ruler and asked if it would be permissible to overthrow him, Mengzi replied: "Such a man does not deserve to be called a 'ruler.' He is a tyrant. I would not condone overthrowing a ruler, but to over-throw a tyrant is just" (*The Book of Mencius*, Book 1B, Chapter 15).

Mengzi's distinction between a "ruler" and a "tyrant" highlights what Confucians call the "rectification of names" (正名, *zhengming*): the idea that one is not merely role-playing as a "father," "mother," "son," "daughter," "husband," "wife," "teacher," "student," "ruler," or "subject," but that one should recognize each of these names as being endowed with significance and meaning, as titles deserving respect. As a Confucian, my life-long goal is to "live up to the name" that defines me – or the various names or capacities that I try to fulfill at various stages of my life. Confucius said: "A parent is someone who parents, a ruler is someone who rules, a teacher is someone who teaches," and so on – obvious points, perhaps, but all requiring knowledge, seriousness of purpose, conscientiousness, and care. I do not just possess a title; I must earn it (*Analects*, "Yan Yuan, chapter 11). I earn the name of that title through deliberate self-cultivation, and I become a better father, daughter, teacher, student to the extent that I take these roles seriously and do my best to *realize* them – to make them *real* – in my own life.

In this chapter we have examined the contexts in which the Confucian values of *li* and *ren* are put into practice. At the same time we have looked at what makes someone a "person," that is, how one can fulfill one's human potential. This is done through the conscientious, deliberate cultivation of personal virtues within a web of relationships, beginning with family and friends and extending outward to community and nation. There is an important book of the later Confucian tradition called the Great Learning (大學, *Daxue*) – a book of directives to rulers. It is too long to quote in full, but the basic premise is that a ruler who wishes to govern well must first find harmony within his own household; one who wishes to find harmony in one's own household must first practice self-cultivation; in order to practice self-cultivation, one must first pacify one's mind; in order to pacify one's mind, one must first be sincere in one's thoughts; and in order to be sincere in one's thoughts, one must strive for knowledge of oneself and of the world. So, contrary to what many Westerners think of the "group-mindedness" of Confucian cultures, Confucian cultivation begins with the self.

6

Learning to Be Human

Although Confucian relationships are hierarchical, perhaps the greatest contribution that Confucius made to his society was the commitment to human equality or "equal opportunity." Self-cultivation and human flourishing, indeed human "perfection," are accessible to anyone, regardless of social class. One of his most admirable traits as a teacher was his willingness to accept any student, regardless of his or her ability to pay; he said in the *Analects* ("Shu Er," chapter 8): "I will take any student who, given three corners of a square, can give me the fourth" (that is, anyone capable of rudimentary logical thinking). He also showed great personal humility as a teacher: "If I see three persons walking, I know that one of them could be my teacher" (*Analects*, "Shu Er," chapter 22). This is testament not only to the fact that Confucius could recognize anyone as a teacher, but also that he himself regarded learning as a life-long pursuit.

Confucius expressed his egalitarian ideal through the model of the *junzi* (君子) – an ideal, he said, that anyone could achieve. This was a remarkable statement and at first must have seemed perplexing, because the traditional definition of a *junzi* was a man of high birth: the two characters literally mean "son of a nobleman." In feudal societies, where class was a birthright, the "son of a nobleman" would be, simply, a nobleman! So how could Confucius have asserted that *anyone* could become a *junzi* – not by birth, but by means of self-effort? Clearly, he was using the term in a new way. The traditional English translation of *junzi* is "gentleman": a good choice, because, while in Victorian England the word may have referred to a certain social status, today we see it as being descriptive of *character*, not of a birthright. When I was growing up, I was taught by my own father to be considerate, polite, assertive but humble, respectful and self-possessed; he was a "gentleman" though he had been born in impoverished circumstances and never enjoyed great wealth or high social standing. Having studied Confucianism later in my life, I realized that my father had been a *junzi*; and I have tried to emulate him.

Asian Religions: A Cultural Perspective, First Edition. Randall L. Nadeau.
© 2014 John Wiley & Sons, Ltd. Published 2014 by John Wiley & Sons, Ltd.

Confucius' target audience consisted only of men, and the word *junzi* is certainly masculine. Social values of the time dictated that women dedicate themselves to child-rearing and domestic labor, not to activities outside the home. Nevertheless, contemporary feminist thinkers have found incipient ideas within Confucianism that support male–female equality, ideas not unlike those of the "ethics of care" of feminist ethical theory. Some have therefore adopted a translation of *junzi* as "exemplary person" rather than "gentleman." I applaud this translation, but it is true that the word *junzi*, even today, is generally applied only to men – in fact the title remains, some 2000 years after the time of Confucius, the highest compliment that one can give a man. Still, the qualities of a *junzi*, as well as the means to cultivate those qualities, are certainly as applicable to women as they are to men, being accessible to all.

For Confucius, a *junzi* has two defining qualities. The first is education: a *junzi* is educated in the arts and literature, history, and the rites. The second is character: a *junzi* is conscientious, self-critical, and co-human. On this last quality, Confucius said:

A *junzi* has nine wishes:

- that his vision be clear,
- his listening sharp,
- his appearance gentle,
- his expression reverential;
- he will be true to his word,
- and conscientious in his affairs;
- when in doubt, he will inquire;
- when he loses his temper, he will regret it;
- when he sees something he can attain, he will think first of what is right. (*Analects*, "Ji Shi," chapter 10)

Confucians believe that these two attributes of a *junzi* – education and character – are not really "two," but "one." That is, they are inseparable. One great Confucian thinker of the Ming Dynasty, Wang Yangming (王陽明, an important figure not only in China, but also in Korea and Japan), called this "the unity of knowledge and action" (知行合一, *zhixing heyi*). One's actions and behavior are informed by one's education. As a teacher, I share this conviction – not that educated people are necessarily "better" people, but that, ideally, they should be! A university education, for example, should not simply consist of the accumulation of facts or skills; rather it should be personally transformative. This is why an educated person should have some exposure to the arts, to social science, and to the natural world. He or she should apply this knowledge to the real troubles of our world and suggest solutions to global concerns – through ethical action, aesthetic expression, or technological improvements to our living environment. These goals of higher education are consistent with those of the Confucian tradition, and this is why, to this day, Confucian cultures demonstrate respect and admiration toward those who pursue higher education in any field.

The contemporary Confucian scholar Tu Weiming has summarized the steps by which any person can become a *junzi* in several of his published works. One was a talk given at the University of Singapore entitled "Core Values in Confucian Thought";[1] another was a published essay entitled "A Confucian Perspective on Learning to be Human."[2] In these and other essays, Tu Weiming has described the Confucian self as a "center of relationships": "Confucian self-cultivation is a deliberate communal act. Confucianism conceives of the self neither as an isolated atom nor as a single, separate individuality, but as a being in relationship." Of course, we exist in not just one relationship, but in many, and these various roles mutually inform and reinforce one another. In one touching line, Tu Weiming says that it was only when he himself became a father that he really understood what it meant to be a son. And in "growing into" the roles of father and son, in "rectifying the names" in a Confucian sense, Tu became a more sensitive, self-aware, and compassionate individual. Moreover, "[m]y being a son and a father is also informed and enriched by being a student, a teacher, a husband, a colleague, a friend, and an acquaintance."[3] Consequently we are "learning to be human" throughout our lives. This lifelong process of self-cultivation is fundamentally transformative (of both oneself and one's community), and in this sense it fits our definition of a consciously religious life. "To be religious, in the Confucian sense, is to be engaged in ultimate self-transformation as a communal act. Salvation means the full realization of the anthropocosmic reality inherent in our human nature."[4]

How different this religious vision is from the model of the isolated individual in the Christian West! In his *Confessions*, the autobiography of Augustine of Hippo (written in the year 389 CE), Saint Augustine (Figure 6.1) describes his conversion to the Christian faith. As a young boy he had led a dissolute life, and he recalls one particular example of his "sinful nature" when he, with a group of other young troublemakers, stole a basket of pears from a neighbor's orchard. He did so not for the sake of their color or taste – in fact he discarded them as soon as he had picked them – but because he was drawn to wrongdoing, "seeking nothing from the shameful deed but shame itself."[5] And he recognized that it was peer pressure – his association with a group of young delinquents – that spurred him into action.

> Why did I find such delight in doing this, which I would not have done alone? . . . Yet alone I would not have done it – alone I could not have done it at all. (Augustine, *Confessions*, 2.6)

Figure 6.1 Engraving from the anonymous *History of the Church*, circa 1880. Augustine of Hippo (Saint Augustine) is represented in the middle. © Bocman1973 / Shutterstock.

Later, when he experienced his conversion to Christianity, Augustine felt that God had saved him from his innately sinful state and that his salvation was highly personal. At the instant of conversion he wrote: "Let me know thee, O my Knower; let me know thee even as I am known" (*Confessions*, 2.1).

To the extent that Augustine is representative of a Western understanding of the self, we see the true self – the soul – in contrast to the self of worldly (that is, social) existence. I describe this as the *vertical* conception of human nature, drawing a line between self and God. By contrast, the Confucian self is understood *horizontally*, in relation to the world, as a social being. The self as an isolated entity is impossible to conceive.

Tu Weiming's assertion of the anthropocosmic reality of human nature speaks to character – that is, to the development of virtue within oneself through its application in the world. Tu Weiming also discusses the complementary dimension of "education" in cultivating the life of a *junzi*. Learning, Tu writes, "means becoming aesthetically refined, morally excellent, and religiously profound."[6] He describes five areas of learning that are vitally important to the Confucian tradition:

1 *Poetry, art, and music*   Appreciation of the arts and the ability to express oneself aesthetically create a "vibration between the person and the larger

world."[7] Moreover, artistic appreciation and expression refine human feelings and sentiments, enhancing our interactions with others. Roger Ames, the foremost Confucian scholar in the West, describes *li* (ceremonial living) precisely in this aesthetic sense, when he says that mastery of *li* "gives ornamental expression to the emotions that otherwise would have no proper outlet and would become socially dangerous."[8] The arts give us the tools both to express and to *elevate* our innermost feelings.

2   *The ritualization of the body*   Here Tu Weiming refers to the way we communicate our character and convictions to others, often non-verbally. The way we carry ourselves, our personal habits of dress and appearance, even the way we eat or sit (especially in public) reflect our attitudes toward others and our upbringing (see Figure 6.2). When my children were young, I taught them to look others in the eyes when speaking with them. The reason is that, when one looks directly into another person's eyes, one is showing interest and respect. If one is looking down, one is demonstrating

Figure 6.2   "Confucius would not sit unless his mat was straight." Source: Tanyu, Kano (1602–1674). Private Collection / Peter Newark Pictures / The Bridgeman Art Library.

a lack of interest or of self-confidence; if one is looking over the shoulder of one's conversation partner (perhaps to see who else is in the room, someone more "important" or more worth talking to), one is demonstrating a lack of respect. Non-verbal communication is an important expression of ceremonial living and of co-humanity.

3 *History* Confucians emphasize the importance of studying history both to learn from the past and to honor one's roots. Tu Weiming describes history as "collective memory, a knowing from whence we came."[9] When the early Confucians argued against the Mo-ist notion of universal love, they were affirming a strong sense of personal identity rooted in culture, nation, ethnicity, community, and family. To be sure, "rootedness" can also lead to closed-mindedness, and potentially to negative expressions of belonging – such as nepotism, parochialism, racism, nationalism, and cultural bias. Such tendencies have not been absent from East Asian societies and can still be seen today. But a healthy sense of belonging and of personal identity are core dimensions of being fully human.

4 *Social and political participation* Confucianism encourages meaningful, significant participation in the political process. In fact there are historical precedents for advocating freedom of expression and democratic empowerment *within* the Confucian tradition; these ideas do *not* need to be imported from the West. Several years ago I published an article in which I argued that human rights are consistent with Confucian principles and are not philosophically dependent on Western individualism.[10] This point is important if we are serious about promoting human rights in China and elsewhere – not as a "colonialist" or "hegemonic" imposition, but as the expression of internal cultural values. The human rights debate has a much higher chance of success if we in the West will simply acknowledge the democratic principles *inherent in* East Asian societies.

5 *Ecological consciousness* Tu Weiming writes: "A human being does not exist only in the anthropological world of other human beings. Beyond this human world is a larger universe."[11] This is a point not often expressed in Confucianism, and Tu Weiming is to be applauded for bringing it forward. Confucius himself showed a rather callous lack of concern for the natural world. (As recorded in the *Analects*, "Xiang Dang," chapter 12: "When he heard about a stable fire, Confucius asked, 'Was anyone hurt?' He did not ask about the horses.") Ecological consciousness as a whole is not well developed in East Asian societies, and some of the worst ecological abuses in the developing world can be found in contemporary China. It is hoped that Tu Weiming can be a prophetic voice (a role certainly consistent with Confucianism) in drawing attention to the impact of economic development on the natural environment.

Survey 1   The Confucian Values of Li (禮) and Ren (仁)

You can access a survey based on the principal values of the Confucian tradition through the following link: http://goo.gl/ayZPwn. Upon submitting your responses, you can see how other readers have responded to the same queries.

Notes

1 Published in *Confucian Ethics Today: The Singapore Challenge* (Singapore: Federal Publications for the Curriculum Development Institute of Singapore, 1984), pp. 2–38.
2 Published in *Confucian Thought: Selfhood as Creative Transformation* (Albany, State University of New York Press: 1985), pp. 51–66.
3 Tu Wei-ming, *Confucian Thought*, p. 58.
4 Tu Wei-ming, *Confucian Thought*, p. 56.
5 St. Augustine, *Confessions and Enchiridion*, trans. Albert C. Outler (Philadelphia: Westminster Press, 1955). The full online version of the *Confessions* can be found at http://www.ccel.org/ccel/augustine/confessions.v.html (accessed 23 July 2012), in the Christian Classics Ethereal Library.
6 Tu Wei-ming, *Confucian Thought*, p. 52.
7 Tu Wei-ming, "Core Values," p. 6.
8 Roger T. Ames and Henry Rosemont, *The Analects of Confucius: A Philosophical Translation* (New York: Ballantine Books, 1998), p. ix.
9 Tu Wei-ming, "Core Values," p. 7.
10 Randall Nadeau, "Confucianism and the Problem of Human Rights," *Intercultural Communication Studies* 11: 2 (2002), pp. 107–119.
11 Tu Wei-ming, "Core Values," p. 8.

7

The Lasting Influence of Confucianism in Modern East Asia

Despite the radical political disruption of the Confucian tradition in the last 150 years, its values remain strong in East Asia, and in China they have experienced a fundamentalist revival. As a cultural system, Confucianism is, in several respects, the bones and marrow of the East Asian region, through its emphasis on:

- education;
- political authoritarianism;
- family values;
- filial piety;
- civic values;
- public support for the arts and civil religion;
- ceremonial living, politeness, and decorum.

Education as a Primary Indicator of Social Status and Achievement

The emphasis on education in modern East Asia is one of the most abiding cultural values of the Confucian tradition. Children in China, Korea, Japan, and Vietnam demonstrate a Confucian work ethic that is astoundingly rigorous. Most go to tutors or private "cram schools" at the end of the regular school day and do homework late into the night. These practices continue to be upheld by East Asian immigrants in the West, as evidenced by the high rate of success on standardized tests and in college admissions, even among students whose first language is Chinese, Korean, Japanese, or Vietnamese. Teachers are highly respected and honored for their work. As a cultural value and institutional

Asian Religions: A Cultural Perspective, First Edition. Randall L. Nadeau.
© 2014 John Wiley & Sons, Ltd. Published 2014 by John Wiley & Sons, Ltd.

priority, education is Confucianism's most obvious legacy and the Confucian remnant that has been least affected by the winds of change. Whether rumor or fact, it is certainly believable that the University of California at Berkeley must turn down thousands of qualified applicants of Asian descent. Nationwide, children of East Asian immigrants are at the top of the class, and are often accomplished in a musical instrument as well.[1]

The Reluctance to Adopt Democratic Institutions, an Uncritical Acceptance of Political Authority, Conservatism in Politics and Economics

Despite the overthrow of the imperial system in China and its weakened state in Japan, the East Asian political ethos remains authoritarian and averse to change. Political leaders are trusted to represent the best interests of the nation, and many East Asians express nationalism and loyalty to the governments that represent them. While communism is frequently cited as the cause of political authoritarianism in China and Vietnam, the power of East Asian governments is equally attributable to Confucianism. Today authoritarian governments from Beijing to Singapore have appealed to the Confucian tradition as the basis for their hold on power.[2]

Filial Piety, Active Participation of Parents in Children's Affairs, Support of Parents in Old Age, Strong Extended Family Identity

From the home radiate moral values, spiritual beings, and ritual action. The primary moral tie is the one between parents and children, and moral consciousness begins with training in the Confucian virtues, especially *xiao* (孝), filial piety.

Among family relationships, the vertical/generative always takes precedence over the horizontal/affiliative. Thus the parent–child relationship is emphasized over the husband–wife relationship, the latter being patterned after the former but always secondary to it. This is reflected historically in the private writings of Confucian intellectuals – the scholar–official class – who wrote of their mothers without fail and at length, but rarely if ever of their wives. And it remains true today, when parent–child relationships are given much greater attention than marital relationships. Up until the twentieth century East Asian marriages were arranged by parents. Although this is no longer the case, parents still play a significant role in their children's choice of marriage partners, and divorce brings shame to the family as a whole, not just to the husband

and wife. Divorce rates in China and Japan, while on the rise, are only about one tenth of those of Europe and America.

Of the five lasting relationships of classical Confucianism, three are related to the family: parent–child, husband–wife, and sibling–sibling. These ties are stronger than ever. As people have become disillusioned with the grand promises of communism and are equally distrustful of Western individualism, the family remains the principal source of personal value in every country of the East Asian region.

Persistence of Filial Piety as an Abiding Cultural Value, though under Threat from New Family Models, Declining Marriage and Birth Rates, and Economic Changes

The religion of China (including the Chinese-dominant states of Taiwan, Hong Kong, and Singapore) and of Korea, Japan, and Vietnam is, first and foremost, a family religion. Throughout East Asia, the most revered of all spiritual beings are the family ancestors. Families make offerings of incense, rice, meat, and fruit every morning at the family altar and on anniversary days at the family gravesite. The cult of the ancestors makes the home the most central "sacred space." Periodic rites at local shrines and temples are also for the benefit of the family: its health, its harmony, and its preservation.

While still strong as a ritual tradition and as a social value, filial piety – indeed the traditional family model – is under threat. In China, a generation of universal birth control (in the form of the "one-child policy") has radically altered traditional demographics; in the developed economies of Hong Kong, Taiwan, and Japan, changing values, economic factors, and educational and economic progress for women have delayed the age of marriage as well as birthrates, which are now among the lowest in the world. The result: rapidly aging populations in the entire East Asian cultural area and projections of a significant economic slowdown (even halting the Chinese economic juggernaut) in the coming decades.[3]

Self-Sacrifice for the Benefit of Others and the Rejection of Western Individualism, Privacy, and Self-Interest: An Ethic of Conformity

Communitarian values, advocated cynically by authoritarian governments as a buttress to their suppression of individual rights, are still viewed positively at the grassroots level. Many Chinese and Japanese see American-style individualism as extreme and socially divisive, and even as harmful to individuals themselves. Individualism is associated with isolation, loneliness, and "outsider" status. For contemporary East Asians, a person's social identity is far more important than his or her sense of privacy or individuality. Some would argue that Confucian communitarian values have created an East Asian ethic of conformity – an ethic frequently observed by sociologists studying Japan in particular. But this characterization is highly Western: from a Chinese or Japanese point of view, Confucian communitarianism provides individuals with a strong sense of meaning and purpose in their lives.

At the same time, it cannot be denied that globalization has inspired a yearning for greater freedom and individual expression, on the part of Chinese and Japanese in particular. In the midst of a political crackdown on dissidents in China – including the long-term imprisonment of Nobel Peace Prize winner Liu Xiaobo (劉曉波) and the temporary kidnapping of outspoken architect and rights-activist Ai Weiwei (艾未未) – thousands of people have made use of social networking sites to express both political and personal concerns, often anti-communitarian in tone.[4]

In Japan, the traditional constraints have been less political than cultural. As Gordon Mathews, a sociologist and an expert in Japanese society, remarked in an essay on the Japanese concept of *ikigai* (what makes life "worth living"): "Perhaps as a way of resisting their societies' dominant pressures, the most vociferously individualistic pursuers of *ikigai* among those I interviewed were not American but Japanese."[5] In the face of political or cultural oppression, Chinese and Japanese people are more and more individualistic in dress, artistic self-expression, and legal and political advocacy. Still, communal values remain strong.

Public Support for the Arts and Civil Religion

In keeping with the Communist revolution's general condemnation of Confucius and Confucian values, the Confucian rites all but disappeared in the early years of the Peoples' Republic of China. However, state sponsorship of religious ritual, once described by the People's Republic of China as an expression of "feudal superstition," has enjoyed a dramatic revival in contemporary China, with government-sponsored birthday celebrations of the Grand Master in his hometown of Qufu beginning in 2004.

Public performances of Confucian rites now enjoy government support in China. This reflects an emerging nationalism based on traditional Confucian values. Moreover, the "civil religion" of China, Korea, Japan, and Vietnam is highly ceremonial, and public gatherings such as school assemblies, graduations, inaugurations, and other commemorative events are promoted by state and local governments and are generally well attended. People enjoy and appreciate public ceremonies, and the kind of cynicism and lack of interest so often seen in the West is almost completely absent in East Asian contexts. Public ceremonial is highly valued in the East Asian cultural region.

Another remnant of Confucianism is an emphasis on artistic education and public support for the arts. China, Japan, Korea, Taiwan, Singapore, and Hong Kong all boast grand national theaters featuring some of the world's greatest musical and theatrical performers. Government-funded arts institutions can also be found in Japan (the Japan Arts Council), Taiwan (the National Culture and Arts Foundation), Korea (the Seoul Foundation for Arts and Culture), Hong Kong (the Hong Kong Arts Development Council), and so on. As a socialist state, China has consistently supported artistic expression, though severely curtailed by restrictions on artistic freedom.[6]

Hospitality, Social Grace, Emphasis on Social Identity

The traditional Confucian vision sees the self as a "center of relationships," internalizing societal norms of etiquette and cooperation. Relationships are constitutive of individual identity. As a result, the maintenance of harmonious family and social relationships is a deeply held personal commitment. Confucius extended the traditional meaning of *li* (narrowly defined as "rites" or "ceremonies") to a normative pattern for everyday life. *Li* refers to the proper patterns of behavior in all social encounters, in a living human context. The individual-in-community regards his or her personal relationships as essential to individual and social well-being and adopts a "ceremonial attitude" toward all persons.

The *li* of everyday life are so highly regarded in the East Asian cultural region that they are taken to be obvious. They are fundamental, so much so that they are not labeled as "Confucian," but simply as "human" and "right." In the details of social life, in the lessons taught to children, and in the patterns followed by adults, modern-day East Asians are unselfconsciously Confucian, as they have been for two millennia. The patterns of *li* are the social code or behavioral idiom of East Asian society. Once, in a public address sponsored by the Asia Society in Washington, DC, the Japanese ambassador to the United States was asked by a member of the American audience about reports of bullying among Japanese teenagers. "Are they really Japanese?" he asked, rhetorically. Acting in such a manner represents a rebellion against their cultural heritage.

The observance of *li* (as personal comportment) is so important that it plays a role in political disputes. One of the arguments advanced by the Taiwanese Independence Movement to promote a formal separation from Mainland China (China and Taiwan agreed in 1994 to a formula of "one China, two systems") is that the Mainland has "abandoned" the *li* of personal habits. Hong Kong and Taiwanese citizens complain that Mainland Chinese tourists are rude and impolite; this charge has received a fiery response from a popular Beijing professor, who has asserted that it is in fact the "renegade" provinces that have abandoned Confucian norms.[7]

Confucian Fundamentalism and the "National Studies Craze"

From the May Fourth Movement of the late 1910s to the Communist Great Leap Forward of the 1950s and 1960s, Confucianism was rejected as a dragon to be slain. So strong was the revolutionary condemnation of the Confucian tradition that any mention of Confucius or Confucianism would lead to imprisonment and black-listing, a situation that persisted well into the 1970s and 1980s. Since the mid-1980s, however, and especially in the decades since 1994, Confucianism has enjoyed a dramatic reversal of fortune, beginning with government support for the traditional rites. These include birthday celebrations of the Grand Master in his birthplace and provincial capitals, the production of children's primers on Confucian principles for elementary schools, and the establishment of programs in "national studies" (國學, *guoxue*) at the country's most prestigious universities. Some schools have found that special programs in national studies have been financially profitable in continuing education and community outreach initiatives.

The national studies movement is indicative of general trends in contemporary Chinese society:

- the revival of cultural Confucianism as a symbol of Chinese uniqueness;
- intense nationalism, expressed in neo-Confucian terms;
- political Confucianism as the foundation for government restrictions on social freedoms;
- assertion of Confucianism as the solution to global problems and as a corrective to (if not as a direct replacement of) democratic institutions.

Confucian fundamentalism and the "national studies craze" are controversial even within China itself, but it is doubtlessly true that Confucian values, for so long regarded simply as a remnant of China's feudal past, are now expressed openly and forcefully, as the driving ideology of China's political and cultural future.[8]

Notes

1   On the recent history of admissions at the University of California, Berkeley, see, for example, PBS Frontline, "History of Admissions at UC Berkeley," at

www.pbs.org/wgbh/pages/frontline/shows/sats/etc/ucb.html (accessed July 22, 2013). Numerous articles and books address the educational achievements and hurdles faced by America's "model minority," descendants of East Asian immigrants. One of the most talked about is Amy Chua's book *Battle Hymn of the Tiger Mother* (Oxford and New York: Penguin Press, 2011).

2   One of the most direct statements of the contemporary application of Confucian-inspired "soft authoritarianism" was articulated by the former president of Singapore, Lee Kuan Yew. See Fareed Zararia, "A Conversation with Lee Kuan Yu," *Foreign Affairs* (March/April 1994). On the growth of Confucian dialectic within today's Chinese government and educational system, see, for example, Andy Yee, "China: The Coming of the Age of Political Confucianism?" *Global Voices*, February 5, 2011, at http://globalvoicesonline.org/2011/02/05/china-the-coming-of-age-of-political -confucianism/ (accessed February 29, 2012).

3   Many sources can be consulted for greater detail. Some interesting ones are Judith Banister, David Bloom and Larry Rosenberg, "Population Aging and Economic Growth in China, at http://www.hsph.harvard.edu/pgda/WorkingPapers/2010/ PGDA_WP_53.pdf; *The Economist*, "Asian Demography: The Flight from Marriage," at http://www.economist.com/node/21526329; Mari Tsuruwaka, "The Declining Birthrate and the Aging Population in the East Asian Region: From the 13th Conference on the Aging Population in the East Asian Region," at http://www .jarc.net/int/?p=68 (all websites accessed February 29, 2012).

4   See ongoing investigative reports by the China Media Project, a Project of the Journalism and Media Studies Centre of the University of Hong Kong (http:// cmp.hku.hk/, accessed February 29, 2012).

5   "The pursuit of a life worth living in Japan and the United States," *Ethnology* 35: 1 (1996), p. 51ff.

6   For an overview of public funding for the arts in China, see Tobias Zuser, "How the Cultural Sector Works in China," at http://www.hitangandccc.com/blog/2011/11/ financing-funding-cultural-projects-china (accessed February 29, 2012).

7   This hot-button issue in 2012 has received extensive press coverage. For example, see Jens Kastner, "Hong Kong Clash Stirs the Pot for Taiwan," *Asia Times Online*, February 9, 2012, at http://www.atimes.com/atimes/China/NB09Ad01.html (accessed February 29, 2012).

8   For further reading on the Confucian revival in China, see Ruiping Fan, editor, *The Renaissance of Confucianism in Contemporary China* (Dordrecht: Springer, 2011).

Part III
The Taoist Tradition

8

What Is Taoism?

"Taoism" refers to a religious and philosophical system that promotes holistic well-being and ritual mastery of the spirit world. Taoism is often contrasted with Confucianism, but it is better to think of Taoism and Confucianism as two aspects of a single religious tradition; Chinese themselves, throughout the centuries, have regarded Taoism and Confucianism in complementary terms. Taoism arose in China, but now can be said to be a "world religion," with adherents in Europe and America as well as in East Asia.

Until recent years, the Western encounter with Taoism was focused on the literary and philosophical tradition of the Zhou Dynasty, the same period in which Confucius and the early Confucians Mengzi and Xunzi lived. This tradition was associated with the writings of a "hermit intellectual" named Zhuangzi (莊子) in a book by the same name and with the writings of a "wise sage" named Laozi (老子) in a book attributed to him and known by the title *Daodejing* (道德經). For many decades, Western knowledge was limited to these books in English translation, and the entire rich history of religious institutions, rituals, and individual practice of Taoism was all but ignored. This situation has been rectified, and, for the past 25 to 30 years, the study of Chinese religions has been focused, quite rightly, on the history of Taoism over its two millennia of development and elaboration.

Scholars have been divided on the issue of how to relate the "philosophy" of the early sages with the "religion" of the ritual tradition; even in Chinese, they are referred to differently, as *Daojia* (道家, the "school" of the Tao) and *Daojiao* (道教, the "religion" of the Tao). Simply for purposes of organization, the present book will treat these two aspects sequentially; but it should be understood that they are interpenetrating. Both the *Daodejing* and the *Book of Zhuangzi* anticipate the subsequent religious tradition, and this tradition, in turn, refers back to the early sages with reverence, deifying Laozi as "Lord Lao."

Asian Religions: A Cultural Perspective, First Edition. Randall L. Nadeau.
© 2014 John Wiley & Sons, Ltd. Published 2014 by John Wiley & Sons, Ltd.

Still, historians cannot find evidence for a fully developed Taoist religion at the time of the early books, and so it makes sense to treat them separately here.

We should remind ourselves, as we did in Chapter 1, that the words and names that we employ to describe Asian religions all originated in the West – they appeared first in English, German, or French, and they were translated into Chinese and Japanese only later. So the labels we use – "religion," "philosophy," even "Confucianism" and "Taoism" – are Western inventions, imposed upon Chinese culture to make sense of its history in familiar terms. "Taoism" is an especially amorphous name, and I have intentionally retained the traditional English spelling "Taoism," as opposed to the preferred Romanization today ("Daoism"), in order to underscore the fact that the designation is not indigenous to China. It is not autochthonous, to use a scientific term, and "Taoism" is not an autonym – it is not a word used by Chinese to describe their religion. In fact I can say that I have never met a Chinese who identified him- or herself as a "Taoist" or as a "Confucian," except in very special circumstances.

Not only are the Taoist religion and Taoist philosophy difficult to differentiate; so, too, are Taoism and Confucianism. The use of these names should not suggest two completely distinct entities. At the elite, intellectual levels of Chinese culture, members of the scholar–gentry class were as likely to cite the Taoist classics as the "Four Books" of Confucianism, and they incorporated both Taoist and Confucian modes of living into their daily lives. At the level of popular culture, the same was and remains true: enter any community temple and you will find both traditions represented without differentiation – an image of the deified Laozi next to placards promoting social harmony, righteousness, and other Confucian virtues; ritual practices that borrow from both traditions; and temple talks citing both Taoist philosophy and Confucian learning.

Confucianism and Taoism interpenetrate to such an extent that it is more accurate to describe them as a single "Chinese religion." Notably, in the Chinese case, there is no one word parallel to "Hinduism" – a label simply designating the "religion" (in fact, religions) of the people of India. Just as the word "Hinduism" suggests a false unity in India, the words "Confucianism" and "Taoism" are equally misleading in that they suggest a conceptual separation in Chinese religious thought and practice.

As for Buddhism, the third of the "great religions" of China, another abstraction can be made, and this book will treat Buddhism (including its Indian, Chinese, and Japanese forms) as a separate entity in Parts V and VI. In China's case this is acceptable, as the culture itself has tended to perceive Buddhism as a discrete entity. It is the only one of the three traditions that was not indigenous to China, and it arrived relatively late in Chinese history – in the first century CE. Certainly Taoist and Buddhist institutions – temples, abbeys/monasteries, and so on – are readily distinguishable. But, once again, there is no doubt that scholar–gentry and contemporary intellectuals fully embrace Buddhism as part of a single cultural tradition and that common folk fully incorporate elements of all three forms into their lives. We can only say that the demarcations presented in this book are heuristic devices – useful for thinking, but highly inaccurate at the level of everyday belief and practice.

With these cautions in mind, we can now turn to the organization of this part of the book and to the topics we will explore under the general rubric of "Taoism."

After some introductory notes in Chapter 8, Chapter 9 summarizes the principal themes of the two great classics of Taoist philosophy: the *Book of Zhuangzi* and the *Daodejing*. These texts are the ones best known to generations of Western students of Taoism, and they still are of major significance to Taoism as a global religious phenomenon.

Chapters 10 to 12 discuss three dimensions of religious Taoism, employing yin–yang cosmology as the organizing principle: the temporal, the spatial, and the personal.

Chapter 13 examines Taoism as a global religion and its contemporary relevance to the twenty-first century.

Philosophical Taoism

The phrase "philosophical Taoism" is usually applied simply to the ideas presented in the Taoist classics of the pre-Han period, especially the *Book of Zhuangzi* and the *Daodejing*. In the following chapter we will look at the major themes of these two works; but, since so much has been written and speculated about their authorship, we should begin with a brief look at the history of the texts themselves.

The *Daodejing* is usually given first billing as the seminal text of the Taoist tradition, and several scholars have claimed that it is the most translated text in human history, outnumbering even the translations of the Bible. This is a somewhat deceptive claim – the *Daodejing* is certainly not as widely read as the Bible – but the sheer number of different translations attests both to its worldwide popularity and to its impenetrability: it is an extraordinarily abstruse work. Here are a few translations just of the first sentence of the first chapter: 道可道非常道 (*Dao ke dao fei chang dao*).

- "The tao that can be described is not the eternal Tao." *J. H. McDonald*
- "The Way that can be told of is not an unvarying Way." *Arthur Waley*
- "The Tao that can be followed is not the eternal Tao." *Charles Muller*
- "The Way that can be experienced is not true." *Peter Merel*

- "The Tao that can be trodden is not the enduring and unchanging Tao." *James Legge*
- "Even the finest teaching is not the Tao itself." *Stan Rosenthal*
- "What we call 'The Dao' is not the Dao forever." *Randall Nadeau*

Multiply this perplexity at least by the number of the book's chapters (81), and you can get some idea of its "mysterious power" (to use a phrase employed in the book itself, 玄德, *xuan-de*, to describe the Dao).

Of "Laozi" himself, the purported author of the *Daodejing*, the only thing that can be said with any certainty is that no such person ever existed or put the *Daodejing* into writing. Legends began to circulate as early as the fourth century BCE of an extraordinarily wise sage, born at the age of 81 (hence his name *Laozi*, 老子, "Old Infant"), who so disdained the world's ways that he mounted an ox and retired to the barbarian reaches of the West.

This was not before meeting up with Confucius, whom Laozi called a "dead branch." (Their meeting is depicted in Figure 8.1.) According to the legendary biography of the Taoist master, Confucius asked Laozi about the *li* (禮) and was so impressed by the Old Infant's enigmatic responses that he described him as a "soaring dragon."

As he departed from the Middle Kingdom through a mountain pass, Laozi deigned to share his wisdom in a text of 5,000 characters – another name for the *Daodejing* in Chinese is the *wuqianzi jing* (五千字經), "the 5,000-character classic" – expounding the Way (道, *Dao*) and its Power (德, *De*). To compound the legend even further, Taoists of the fifth and sixth centuries CE claimed that

Figure 8.1 Statue depicting the legendary meeting between Confucius and Laozi. Photo taken by the author at Qingyuan shan (清源山), Fujian Province (June 2009).

Laozi ended up in India, where he "transformed himself" into none other than Śākyamuni Buddha and "converted the barbarians" to Taoism! This legend arose during a period of intense Buddhist–Taoist rivalry in China, but it is still repeated today, being used now to promote the underlying harmony and compatibility of the two traditions.

These are certainly fantastical stories, with no bearing in reality. Moreover, the *Daodejing* itself – as it is currently known and has most often been translated – dates to no earlier than the third century CE, some 500 to 1,000 years after the Sage supposedly lived. However, fragments of the text have been discovered in recent years at burial sites in Mawangdui and Guodian, China – these fragments date to the second and fourth centuries BCE. Though incomplete, the fragments do indicate the existence of a collection of aphorisms that can be attributed to the collective memory of a group of wise persons or elders, who passed on their wisdom orally until some of their sayings were written down, on silk or bamboo strips, well before the time of Confucius. One scholar sees in the name "Laozi" a hint of this collective authorship, translating the name as "The Elders."[1]

More can be said with certainty of Zhuangzi. He did exist, and though the writings attributed to him were substantially written by others, they contain plenty of biographical information. As part of the educated elite, Zhuangzi was well versed in the philosophical traditions of his day. He cites Laozi (7 times, all in the Outer Chapters) as well as Confucius (3 times in the Inner Chapters, 15 times in the Outer Chapters, 13 times in the Miscellaneous Chapters): he certainly allied himself with the former and distinguished himself from the latter. One of the most amusing features of the *Book of Zhuangzi* (as much a book of humor as anything else) is the use of a character named "Confucius" as a Taoist teacher who often says things that Confucius himself would have found abhorrent. Despite his own intellectual attainments, Zhuangzi saw no value in book learning or formal education and rebelled against conventional social norms. He was a "noble recluse," the first in a line of many such figures in Chinese history that extends even to the present day. The *Book of Zhuangzi* reflects an aesthetic sensitivity that celebrates rebelliousness, intuitive insight, mysticism, and irrationality. We will explore these themes in detail in Chapter 9.

Yin–Yang Cosmology

Though the cosmological system of yin and yang originated with the Book of Changes (易經, *Yijing*, conventionally Romanized as *I Ching*) before the Common Era, it was not fully developed until the Song Dynasty (eleventh century CE). From that point on it became a foundational symbol of religious Taoism.

Figure 8.2   Taiji tu (太極圖), "Diagram of the Supreme Ultimate."

Etymologically related to darkness and light, yin and yang represent balanced interpenetrating states of being and potentiality, which are always described in Taoism in dynamic terms: ever moving, ever revolving, ever circulating. Yin represents receptivity, stillness, and regression; yang represents activity, movement, and aggression. Yin is identified with women or with feminine attributes; yang is identified with men or with masculine attributes. Within Chinese religion Taoism is yin-oriented, Confucianism is yang-oriented. However, as the often replicated Diagram of the Supreme Ultimate illustrates (Figure 8.2), these forces are not seen to be in conflict with one another, but rather exist in a complementary relationship; that is to say, one cannot exist without the other. Humans should strive to preserve the two forces in equal measure in their social interactions, in the natural environment, and in their physical selves.

To the extent that social life and the values favored by the Confucian tradition reward the yang attributes of activity and aggression, the Taoist tradition has tended to favor the yin qualities of stillness and receptivity. As a counterbalancing force to the socially dominant Confucian tradition, both philosophical and religious Taoism favor yin over yang. Traditionally, these qualities have been associated with women, and in both theory and practice Taoism has promoted feminine attributes and women's power. The *Daodejing* is especially clear about upholding feminine qualities, and it likens the Dao to a cosmic mother. Within the Taoist religion priestly functions were shared equally between men and women, and even today Taoist abbeys recruit both male and female practitioners. Community temples also feature powerful gods and goddesses, from the imperial Wang Ye (王爺, a collective name for a number of gods) to Mazu (媽祖, goddess of the sea), the Eternal Venerable Mother (無生老母, *Wusheng laomu*), and the Queen Mother of the West (西王母, *Xiwangmu*). We will explore these themes further in the following chapters.

Note

1   Michael LaFargue, *The Tao of the Tao Te Ching* (Albany, NY: State University of New York Press, 1992).

9

Philosophical Taoism

In this chapter we will explore major themes of the classics of Taoist philosophy, the *Daodejing* (道德經), traditionally attributed to the "Old Infant" Laozi (老子), and the *Book of Zhuangzi*, whose first seven chapters (the so-called "Inner Chapters") were written by Zhuangzi (莊子) in the third century BCE. These are unusual and perplexing books, as much aesthetic as they are philosophical, promoting mythic consciousness, intuitive thinking, and a suspension of critical rationality. They are works of poetry and fantasy that express perplexity and doubt about the very words they are written in: their words overcome words, like fire used to overcome fire. They employ imagistic language to disengage the logical, conceptual functions of the mind.

Major Themes of Philosophical Taoism

The themes to be investigated under this heading are:

- anti-Confucianism;
- uselessness (*wuyong* 無用);
- naturalness and spontaneity (*ziran* 自然);
- non-action (*wuwei* 無為);
- intuition;
- transmutability (*hua* 化);
- the "uncarved block" (*pu* 樸).

Asian Religions: A Cultural Perspective, First Edition. Randall L. Nadeau.
© 2014 John Wiley & Sons, Ltd. Published 2014 by John Wiley & Sons, Ltd.

Anti-Confucianism

In the *Zhuangzi* and the *Daodejing*, the highest values and goals of Confucianism are either explicitly rejected or they are subjected to unrelenting ridicule. When Zhuangzi has a character named "Confucius" speak his mind, the "master" advocates empty-headedness – literally "the fasting of the mind." Zhuangzi's "Confucius" says that we should close our eyes and practice "quiet sitting," cultivating stillness. As for the Confucian *li* (禮), Zhuangzi says they are best abandoned; he did not even mourn his wife's passing, instead beating on a drum and singing a ditty.

The *Daodejing* expresses similar sentiments: Confucian kindness (仁, *ren*) and righteousness (義, *yi*) reflect the "decline" of the Dao, not its culmination, and "sageliness and wisdom" (at least in Confucian terms) are explicitly rejected. Laozi envisions a country where there are no books or schools, no government institutions, not even writing or record-keeping, and where people are perfectly content with their simple huts and plain clothes. The *Daodejing* turns many Confucian values on their head. Instead of being whole, straight, full, new, famous, and luminous, Laozi says he would prefer to be crooked, bent, hollow, worn, hidden, and receding. "Mine is the mind of a fool – it's empty," he says, and he wishes to be "floating in the dark . . . drifting with the wind."[1]

Uselessness (wuyong, 無用)

The philosophical Taoists were part of an early Chinese eremitic[2] tradition, defined in opposition to government service and Confucian norms. Zhuangzi said he would rather be a turtle dragging his tail in the mud than a high-paid counselor to a mighty lord. He rejected public display and social service in favor of a simple life in a natural setting. Government service just gets you killed. The heroes of Zhuangzi's tales and stories are misfits, cripples, madmen, hunchbacks, gnarled trees, and giant gourds; what these characters have in common is that they can't be "used" for conventional purposes such as going to war, performing hard labor, being cut down for the construction of ships and houses, or being molded into ladles and spoons.

Ironically, such "uselessness" is extremely "useful" – Zhuangzi calls this the "usefulness of uselessnesss" (無用之用, *wuyong zhi yong*). Cripples and misfits live long because they are of no use to the state; gnarled trees live long because they are of no use to carpenters; weak and docile animals are left alone because they are of no use to builders and farmers. Then again, they possess a different kind of utility, if we just know how to look for it: instead of cutting down a giant tree, Zhuangzi recommends that the carpenter have a nap under its shady outstretched limbs; instead of discarding a huge gourd (which is too bitter to eat and too big to shape into a utensil), Zhuangzi suggests that the artisan fashion it into a boat and float merrily down the stream. Similarly, the mind can be put to uses other than rationalistic thinking: dreaming, imagining, creating images and sounds, art and music. We usually think of "schoolwork" (education and learning) as "useful" enterprises, but the Taoists don't see the point. "Stop learning!" says Laozi; "you'll stop worrying."

Naturalness and spontaneity (ziran, 自然)

Both Confucianism and Taoism emphasize "harmony" as a primary goal; but for Taoists, the Confucian scope of harmony is too narrow, extending only to the harmonizing of human relationships. Taoism advocates instead a harmonizing of the self with the cosmos, especially the natural world. The Taoist classics are full of trees, fish, bugs, streams, mountains, oxen, weasels, rabbits, birds. Taoist-inspired landscape paintings, perhaps the most representative and best known of China's contributions to the history of art, show humans in harmony with nature, usually by indicating the vastness of nature towering over tiny human figures who have found their proper place within the natural scene.

In Chinese the word for nature, *ziran* (自然), also designates personal naturalness, "doing what comes naturally," "spontaneity" – literally, the characters mean "self-so-ly," that is, in a manner of self-becoming, self-generating, self-directing, self-evolving. This is the way of nature, and we should pattern our own lives on nature's self-unfolding.

One of my favorite anecdotes from the *Book of Zhuangzi* recounts a conversation between Zhuangzi and his friend Huizi. They are gazing at some minnows swimming about in the shallows below a bridge over the River Hao.

Zhuangzi said:	"How I love the happiness of fish."
Huizi argued with him:	"You are not a fish. How would you know that they are happy?"
Zhuangzi replied,	"You are not me, so how would you know that I do not know that they are happy? In fact, even in asking the question, you knew that I knew it. I know it standing here on the bridge over the River Hao."[3]

From a purely logical point of view, Huizi is probably right, and Zhuangzi's argument is rather spurious. But what he is expressing is a different way of looking at nature, perhaps a more sympathetic or empathic approach, which relies on intuition rather than rational thinking and argumentation. Zhuangzi's "trick" is simply to show the pointlessness of argument – and to enjoy nature intuitively, "just as it is."

While China in the past century has been hell-bent on catching up with the industrialized world, with horrendous consequences for the natural environment, we have in Taoism a home-grown system of values that might one day stem the flow of unbridled growth and its negative environmental impact. One example of this is in the traditional use of *fengshui* (風水, "geomancy") to design and construct human habitations in a way that is environmentally friendly and naturally harmonious; we will look at some examples in Chapter 11.

Non-action (wuwei, 無為)

The doctrine of "uselessness" in civil or social affairs is extended to one's personal self-cultivation through the idea of *wuwei*, "non-action." Partly this means just what it says: simplicity, stillness, quiescence. These are Taoist values, and they are part of the Taoist meditative tradition – think of the slow, peaceful movement of *taijiquan* (太極拳, "shadow boxing"), which, while not literally "not moving," certainly takes physical movement to its most flowing, tranquil level. In fact "flowing" or "going with the flow" is perhaps a better way of thinking of *wuwei* than through its literal meaning of "non-action," and we can consider *wuwei* to be synonymous with *ziran*, "spontaneity." *Wuwei* designates non-purposive or non-manipulative action, non-interference, taking no artificial action, letting things take their own course; spontaneous transformation, non-aggressive manipulation. It means "unforced action" or "unforced living."

As with naturalness, mastery of this "non-active" approach is quite powerful. Laozi likens it to water. Though water is "soft and yielding," nothing in the world is stronger. Water "dwells in the lowest places," yet it can wear down the hardest rock. To be "like water" means to be yielding, supple, receptive, and yet powerful, strong, and successful.

An interesting twist on "non-action" is its application to governing and to physical conflict. In fact it became a principle adopted by kings and warriors. In the case of government, the application of "non-action" is what we might call a doctrine of *laissez faire*, where the light hand of government produces a more robust society; in the case of physical combat, the idea of "uselessness" is applied in the "soft method" (the literal meaning of *judō*) whereby the aggressor's action is used against him. As the *Daodejing* states, "with non-action, there is nothing that cannot be done (無為而無不為, *wuwei er wu bu wei*)."[4] There have been points in history when the *Daodejing* was employed as a manual for governing, and some scholars speculate that the book was originally written for this purpose.

Intuition

We have seen how much Zhuangzi admires intuition over discursive rationality in his appreciation for the "happiness of fish." The *Book of Zhuangzi* employs myths and fabulous stories, humor and paradox, to frustrate the "thinking" mind and to cultivate a "feeling" mind. The heroes of the book are not only "crippled in body" but also "crippled in thought": they are madmen or simpletons. This is consistent with Laozi's wish to "return to infancy" in the *Daodejing* and to be an "idiot" or a "fool."

The use of intuition is not so much a *rejection* of thinking as it is a *new way* of thinking, a "right-brained" approach to solving problems. The *Book of Zhuangzi* tells one story of a meeting between a powerful ruler, Lord Wenhui, and a cook named Ding. Cook Ding explains how he uses "spirit" rather than "thought" when butchering an ox. He is so skillful and experienced that he never hacks into the bone, and he needs to sharpen his knife only once every 19 years! He is like a dancer moving to music. He plays in "nothingness." Lord Wenhui is so impressed by Cook Ding's intuitive method that he begs to become Cook Ding's disciple in spiritual self-cultivation.

This kind of knowledge is far superior to our more rationalistic ways of thinking. Concerning factual knowledge, Zhuangzi expresses great doubt, and, at the level of language and learning, he is a thorough relativist. How do I know what I know? Do I really know what I think I know, and not know what I think I do not know? Do I know what is right, what is true, what is beautiful? Zhuangzi presents an illustration. People would not like to sleep in a precarious position high up in a tree, but a monkey would; people would not like to sleep in a damp marsh, but a leech would. People like to eat meat, but deer eat grass, centipedes eat snakes, and hawks eat mice. Men think that "Maoqiang and Lady Li were beautiful," but if deer saw them they would break into a run, if fish saw them they would swim to the bottom of the stream, if birds saw them they would fly away. "The way I see it, the rules of benevolence [*ren*] and righteousness [*yi*] and the paths of right and wrong are all hopelessly snarled and jumbled. How would I know anything about such discriminations?" (book 2, chapter 11).

Transmutability (hua 化)

The imaginative thinking that the Taoist philosophers inspire is flexible, adaptable, and creative. It is thinking that "wanders" and "flows." How do their words stimulate intuitive thinking? How do their words help us to "forget words"? How do they "free" our minds? Zhuangzi's imagistic language and flights of fancy represent an alternative way of thinking and perceiving. The world of Taoist creation is not linear and concrete, but cyclical (even meandering) and abstract. It is a world characterized by "transmutability" (化, *hua*).

Figure 9.1 Ike no Taiga (池大雅, 1723–1776), Zhuang Zi dreaming of a butterfly. Private Collection / Photo © Christie's Images / The Bridgeman Art Library.

Zhuangzi was fascinated by transformation of every kind, and he even seems to have toyed with a kind of early evolutionary thinking. He does not lament his wife's death because he imagines that she has "changed into something else," and he looks forward to his own death for the same reason. He is intrigued by transformations that he observes (or imagines) in nature: marsh grasses turning into worms and eels, then, in turn, into rooster tails, and, eventually, into his own arm! Probably one of the most commonly cited stories from the *Book of Zhuangzi* recounts Zhuangzi's "butterfly dream" (Figure 9.1). He dreamt he was a butterfly, flitting and fluttering about, enjoying its unfettered wandering. But when he awakened he wondered, "Am I Zhuangzi having dreamt I was a butterfly? Or am I a butterfly, dreaming that I am Zhuangzi? Such is the 'transformation of things' (物化 *wuhua*)" (book 2, chapter 14). Perhaps Zhuangzi was drunk: drunkenness is another state of mind that he celebrates. "He who dreams of drinking wine," he laments, "will weep when morning comes." But he also predicts a "great awakening" (an "ultimate transformation," in Frederic Streng's words), when we will all realize that "this has been but a dream," and we will see things as they truly are (book 2, chapter 12).

In the very first chapter of the *Book of Zhuangzi* the myth is told of a great creature, a fish the size of a whale, whose name is Kun (鲲). The name itself is ironic and mind-boggling, as the word *kun* refers to fish roe, which is generally very tiny, but here it names a fish larger than any fish we can imagine. Kun is so big that, when it swims by, ships are raised above their moorings. Kun swims about, unobstructed and free, and then, rising up, it transforms itself into a great bird named Peng (鵬), whose wings are so wide that they are like clouds traversing the sky. Peng flies to the Lake of Heaven, far to the south. Looking up, a tiny dove and a cicada marvel at the creature flying above them. It is an incredible sight, and they are amazed. But they are also disdainful; they are content with their own short lives and limited range. "Where does he think he's going?" they ask. Zhuangzi comments: "The short-lived cannot live up to the long-lived; those with little understanding cannot live up to those with great understanding" (book 1, chapters 1–2). Clearly Zhuangzi is no relativist: the power of creative self-transformation gives one the ability to "soar above the world's ways" and to adopt a higher, all-encompassing point of view.

The "Uncarved Block" (pu, 樸)

Perhaps the whole of Taoist philosophy as a system of thought and as a system of values can be summed up in one word: *pu* (樸), the "Uncarved Block." Literally the term refers to an uncarved block of wood, a natural object in its original state, before it has been cut, whittled, shaped, or molded by outside forces. Both the *Book of Zhuangzi* and the *Daodejing* advocate becoming "uncarved" – going back to a state of being without knowledge, without language, without thinking and calculating, without concepts of good and evil, without desires. The character *pu* (樸) is used in modern Chinese to mean "plain, unadorned, basic." It also means "unbridled, untamed": a wild horse is a *pu-ma* (樸馬). To "practice *pu*" means to be simple, honest, and unsophisticated.

These are not just philosophical ideas: they are lessons in living. Laozi says he wishes to become like "dry wood" – without desires, without worries, without frustration. He seeks to cultivate a state of being that is "empty," "unmoving," focused, and still: "I reach for emptiness and hold firmly to stillness" (*Daodejing*, chapter 16). The *Daodejing* directs its readers to "manifest simplicity, embrace the uncarved block, reduce selfishness, have few desires" (*Daodejing*, chapter 19). Similarly, the *Book of Zhuangzi* contains hints of early meditation practices that were later cited in Taoist religious texts and may eventually have come to influence Zen Buddhism: Zhuangzi would have us cultivate a "mind like a mirror," with no "active thinking" of its own, and he would have us "sit in emptiness"; this, he says, is the "fasting" of the mind (book 6, chapter 9).

Let us finish this chapter with a longer quotation from the *Daodejing*: here Laozi, the imagined author of the text, describes the terms *Dao* (道, "Way") and *De* (德, "Power") that make up its title:

> When superior persons hear about the *Dao*, they do their best to put it into practice. When average persons hear about the *Dao*, they preserve it for awhile,

but then it disappears. When the lowest persons hear about the *Dao*, they laugh at it. If they didn't laugh, it wouldn't be the *Dao*. That's why it's been said,

> Brightening the *Dao* is more like darkening it;
> Advancing the *Dao* is more like pushing it back;
> Universalizing the *Dao* is more like differentiating things.
> Raising *de* is more like troughing it;
> Ennobling *de* is more like discrediting it;
> Enlarging *de* is more like diminishing it;
> Strengthening *de* is more like exhausting it;
> Witnessing for *de* is more like making a retraction.

A great square has no corners. A great vessel is completed only after a long time. A great note produces a weak sound. A great image has no shape. The *Dao* hides in namelessness. So, the *Dao* alone excels in endowing and in bringing things to completion. (*Daodejing*, chapter 41)

Notes

1   Laozi, *Daodejing*, ch. 20. Chinese Text Project. At http://ctext.org/dao-de-jing (accessed July 17, 2013). All translations from the *Daodejing* are by the author. Among the many good translations of the *Daodejing*, I would recommend Michael LaFargue, *The Tao of the Tao Te Ching* (Albany, NY: State University of New York Press, 1992).

2   The word "eremitic" is etymologically related to the English word "hermit" – a recluse, one who has rejected civil society, its duties, commitments, and entanglements. The common point of origin is the ancient Greek *erēmos*, "solitary, empty, deserted."

3   *The Book of Zhuangzi*, "Autumn Floods," ch. 13. Chinese Text Project. At http://ctext.org/zhuangzi (accessed July 17, 2013). All translations from the *Zhuangzi* are by the author. For a complete translation, I would recommend Burton Watson, *The Complete Works of Chuang Tzu* (New York: Columbia University Press, 1968).

4   Laozi, *Daodejing*, chs. 37, 48.

10

Temporal Dimensions of Yin–Yang Cosmology

Having reviewed some of the predominant values of philosophical Taoism, we turn in the next three chapters to Taoism as a religious system. Our goal here is not to review the history of Taoism or to describe its rich liturgical traditions, which are the focus of much contemporary scholarship on Taoism. Here we will examine Taoism as a lived and living tradition, as it is practiced by people in China and around the world. We will use yin–yang cosmology to organize this overview: yin–yang cosmology in its temporal dimensions (relating to time), in its spatial dimensions (relating to space), and in its personal dimensions (relating to physical and spiritual self-cultivation).

The Beginning of Time

In the Abrahamic traditions of Judaism, Christianity, and Islam, when we think of the temporal dimensions of religion, we tend to think first of the "beginning" of time, that is, the myth of the creation of the cosmos in seven days.[1] This myth is of primary importance; after all, adherents of these traditions identify the Supreme Being first and foremost as the Creator of all things. God is mighty and powerful, and, perhaps most importantly of all, our very existence depends upon God. Consequently the myth of creation takes pride of place at the beginning of the first book of the Bible, in the first chapters of the book of Genesis.

Most of us in the West are familiar with the basic contours of this myth, which tells of six separate acts of creation over six days, culminating in a "day of rest" on the seventh day: light on the first day, land on the second, vegetation on the third, the heavens on the fourth, animals on the fifth, and humans on the sixth. Significantly, each of God's acts of creation involves *differentiation*.

Asian Religions: A Cultural Perspective, First Edition. Randall L. Nadeau.
© 2014 John Wiley & Sons, Ltd. Published 2014 by John Wiley & Sons, Ltd.

That is, God creates by separating one thing from another: on the first day, light from darkness (Genesis 1: 4); on the second, water from land (Genesis 1: 10); on the third, seed-bearing plants from fruit-bearing plants (Genesis 1: 12); on the fourth, the light of the day (the sun) from the light of the night (the moon) (Genesis 1: 16); on the fifth, animals that fly from animals that swim (Genesis 1: 20); and on the sixth, male humans from female humans (Genesis 1: 27). Therefore *duality* is a fundamental characteristic of Western thinking – "from the very beginning." No wonder that, even today, the Chinese describe the West as an "oppositional culture" (對抗文化, *duikang wenhua*): our tendency to think in dualistic terms is evident in politics, the arts, gender relations, morality and ethics, and virtually every other aspect of life. In his *Patterns of Faith Around the World*, Wilfred Cantwell Smith describes the "conflict dualism" of Western cosmology:

> We in the West are familiar with [a] type of dualism, which we may call *conflict dualism*. In this, two basic forces are in collision, as opposites that struggle and clash: good and evil, right and wrong, black and white, true and false. This type of dualism . . . found its way into the Jewish, Christian, and the Islamic traditions . . . In our religious traditions a Devil, over against God, was long accepted; Heaven and Hell are postulated; and the saved and the damned, the sheep and the goats . . . If not God and the Devil, at least God and the world, man and nature, matter and spirit, either/or.[2]

In Taoism, myths of creation are not as important as they are in the West.[3] The gods of Taoism are not creator gods; rather they are gods of health and longevity, of weather, of wealth, of community service and martial heroism, of fidelity and friendship – responding to the everyday lives of their devotees. Still, we do find a cosmogonic myth in the yin–yang cosmological texts, and, though it is not widely known by Chinese today, its principles are certainly fundamental to Chinese thinking about life, nature, and personal well-being. So the myth is worth investigating from a comparative point of view. How does the Genesis myth compare with the traditional Chinese cosmological conception? How does the Chinese cosmogonic myth illustrate the idea of opposing forces that are *complementary* rather than *conflicting*?

According to the *Huainanzi*, a cosmological treatise composed in the Han Dynasty (around the time of Christ), the universe came into being not by virtue of the acts of a divine being, but in a thoroughly naturalistic way. At the beginning of time there was simply a great sea, lacking differentiation, shape, or form. The text describes this sea as *hundun* (混沌), "chaos." The Chinese characters 餛飩 are better known in English as "wonton": it is both appropriate and amusing that, in a culture that has so much pride in its cuisine, the cosmos began as soup! Note, also, that wontons are egg-shaped dumplings, and the idea of the world emerging from a "cosmic egg" is a theme shared by many cultures.

Emerging from this amorphous, vague, and chaotic sea there rose a vapor or steam, called in Chinese *qi* (氣). *Qi* is an extraordinarily important concept in Taoism, as we will see further in Chapter 12. The character for *qi* shows a steaming pot of rice: as the water boils in the pot, the steam's energy causes the heavy lid to shake and rattle. So, while concretely *qi* means vapor, steam, or breath, the character symbolizes energy, strength, and vitality; its constant flow and circulation is essential to physical and spiritual well-being.

Returning to the myth, as the *qi* rises from the sea of *hundun*, it separates into two forces or potentialities, called *yangqi* (陽氣) and *yinqi* (陰氣), yang energy and yin energy. The *yangqi* is light and airy, energetic and hot: it forms fire, and from fire comes the heat of the sun and stars. The *yinqi* is heavy and cool: it sinks and precipitates, forming water and the earth. The oscillating energy of *yangqi* and *yinqi* creates a cosmic breath, whose yang-exhalations and yin-inhalations are vital for the creative unfolding of the cosmos. This pattern of oscillation and of the eternal dynamic of cosmic breath creates a wave of energy: the Way, Path, or *Dao* (道) of the universe (Figure 10.1).

What mysterious power the universe contains, evolving from creation and sustaining all life! This process, this *Dao*, is, for Laozi, the One, the Mother, the Beginning, the Great Storehouse. Coming into existence before the "ten thousand things," it is "vague, elusive, impossible to grasp." It is beyond description; all that Laozi can say is that the *Dao* is "profound, distant, and vast" (*Daodejing*, chapter 25). Unlike the Creator God of the Abrahamic traditions, the *Dao* is not anthropomorphized – it has no human form or attributes. Moreover, the *Dao* is not identified with the moment of creation but with the vitality of the creation as a whole, in its whole temporal scope; it is continually coming into existence, and it is never complete. The Chinese character for *Dao* (道) shows a running animal. How is a running animal related to a "path" (the literal meaning of *Dao*)? Because natural paths – paths made by animals in the forest

Figure 10.1   *Dao*: The Path, Way, cosmic motion or principle.

or along a stream – are never finished; they are constantly coming into shape as they are used, as they evolve. Taoism, like the cosmogonic myth from the *Huainanzi*, is a tradition that emphasizes unfolding processes over static states, verbs over nouns, motion and adaptation, transformation and change. It is evolutionary and dynamic.

Certainly there is a kind of dualism here: the dualism of yin and yang. But Chinese dualism is complementary. Without yin and yang working together – harmonized and balanced – there can be no life, just as there can be no life without breath – that is, without both inhalation and exhalation. This is the cosmic breath, the ebb and flow of the universe.

Putting these two cosmogonic myths side by side, we see how differently Taoism conceives of life and the universe: dynamic rather than static, emphasizing becoming over being, a self-contained and self-generating universe with no external creator. And, so far, there is no mention of humans: unlike the Abrahamic traditions, Taoism affirms neither anthropomorphism (a creator with human characteristics) nor anthropocentrism (a conception of humans as the center or culmination of creation). But humans do have a role to play in this dynamic process, as seen temporally in the celebration of seasonal changes – that is, in the ritual calendar.

The Ritual Calendar

We have examined one dimension of religious time: the myths of origins, or of the beginning of time. Another dimension is that of movement through time, especially the annual calendar of religious festivals and holidays. Here, too, we see the operations of yang and yin, the constant interplay of positive and negative energies, activity and quiescence, heat and cold. And in this annual cycle humans do play a vital role.

The oscillating pattern of the *Dao*, while assuring a cosmic balance and harmony over the course of time, is characterized by ebb and flow, seasons where yin is dominant (winter), where yang is dominant (summer), and where they are in equilibrium (the spring and autumn equinoxes). As in European cultures, winter is traditionally associated with death, spring with rebirth, summer with life; so spring is the time of renewal, bridging the worlds of death and life. In the Chinese lunar calendar the most celebrated festival of the year is the Spring Festival (春節, *chunjie* – or New Year's Festival). Unlike the Western new year, which comes in the dead of winter, the Chinese New Year Festival is celebrated on the first day of the first lunar month, which can fall as early as January 22 and as late as February 19, that is, on the second new moon after the winter solstice (the first day of a lunar month is a new moon, and the fifteenth day is a full moon). While this is still winter – still the cold season in a northern climate – nevertheless the first stirrings of spring are present: the winter ice is beginning to thaw, the soil is beginning to soften, new life is beginning to emerge from the ground. Humans encourage this re-emergence by counterbalancing the yin forces of darkness and quiescence with yang forces of brightness and activity. This is why, on the Chinese New Year's eve, lights are blazing and children try to stay up all night, a great feast is served, and fireworks are set off to waken the sleeping world to the coming of spring. The staple food of Spring Festival is dumplings, which are perhaps reminiscent of the *hundun* "soup" at the beginning of time, and people stay up much of the night, preparing the wonton skins and fillings and wrapping the dumplings as a family activity.

Clearly, then, humans have a role to play in the harmonizing or re-balancing of yin and yang forces. This is evident again in mid-summer, when yang reaches its peak on the fifth day of the fifth lunar month (May 26 to June 23, corresponding roughly to the summer solstice on June 21 – this is the date when the Earth's axial tilt brings the northern half of the Earth closest to the sun). Today this festival is called the Double-Five (端午, *duanwu*) or the Double-Yang (重陽, *chongyang*) Festival, but in ancient times it was called the Cold Food Festival (寒食節, *hanshi jie*), because, since there was already "too much yang" (the heat of the summer sun), cooking fires should be extinguished. To compensate for the excess of yang energy and simply to escape the heat, the Double-Five Festival celebrates yin with water activities such as splashing contests, spraying water jets, and boat races. In English, this festival is known as the Dragon Boat Festival, on account of the dragon boat races taking place throughout the day and into the night.

A final illustration of the relationship between human actions and the balancing of yin and yang are the festivals associated with the spring and autumn equinoxes, when day and night are in perfect balance. The first of these falls on the fifteenth day after the spring equinox, that is, on April 5, and is called the Pure Brightness (清明, *qingming*) Festival. The second falls on the fifteenth day of the seventh lunar month (usually in August) and is called the Ghost Festival or the Ullambana Festival (盂蘭, *yulan*), after a Buddhist rite for the dead. These two festivals parallel each other in the performance of rituals for the dead: in the first, the family dead (that is, the ancestors); in the second, the non-family or unvenerated dead (that is, "hungry ghosts" having no descendents). While momentarily in balance, Chinese cosmological concepts recognize the equinoxes in dynamic terms: whereas in spring yin has completed its six months of ascendency and yang will begin its six months of ascendency, in fall it is the opposite: yang has completed its six months of ascendency and yin will begin its six months of ascendency. Yin is associated with death: the ancestors are "welcomed" at the end of the yin-dominant fall and winter, to remain close to the family and not to depart during the yang-dominant spring and summer; by contrast, the ghosts are "sent off" at the beginning of the yin- or death-dominant fall and winter and asked not to return. On the Ghost Festival, offerings normally reserved for ancestors are provided to the ghosts, but with two significant differences: first, they are placed outside the main gate (rather than within the house); second, they are left uncooked, consisting of dry rice and raw meats, and are discarded at the end of the day (as opposed to the offerings to ancestors, which are cooked and consumed by the family).

Festivals to the many Taoist gods of Chinese popular religion also demonstrate yin and yang cosmological conceptions. These holidays are also perennial, but not necessarily annual: some temples celebrate significant festivals only every three years, or every ten. I have heard of one major temple festival that is celebrated only once every 19 years, for reasons having to do with the particular god who is worshipped there. Indeed Chinese religion recognizes tens of thousands of gods, ghosts, and ancestors, and the spirit world is present within the human and natural world of everyday life. Just as yin penetrates yang and vice versa, the world of the dead penetrates the world of the living, forming one cosmological whole. This is why, in Chinese religion, there is no concept of "supernaturalism" – of another world, separate from that of everyday life. We will explore these themes further in Chapter 12, which deals with the personal dimensions of yin–yang cosmology.

Notes

1 A creation myth is called a cosmogonic myth. It should be noted that this is a term of comparative analysis: the word "myth" does not designate a "false story." For scholars of religion, a "myth" is a narrative with symbolic meaning, containing themes of cosmic importance. A myth is never merely historical.

2 Wilfred Cantwell Smith, *Patterns of Faith around the World* (Oxford: Oneworld Publications, 1998), p. 72.

3 Creation myths are present in virtually every religious system in the world, but they are not of equal importance. Hindu creation myths are virtually "meaningless," as the cyclical nature of creation and destruction means that creations are perennial, endless, even infinite in number. The Abrahamic traditions place an especially heavy emphasis on the story of creation.

11

Spatial Dimensions of Yin–Yang Cosmology

The characters yin (陰) and yang (陽) are etymologically related to space, that is, to topography: they refer literally to the "shady" side and the "sunny" side of a mountain. This fits our theme of complementarity: there can be no shade without sun, and thus the two dimensions of reality are interdependent. Moreover, since the sun appears to move across the sky, sunshine and shade are shifting and alternating, like the cosmic breath of creation. That is, sunshine and shade are dynamic states of light and darkness.

Fengshui

Since humans participate in the balancing of yin and yang forces, their interventions in space have a causative relationship of pattern and response. Humans intervene in the natural world by constructing homes, villages, cities, roads, and bridges. Their interaction with nature and with the "veins and arteries" of natural energies is the object of geomantic prognostication, that is, of *fengshui* (風水). *Fengshui* is the art of "wind and water," whereby humans seek to understand, both practically and aesthetically, the impact of their activities on the natural landscape. It is, to put it in more modern terms, a traditional form of ecological architecture. How should a town or city be situated? On which side of a river or mountain? Which direction should my house be facing? How high should it be, of what materials, and how should the entrance and rooms be configured for cooking, sleeping, dining, and entertaining? Where should I bury a beloved parent or grandparent? What is the optimal shape and size of the tomb, and in which direction should it be oriented? These questions are all

Asian Religions: A Cultural Perspective, First Edition. Randall L. Nadeau.
© 2014 John Wiley & Sons, Ltd. Published 2014 by John Wiley & Sons, Ltd.

addressed by *fengshui* and demonstrate a traditional environmental awareness. Though there are *fengshui* experts who are consulted and paid handsomely for major construction projects, it is safe to generalize that every Chinese has an intuitive appreciation for the aesthetic interaction between human habitations and the natural environment, an appreciation grounded in many centuries of *fengshui* practice.

Not surprisingly, Western missionaries and modernizers in the nineteenth century found *fengshui* to be pointless and irrational: "a mere chaos of childish absurdities and refined mysticism, cemented together, by sophistic reasonings, into a system, which is in reality a ridiculous caricature of science"; "an abyss of insane vagaries"; "a perverse application of physical and meteorological knowledge"; "the biggest of all bugbears."[1] Certainly, if *fengshui* opposes the construction of steeples and towers, the blasting of tunnels and passes, and the straight line efficiency of train tracks and telegraph lines, then it can easily be perceived to be standing in the way of progress. But *fengshui* is born out of a keen sensitivity to the natural makeup of the land, to the flow of "wind and water," and to the interplay of prominences and mountains (yang) with recessions and valleys (yin). It is this effort – not to disturb the natural balance, or even to augment the harmonizing of opposites – that distinguishes urban planning based on *fengshui* principles from the construction methods of rapid industrialization, which sees nature as a force to be "conquered" rather than harnessed.

Fengshui does not depend upon antiquated thinking or design. Contemporary Chinese architecture also seeks to integrate human spaces into their larger environments. When I was living in Hong Kong as a visiting professor at Lingnan University, I frequently passed the apartment block in the New Territories represented in Figure 11.1. Notice the undulating form of the building (not only in height, but even in its serpentine shape), mimicking the contours of the mountain behind it. A touch of yin emptiness is also seen in the 10-story opening at the 5th floor, which allows a glimpse of the natural terrain behind it.

Even ultra-modern buildings, such as the Bank of China Building on Hong Kong island, unite sea and sky by blending creatively into the background (see Figure 11.2). The vast glass panels of the building are so reflective that at times they seem to "disappear" into the sky.

For a final example, look at the design work of I. M. Pei, perhaps the best known Chinese architect in the world, in his construction of the East Wing of the National Gallery of Art in Washington, DC (Figure 11.3). Here it is not so much the natural environment that is emphasized, but the uniquely spoke-shaped urban design of the nation's capital, a design dating to the late eighteenth century. Pei has ingeniously created a building that blends into its artificial landscape, mimicking its distinctive geometry.

Figure 11.1 Apartment complex, New Territories, Hong Kong. Photo by the author (May 2003).

Figure 11.2 Bank of China Tower, Hong Kong. © Norman Chan / Shutterstock.

Figure 11.3 Aerial view of the National Gallery of Art's new East Building. © James A. Sugar / National Geographic Stock.

Fengshui is not superstition as much as an acute sensitivity for the interaction between the natural and the artificial – that is, for the impact of human handiwork on the natural landscape. It expresses these Taoist values:

- a conception of nature as a living, complementary force;
- an appreciation for natural beauty and form;
- architectural design based upon natural topography, forms, and elements;
- an ideal of cosmic, social, and ecological harmony.

Chinese "Elemental" Theory

A marvelous illustration of the dynamic quality of existence – what philosophers would describe as a metaphysics of *becoming* rather than a metaphysics of *being* – can be found in early Chinese understandings of the constituent elements of the natural world, the so-called "five phases" (五行, *wuxing*), traditionally represented as fire (火), earth (土), metal (金), water (水), and wood (木).

The early Greeks also had an elemental theory based on the idea that all things could be analyzed in terms of a few constituents that could be isolated from one another in the mind. One of the key characteristics of these elements was that, one way or another, they were indestructible at the most basic level. The Chinese "phases" cannot be isolated in the mind and are not indestructible; they are interactive and dynamic. In fact, it is more accurate to define them not as elements at all, but as "activities": burning, enveloping, hardening, moistening, and growing (the active characteristics of the elements).

Moreover, the five phases produce "the ten thousand things" by virtue of their *interactions* – as opposed to their *combinations* (as in molecular theory). These interactions are described as the "yang order of production" and the "yin order of overcoming." The yang order of production can be represented as in Figure 11.4:

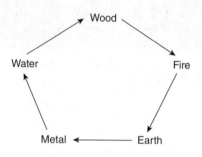

Wood produces fire	Growing things fuel burning (fire depends upon plants and plant-products)
Fire produces earth	Burning creates the earth (mountains and valleys depend upon volcanic activity)
Earth produces metal	The "enveloping" of the earth creates minerals and metals (through pressure and long processes of geological formation and sedimentation)
Metal produces water	Metals existing below the earth's surface produce springs (an ancient assumption about the origins of subterranean sources of water)
Water produces wood	"Growing" things depend upon "moistening" – they consume and transform water into living matter

Figure 11.4   Yang order of production. Drawn by author.

The yin order of overcoming can be represented as in Figure 11.5:

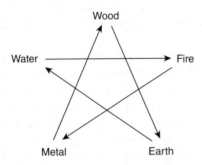

Metal overcomes wood	Growing things can be cut and crafted with the use of hard metallic instruments
Wood overcomes earth	The earth can be moved or penetrated by growing plants and by their root systems
Earth overcomes water	Waters (rivers, streams, and irrigation canals) can be directed through the construction of weirs and dams
Water overcomes fire	Fires are extinguished with water
Fire overcomes metal	Metal is made molten and can be shaped into implements and utensils in kilns and cauldrons

Figure 11.5   Yin order of overcoming. Drawn by author.

It is the dynamic and interactive dimensions of the phases that are emphasized. Notably, human activity is also part of this process; we make use of the natural way of things to harness their power – a basic Taoist theme. Humans are active participants in yin–yang cosmological balancing, not in a way that *violates* the basic nature of things, but in a way that *harmonizes* with it.

Spatial Dimensions of Liturgical Taoism

Taoism has evolved historically and has interacted in complex ways with Chinese popular religion or what Chinese scholars now call *shendao* (神道), the religion of spiritual beings.[2] Some scholars have been insistent that Taoism represents a completely separate tradition, with very elite forms of expression (written scriptures, liturgical manuals that are reserved for Taoist priests and their disciples, secret formulas, and esoteric symbols), but in terms of practice religious Taoism is very much the religion of the people, tied to local temples dedicated to a wide range of gods and spirits, all having distinct, local characteristics. So it is not unreasonable to use Taoism and *shendao* synonymously.

All religions have both temporal and spatial dimensions. Borrowing from the work of Mircea Eliade (see Chapter 2), all religions distinguish between a "sacred time" and a "profane time" and between a "sacred space" and a "profane space." Whereas profane time and space are ordinary and unremarkable and can be measured in minutes and meters, sacred time and space are in some ways "outside" time and space, insofar as our participation or immersion in sacred times and places creates experiences that seem to suspend, contract, or expand our time–space perceptions. A holiday is not just a day of the year; rather it is an occasion of family gathering, of religious remembrance, and of spiritual self-cultivation that suspends our ordinary sense of the passage of time. Similarly, a sacred mountain is not just a hill of certain physical dimensions, measured from base to top; it is rather a separate world, a place of mystery and spirituality, evoking an experience of encounter with sacred reality.

With respect to these two dimensions – of space and time – it is safe to say that Chinese religion is, primarily, spatially oriented. The Chinese landscape is full of sacred significance. The Chinese word for "society," *shehui* (社會), refers to a "gathering around a *she* (社), or sacred altar," traditionally a tree at the center of the village. Today most towns and villages have a temple dedicated to both local and more widely worshipped gods and goddesses, and the center-piece of the temple is an incense burner where worshippers offer incense and prayers. The temple courtyard is a gathering place for the community, and the architectural shape of a temple is that of an imperial palace, linking the community to its cultural history. In this sense the temple is the place where the community comes together, where past and present meet, and where the yang world of the living joins the yin world of the dead.

Temples represent not only cultural centers, but also nodes of inter-regional contact, done on a local, ad hoc basis (there is no overarching ecclesiastical authority in Chinese religion). Ritually, these contacts take the form of periodic visitations, whereby the local deity of one temple is brought to "call upon" the local deity of another temple and to receive some of its spiritual power (靈, *ling*). In some temples these visits have been going on for decades or centuries and represent "parent–child" relationships between the two temples or trade alliances between the two communities. Pilgrimages between temples are a major event of the festival year. Since 2000, pilgrimages between temples on Taiwan and in Mainland China contributed to the thawing of relations between the two governments and are now a regular occurrence.

The most recent temple fair I visited, in spring 2012, involved the transfer of a god's image from one temple to another, about 50 kilometers away; the image was initially located in a village that had seen some miraculous events. The visit would last three months, and the god's image was welcomed by the host temple in a "god's invitation" (神迎 *shenying*) rite. To display the god's presence, a shaman was possessed by a martial god named San Taizi (三太子, "the Third Prince"). The shaman inhabited by the Third Prince, also known as Nezha (哪吒), demonstrated his spiritual power by drawing blood from his own body with a sword and nail-studded club.

From this example we can see that Chinese religion – whether in its Confucian or Taoist forms – recognizes a close, immediate, and intimate relationship between humans and the divine. Gods, ghosts, and ancestors are primarily spirits of the dead, but the dead remain close; they do not occupy some distant, inaccessible world. In fact the gods – and the shamans or priests who interact with them so closely – move between the yin realm (the spirit realm) and the yang realm (the realm of everyday life) freely and quite readily. Our ancestors, too, are near to us and stay close to home. This is why Chinese who have migrated abroad see it as their responsibility to return home to visit their deceased parents. After the disruptive Communist Revolution ending in 1949 and leading to migrations to Hong Kong, Taiwan, and the rest of the world, tens of thousands of Chinese have been sure to visit their ancestral homes as they themselves have aged.

In these and other respects, then, Taoism is a religion of "immanence" – the integration of yin and yang, of death and life, humans and spirits. We will explore this theme further in Chapter 12.

Notes

1   Richard J. Smith, *Fortune-Tellers and Philosophers: Divination in Traditional Chinese Society* (Boulder, CO: Westview Press, 1993), passim.

2   Not to be confused with Japanese Shintō, which uses the same characters. What to call the "religion of the people" has been debated for several generations. In addition to "popular religion," scholars have employed the expressions "folk religion," "common religion," "local religion," and "community religion"; it is this spatial dimension of locality and community that we will emphasize here.

12

Personal Dimensions of Yin–Yang Cosmology

Taoism emphasizes a holistic conception of personal identity, that is, a conception that sees the various aspects of personal identity as whole and unified. This is less the case in Western religious thought, which has (at least traditionally) regarded the self as "bifurcated" – divided by two opposing forces, spiritual and material, which are often at odds with each other. When the New Testament writer Paul said that "the spirit is willing but the flesh is weak," he was talking about a personal struggle for dominance within the self – his hope being, of course, that his spiritual aspect would be dominant and that he would be able to overcome physical temptation and live a good and pure life.

In Taoism the self is not at war with itself. Rather the constituent parts of the self – physical, mental, and spiritual – are integrated. In fact they are composed of the same "substance," *qi* (氣), the matter-energy that underlies all things. Recall from the Chinese cosmogonic myth that the primordial *qi* at the time of creation manifests itself in two kinds of energy: active yang energy and receptive yin energy. Within a person, too, *qi* expresses both yin and yang energy, and it does so in all three facets of the self: body, mind, and spirit. This holistic conception is one of the reasons why it is difficult to pull out the religious dimensions of Taoism and separate them from the physical or the psychological ones: the Chinese see these as complementary, interpenetrating parts of a whole.

The Self as a Psychosomatic Whole

It is almost a "new discovery" in the modern West that body and mind impact each other. Emotional states can have long-lasting effects on our physical health, and, in the "reverse" direction, continuing refinement of psychoactive drugs is proving successful in treating psychological disorders. In terms of

Asian Religions: A Cultural Perspective, First Edition. Randall L. Nadeau.
© 2014 John Wiley & Sons, Ltd. Published 2014 by John Wiley & Sons, Ltd.

spiritual self-cultivation, Westerners are experimenting with "embodied" forms of religious practice and are learning to appreciate the spiritual value of physical exercises such as yoga and *taijiquan* (太極拳, "shadow-boxing").

Chinese have recognized these interconnections for centuries, and holistic awareness is a major theme of Taoist texts and ritual practices. Much of the Taoist Canon – a voluminous body of texts that has only recently been catalogued for Western scholars – is medical in nature, describing medications, exercises, and rituals designed to improve and extend one's life. Chinese medicine emphasizes the interrelationships between physical and mental health: a traditional doctor is likely not only to observe one's acute symptoms, but to check the breath and the pulse, to examine the body's extremities (hands and feet), and to query the patient and his family about diet, sleep, exercise, work, family life, and other personal matters of a "psychological" nature. The doctor's prescription will include herbal medications that are boiled into a soup, yoga and exercise, and family counseling designed to address conflicts or strains that impact both the mind and the body.

Taoism also promotes a healthy attitude toward sexuality. Taoist "sex manuals" have made a splash in the West, and, while their importance is somewhat exaggerated with regard to the history of Taoism, they certainly are consistent with Taoist principles and precedents. Sex enhances life, not only emotionally but also physically. Taoist sexual practices are controlled, even "unimpassioned"; they follow strict ritual guidelines. They are characterized by restraint, not by desire, and they envision love-making as a form of physical, mental, and spiritual self-cultivation, ideally as a cooperative pursuit between two willing partners. People – men especially – can have too much sex, and Taoist manuals prescribe limits; but people can also have too little, and, with the exception of a celibate tradition modeled on Buddhist monasticism – Quanzhen (全真) Taoism, still practiced in a few secluded abbeys in the mountains – Taoism has never condemned sex as such. Sex life, as long as it is healthy – not profligate, overly passionate, or too physically draining – is a basic principle of Taoist practice. Sex and spirituality are perfectly consistent, even inter-connected.

Once, when hiking in the mountains, I spent a few nights at an inn "between the waters and clouds" (水雲間, *shuiyunjian*), as it was so fittingly named. The proprietor, an 80-year-old gentleman who did not look one day over 60, told me how he had left his successful dental practice in a big city to retire to this mountain retreat, with its foggy evenings and crisp mornings. Whenever I came upon him, he was carrying a pair of paring shears, clipping and pruning, walking up and down the mountain paths. He was certainly a recluse in the modern world, wearing a constant smile of satisfaction and wellness. His wife, a woman of indeterminate age with a ruddy complexion and an addictive recipe for rose-hip-flavored peanuts (which she stir-fried at breakfast time), also commented on her husband's improved health since his retirement. And she noted without a touch of embarrassment: "our sex life is better now than it was in our 20s."

The conception of the body as a psychosomatic whole means that "health" is multidimensional. Just as an unhealthy sex life (too much or too little of it) affects one emotionally (one may feel lonely, or obsessed, or out of sorts due to sexual dissatisfaction), so other personal habits, too, have effects that are surprisingly broad-ranging. However subtle, these effects do influence one's quality of life. In addition to a robust but regulated sex life, we can cite other Taoist practices that promote physical, psychological, and spiritual well-being:

- sleep regulated by sunshine – going to bed early, getting up early;
- regular exercise – slow, repetitive motions that stretch and extend the body;
- motion exercises of bodily parts (eyes, toes, tongue, teeth-clicking, etc.);
- massage – which stimulates the circulation of blood and *qi* energy, and thereby all the nerves and muscles of the body;
- walking and hiking;
- breathing mountain air;
- breathing sea air;
- praying to gods of health and longevity;
- tea culture – preparing tea, drinking tea, conversation and relaxation;
- artistic expression – Taoist arts include calligraphy, ink painting, and traditional handicrafts (knot-tying, molding and sculpting, flower arranging, puppetry, and kite-building);
- leisure activities;
- mind-emptying activities such as meditation and deep breathing;
- alcohol – consumed in moderation;
- reclusion – spending some time alone for quiet and contemplation.

If we limit ourselves to a more traditional definition of religion as supernaturalism, then there would appear to be only one truly "religious" activity among these practices. But Taoism is a holistic spiritual discipline that is much more inclusive than worship and prayer.

Yin–Yang Souls and Spirits

Chinese conceive of the body as containing not just one soul, as in the West, but ten: three yang souls, called *hun* (魂), and seven yin souls, called *po* (魄). This formulation can be dated to a group of "neo-Confucian" texts in the Song Dynasty, but it was fully integrated into Taoist theory and practice. Literally *hun* and *po* mean "cloud souls" and "white souls" respectively, but these concepts are more accurately rendered as "cloud-borne souls" and "bone-adhering souls," because the ultimate destiny of the souls is both to dissipate into the heavens and into their own rebirth (which is what the *hun* souls do) and to adhere to the bones and remain with the corpse (which is what the *po* souls do). The coexistence of these two physically and metaphysically distinct destinies explains why Chinese make offerings to their ancestors both within the home and at the graveside. The *hun* souls are represented by a vermillion dot centered on a spirit tablet placed on an altar within the home; here the ancestor receives daily offerings of meals prepared for the family. If the family is strong and prosperous, the spirit tablets are preserved for generations, often in a spirit hall erected specifically for this purpose. Theoretically at least, the *hun* souls receive offerings for centuries.

The *po* souls stay with the body and are buried with the bones. Traditionally, the bones are periodically disinterred, cleaned, and reburied; but I have seen this practiced only on two occasions, once in Fujian Province and once in Taiwan. More commonly, the *po* souls receive offerings at the gravesite, both on the anniversary of the deceased's death-day and on the Qingming Festival in April every year. Since the bones eventually "turn to dust," the *po* souls also disappear, and graveside offerings usually end after three generations.

What is the function of the ten souls for the living? As the body is regarded as a single, multifaceted whole, the souls have both physical and psychological functions. The three *hun* souls are yang-oriented: they are masculine, active, and circulatory. One is located in the brain and is responsible for the activity of the mind; the second is located in the heart and is responsible for the activity of the will; the third is located in the sexual organs and is responsible for conception. Their active circulation is important for good physical and mental health: sexual/conceptual energy flows up the back's *qi* meridians and inspires creative thinking; thinking is put into action by the activity of will. People whose sexual energy is limited to the sex organs, being deprived of the directed flow to the brain, act impulsively and passionately, in a way that is destructive both to themselves and to others. People who "think too much" and are afraid to put thought into action also lack the proper circulation of the *hun* soul's conceptual energies; they suffer blockages that can lead to depression and stomach aches. People who are willful but have no outlet for their passions in the form of healthy sexuality find themselves frustrated and torn; they may suffer from high blood pressure and shortness of breath.

These traditional ideas about the circulation of energy and the correlative impact of the neurological, circulatory, and reproductive organs may strike us as pre-scientific, but it is difficult to deny that they work at a psychological level. It is important to have sexual energy and thoughtful reflection in balance, matched by the "heart" of both action and restraint. Psychologically, if not physically, the proper balancing and circulation of these energies does seem to promote a healthier and happier life.

The seven *po* souls are located in several other organs of the body such as the spleen, the liver, the gall bladder, and the endocrine system. Psychologically, they are associated with seven emotions: joy, anger, pleasure, sorrow, like, dislike, and desire. The Taoist tradition has never tried to suppress emotion, as we will see in Hindu yoga and in Buddhist meditation; nor does it judge some emotions to be positive or desirable and other emotions to be negative or undesirable, as we see in Western philosophical reflections on the "passions" – where joy and pleasure are deemed to be "good" emotions and anger and sorrow "bad." Rather all of the emotions are important and should be experienced and expressed over the course of life in a psychologically healthy way. Although the *po* souls are not "circulatory," like the *hun* souls, they too should be balanced. They are yin-oriented because they are fundamentally passive – or, more accurately, reactive: they represent healthy, natural responses to things we see or hear, to things that others may do or say to us, and even to thoughts, memories, and reflections that we may bring to mind. A healthy emotional life, including both "positive" and "negative" emotions, is both psychologically and physically beneficial to human well-being.

Taoist Long Life and Immortality

If there is a single, overarching goal of religious Taoism across centuries of practice, it is long life and the indefinite extension of long life, immortality. While immortality is not upheld as a practical goal by most Chinese today, long life is certainly valued, not only for the wisdom that comes from old age, but as a result of the inherently positive view of life that Taoists have always promoted. In the Taoist view, whether we are talking about philosophical Taoism or religious Taoism, life is made for living, and to be vital, active, engaged, and youthful well into old age is a universal Chinese aspiration. If I can live to the age of 80 with the youthful vigor of a person half my age, then how much more enjoyable my life can become! And, if to 100, all the more so. A practitioner of Taoist self-cultivation (which involves various exercises and meditation practices) once said to me: "From the moment you begin this practice, if you do it regularly and consistently, your age-appearance will not change. If you begin at 30, you will retain the youthfulness of a 30-year-old well into old age."

Over many centuries, various practices have been recommended for achieving deathless existence. Some of these were "alchemical": they consisted in the consumption of certain herbs and minerals – including some we now know to have been poisonous: the early adepts claimed they produced "fake deaths" – and in the avoidance of others, including rice. While no longer practiced, Taoist alchemy has influenced the Chinese consumption of healthy legumes and dark green vegetables, limitations on the intake of meat and strong vegetables (onions and garlic), and the proliferation of innumerable vitamins and medicinal supplements (which remain very much in vogue among Chinese). Other "alchemical" practices were "internal": the basic principle here was to treat the body as a circulating system, enhancing *qi* energy while not allowing *qi* to dissipate or leave the body. One form of internal alchemy consisted in ritual sexual intercourse, where *qi* or seminal energy should be "stimulated" but prevented from leaving the body: for men, by avoiding ejaculation, and for women, by "slaying the red dragon," that is, by suspending menstruation through the cultivation of the "holy embryo." All of these alchemical practices enhance energy circulation, such that, if they are practiced correctly, the body becomes a self-perpetuating machine.

In Chapter 13 we will explore contemporary manifestations of Taoism as a global religious phenomenon, but we can conclude this chapter by pointing out that, while some traditional conceptions may now seem antiquated and even superstitious, the basic orientation of Taoist self-cultivation is appealing on a number of levels:

- Taoism describes a holistic, balanced, and well-integrated conception of personal identity.
- Taoism promotes healthy living and recognizes the influence of diet, exercise, and sexuality on psychological and spiritual well-being.
- Taoism defines the religious dimensions of life in both supernaturalistic and naturalistic terms.
- Taoism celebrates a "free and easy" lifestyle, in tune with nature and with one's own natural inclinations, while at the same time controlling and harnessing emotional and physical desires.
- Taoism "overcomes death" by promoting healthy attitudes and practices well into old age; elders are treated as vital members of family and society.
- Taoism provides practical, detailed instructions both for the preparation of homeopathic medicines and balanced, delicious meals and for the performance of physical exercises, sexual practices, and religious and ritual behaviors that are spiritually enlivening and ennobling.

Survey 2   Principles of Philosophical and Religious Taoism

This survey can be found at http://goo.gl/PkEJfK and explores your own interest in adapting Taoist models for personal self-cultivation. Which of these values and behaviors strike you as meaningful and important? Which do you think have prescriptive force: not just describing what East Asian cultures have valued in the past, but also prescribing constructive solutions to global disequilibrium and to issues of contemporary concern?

13

Taoism as a Global Religious Phenomenon

Whereas historians used to limit "Taoism" to an ancient philosophy of mystical anti-rationalism, we now know that Taoism continued to evolve and develop. It came to include not just philosophical texts, but also church-like institutions, rites, and ceremonies with hundreds, if not thousands of ritual instruction manuals; a rich tradition of physical and hygienic practices, all with the goal of reaching long life or immortality; a pantheon of terrestrial and celestial deities; and mythologies related to their lives and heavenly existence. Of course, historians have been aware of these religious elements for a long time – and all of these beliefs and practices continue to exist – but in the past we tended to denigrate them as "superstition" or "folk religion," not realizing that they are highly elaborate, intellectually sophisticated, and ritually complex and that they are part of the Taoist tradition. "Taoism" therefore includes much more than the teachings of Laozi and his immediate followers. It is rather a religious tradition with certain identifiable features:

- a priesthood, composed primarily of ritual specialists;
- rituals that benefit individuals or social communities by tapping into the power of the Dao; and
- a canon of religious texts (one of the most voluminous canons in the world's religions), including hundreds of scriptures, commentaries, treatises, and manuals.

The beliefs and values underlying this religion extend far beyond the formal aspects listed above, and many Chinese today exhibit Taoist characteristics apart from these institutional forms. Just as "Confucianism" describes a system of values and behaviors that permeates Chinese society, most Chinese are Taoist to one degree or another, though they may be unaware of the religious

Asian Religions: A Cultural Perspective, First Edition. Randall L. Nadeau.
© 2014 John Wiley & Sons, Ltd. Published 2014 by John Wiley & Sons, Ltd.

origins of their thinking and habits. The Taoistic elements of everyday life can be summarized as follows:

- the sense that reality extends beyond the observable realm and includes spiritual power that has physical effects and manifestations;
- the belief in *harmony*, not only among persons but between persons, the natural world, and the cosmos;
- the practice of meditation and of physical exercises that emphasize the unity of an individual's psychological, emotional, physical, and spiritual identity; and
- the belief that internal and external harmony have practical benefits, from social welfare to individual health and longevity.

Most Chinese today, even after a century of Western influence (not to mention half a century of communist rule), would consider these things to be commonsense; and, while the institutional forms of Taoism almost disappeared in the latter half of the twentieth century, Taoism as an approach to life is still very much alive.

Taoism as a World Religion

Europeans and Americans are increasingly aware of some of the short-comings of Judeo-Christian and Western Enlightenment values. As critics see it, the globalization of Enlightenment values and institutions has had a number of negative consequences:

- violence arising from ethnic and political conflict;
- urbanization and its attendant ills (from crime to unsightly cityscapes);
- ecological degradation and worldwide decrease in forested or virgin land;
- medical technologies that preserve life, but often at great material and spiritual cost;
- greed and avariciousness, expressed both personally and nationally;
- a sexual ethics that is often distorted, on the one hand through demeaning images and attitudes, on the other hand through religiously motivated prudishness;
- lifestyles focused on personal achievement in highly artificial environments, with little opportunity for physical exercise, creative expression, or communion with nature.

There is no one thing, or single factor, to "blame" for these ills, and it would be foolish to think that they are limited to the industrialized West. Increasingly they are global issues, experienced by individuals everywhere. Are they the consequence of technological progress and of a world increasingly unified by new forms of communication and transportation? Do they reflect a breakdown in communal structures, including religious institutions, which leads people to measure their interests in purely individual terms? Are they a function of rampant consumerism, greed, and acquisitiveness, and of global values that "commodify" success, health, happiness, and personal well-being? Are they a consequence of demographic changes, including population growth, urbaniza-tion, and widening income gaps between the rich and poor? Or have they always been with us, in one form or another, as contemporary manifestations of the more selfish inclinations of human nature?

Whatever their causes, many who have observed these ills have seen in Taoism an alternative religious orientation – one that offers tools for understanding and self-cultivation to counterbalance these destructive trends. With its emphasis on naturalism, holistic development of the physical and emotional aspects of human identity, political and ecological harmony, healthy sexuality, non-invasive medicine, and the "feminine" values of nurturing and caring, Taoism has emerged as a viable religious practice for people all over the world. A number of Taoist masters (usually, but not exclusively, of Chinese ancestry) now live in the West and have adapted Taoist alchemy, physical and psychological exercises, and related practices to Western lifestyles and goals. While Taoism has no insti-tutional base either in China or the West, many individuals are investigating Taoist practices on their own, or have joined with like-minded persons in infor-mal groups for study, ritual practice, and support. In the future it is likely that Taoism will be included among the major religions of the West – as well as of the East.

Is Taoism still a viable religious option in the modern world? After 50 years of communist rule in Mainland China, institutional forms of Taoism have largely ceased to exist. Though several Taoist monasteries of the "Complete Reality" (全真, *Quanzhen*) tradition have been restored as tourist attractions – most notably the White Cloud Temple in Beijing, which attracts thousands of foreign and domestic tourists – few Chinese are drawn to Taoist monasticism. However, liturgical Taoism remains vital to contemporary Chinese religious life. It is practiced in rural villages and in Chinese communities in Taiwan, Hong Kong, and Southeast Asia, as part of the "diffused religion" of traditional China, based upon beliefs and practices surrounding human interactions with gods, ghosts, and ancestors. Taoist priests are still subjected to years of apprenticeship and rigorous training and have mastered the arts of Taoist self-cultivation. They are well educated in the history of Taoism, in alchemical practices, in the prepara-tion of talismans and amulets, and in the conduct of religious ritual. The Taoist priesthood is a vital resource for the preservation of traditional Chinese medi-cine, religion, and culture.

On a personal level, Taoist values remain strong. In spite of the Confucian ethic that has dominated Chinese social interactions for centuries, Chinese retain the Taoist belief in individual "ease" and freedom against social constraint, conceived of as a counterweight to everyday duties and responsibilities. Many Chinese practice Taoist forms of physical exercise and make use of traditional medicines, which are still favored over Western pharmaceuticals. And Chinese are becoming more appreciative of nature and natural impulses. Young people in China who may be disenchanted with the political manipulation of Confucianism by authoritarian governments, or who have become less sanguine about the "promise of modernity" represented by the West, find in traditional Taoist practices a viable home-grown solution to personal, societal, and global conflict. Increasingly Europeans and Americans, too, have been drawn to Taoist literature and to practices associated with Taoist self-cultivation, from gymnastics exercises (such as the practice of shadow-boxing pictured in Figure 13.1 and *Qigong*) to herbal medicine and a more naturalistic spirituality.

What Taoist practices and values are still upheld today?

- Modern and contemporary Chinese art is significantly influenced by Taoist naturalism, as it has been throughout Chinese art history.
- Longevity practices are still evident in Chinese cooking (a diet rich in leafy green vegetables, tubular vegetables such as fungi and mushrooms, vitamins, herbs, and spices).
- Chinese people maintain a holistic conception of personal identity and consider a balanced life to be crucial for physical and psychological health:

Figure 13.1 Taoism is, increasingly, a viable religious alternative in the West. © Anna Furman / iStockphoto.

work is balanced with rest and relaxation, sedentary activity with physical activity.

- Physical activity, while strongly valued, is not competitive or sports-oriented, as it is in the West: Taoist-inspired physical exercises are aerobic, yogic, and meditative.
- Nature is idealized. Though modern China is plagued with pollution problems associated with rapid economic growth, Taoism remains a significant cultural resource for ecological thinking. More and more, Chinese show an appreciation for nature, as expressed in the cultivation of plants, pet owning (traditionally songbirds and singing insects, but now also dogs and cats), hiking, nature photography, and family outings.
- While family and profession are prioritized, in keeping with a more Confucian orientation toward life, Taoist ideals of self-expression, freedom from constraint, and recreation are highly valued: Chinese like to have fun and regularly indulge in parties involving alcohol consumption, singing, and composing poetry.
- Sexuality, while constrained by Confucian family and marital obligations, is considered natural and healthy.
- In the siting of homes and graves, Chinese refer to the principles of *fengshui*, though they may or may not make use of the services of a *fengshui* master.
- Temple construction and temple-based activities such as festivals, pilgrimage tours, and community rites enjoy more public support than they have in a century of social and political transformation, and they typically involve the participation of Taoist priests, mediums, and shamans.

Taoism has significantly caught on in the West as well. One indication is a highly successful series of conferences and workshops headed by Livia Kohn, emeritus professor from Boston University, and held in Boston in 2003, on Mt. Qingcheng in Sichuan Province in 2004, in Fraueninsel in Bavaria in 2006, in Hong Kong in 2007, on Mt. Wudang in Hubei in 2009, in Los Angeles in 2010, on Mt. Nanyue, Changsha in 2011, and in Utting am Ammersee, Germany in 2012. These conferences combine workshops on Taoist practice with the latest scholarship on the tradition in all its aspects; and they bring practitioners and scholars together, in a creative dialogue. They are but one example of the increasing interest in Taoism as both a philosophical and a religious tradition that focuses on spiritual self-cultivation.

In these chapters on Confucianism and Taoism I have treated Chinese religion as a living cultural phenomenon, not as two distinct systems of thought or historical relics. My goal has been twofold: to understand contemporary East Asian culture in terms of religious thought and practice, and to recognize Confucianism and Taoism as viable and increasingly popular alternatives for spiritual seekers worldwide. While it is impossible to understand East Asian culture fully without knowing something about these traditions, it is true that their legacy is precarious: ethnic identity politics, nationalism, and consumerism all express values that are culturally destabilizing. These values contradict the highest teachings of Chinese tradition. And these destabilizing forces are not limited to China: more and more people see themselves purely in terms of economic agency, or as winners and losers in a global competition. As a scholar of religion, it is difficult to be a mere by-stander to this materialist surge. Rather I hope that the values promoted by both Confucianism and Taoism still have something to say to twenty-first-century life. Briefly, those shared values include

- the idea that individuals are something more than consumers and that the value of life should be measured in non-economic terms;
- the idea that a person is more than a material being but should also cultivate physical, psychological, and spiritual wellness;
- the idea that religious beliefs and practices, while rooted in particular social and historical origins, also teach universal lessons that can be appropriated cross-culturally;
- the idea that spiritual self-cultivation can take non-institutional forms and is never limited to simply one nationality, one ethnicity, or one culture;
- the idea that the individual can be a powerful source of goodness, integrity, and both personal and social transformation;
- the idea that certain values can and should be made to survive and to prosper: these include the Confucian ideals of ceremonial living, co-humanity, moral virtue, and social responsibility and the Taoist ideals of personal balance and moderation, artistic appreciation and self-expression, environmentally responsible lifestyles, and holistic spirituality.

Taken together, these Confucian and Taoist values have great prescriptive force as models for a healthier life – healthier not only for individuals and communities, but also for the world as a whole.

Part IV

The Hindu Tradition

14

What Is Hinduism?

"Hinduism" refers to "the religion of the Indus Valley" or, more generally, the religion of the Indian subcontinent. There is no term like it for Chinese religion; nor for Japanese religion; nor for any of the Western religious traditions. As a descriptive noun for the religion of a place, the word suggests a false unity. It reflects a failure (on the part of the people who came up with the label) to perceive a remarkable variety of ethnicities, languages, beliefs, practices, deity cults, institutional organizations, worldviews, and cosmologies. In fact it is a stretch even to say that the word describes a single religion at all. The word "Hinduism" was the invention of outsiders, from the Muslim Moguls of the sixteenth century to the British Empire, which ruled India from the early 1800s until 1947. It was employed as a grossly general term to name a religious tradition that has existed, in its numerous forms, for thousands of years.

Should we go so far as to say, as some postcolonialist scholars have done, that "Hinduism" therefore does not really exist, that it is a speculative invention and a forced generalization that has no use or applicability? There are two reasons not to discard it. First, it is useful to have a single term to refer to the religious traditions of a geographic and cultural entity; in fact one might wish that there was such a term for the Chinese religions, which display much greater unity than the separate terms "Confucianism" and "Taoism" would imply – not to mention "Buddhism" or "Chinese folk religion." It is more accurate to say that there is "one religion" of China than that there are "four," and we can be grateful that, at least for India, we do have such a term. Second, at least since the nineteenth century, Hindus in India and around the world describe *themselves* as "Hindu" and, even if they did not invent the term, they have now embraced it. In fact some Hindus – especially those of the modern Hindu Nationalist (*Hindū rāṣṭravāda*) movement – identify themselves adamantly as Hindu and would reject the idea that the term is a foreign imposition. So, whether or not it was invented by others, Hindus today regard it as an

Asian Religions: A Cultural Perspective, First Edition. Randall L. Nadeau.
© 2014 John Wiley & Sons, Ltd. Published 2014 by John Wiley & Sons, Ltd.

autonym, a self-referential term. Moreover, there can be no doubt that the word has entered the common vocabulary, being employed by scholars and seekers alike to describe one of the great religions of the world, now practiced both in India and across the globe.

The Three Margas

Given the great variety of religious institutions, beliefs, and practices that the word "Hinduism" envelopes, difficult choices must be made in a book such as this one when it comes to what and what not to include. Some Hindus are so inclusive in their thinking that they would label virtually every religion that has ever been practiced in India as "Hindu," even Buddhism and Christianity! And in many respects they would be right: Buddhism has so many Hindu elements that the two religions are as interconnected as the three religions of the Abrahamic tradition – Judaism, Christianity, and Islam. Even Christianity takes on a distinctly Hindu flavor in India, adopting the Hindu practices and terminology of the *bhakti* (devotional) tradition. To be sure, though, Indian Buddhists and Christians see themselves as distinct from Hindus, and we will let the self-understanding of religious believers themselves be our guide in naming and describing the Hindu tradition in contrast to other religions that may have been practiced in India, whether Buddhism, Christianity, or Islam.

But, even as a distinct religious tradition, Hinduism is diverse and multifaceted, and not all Hindus do or believe the same things. Scholars have devised a number of ways to address this diversity, all somewhat arbitrary. Since this book attempts to make Asian religions accessible, at the level of both belief and practice, to Western readers, the way we will organize this unit is based on a traditional categorization of Hindu practice. Hindus identify three *margas*, known collectively as the Trimarga ("the three paths") or the three yogas: the path of duty and responsibility (literally, the path of action, *karma-marga*); the path of philosophical insight (literally, the path of knowledge, *jñāna-marga*); and the path of faith and devotion (literally, the path of love, *bhakti-marga*). What unites these three paths is both historical and philosophical. Philosophically, the "three" are unified as "one" in the sense that all three paths lead to a single goal: the experience of a liberated self, in union with sacred reality. Though Hindus vary widely in how they think of sacred reality, in how they represent it in images or words, and in how they interact with the sacred dimension of life, generally they believe that all of these three paths lead to one goal or destination: the experience of unity with something greater than oneself, and the erasure of individuality.

Chapter 15 will address the path of duty and responsibility (*karma-marga*), including a discussion of karma and rebirth and of the law (*dharma*) of personal responsibility, which is based upon one's caste and stage of life – a moral system that Hindus refer to as *varna-āśrama-dharma*.

Chapter 16 will address the path of philosophical insight (*jñāna-marga*) and discuss the ultimate destiny of the soul (*Ātman*) as union with the sacred (*Brahman*), a union experienced as "freedom from embodied existence" (*mokṣa*). In its long path to this realization, over the course of many lifetimes, the soul experiences wants or desires (*puruṣārthas*) that become increasingly "selfless" as the individual matures spiritually. The ultimate realization – "liberation" – reveals that this world of embodied, material, and separable persons and things is an illusion that springs from ignorance of the true nature of reality.

Chapter 17 will address the path of faith and devotion (*bhakti-marga*), discussing two of the most widely venerated Hindu gods: Krishna (Kṛṣṇa) and Shiva (Śiva). In both instances the symbolism, iconography, and worship practices associated with the sacred help the devotee to overcome individuality or independence – or, more accurately, the illusions of individuality and independence. Devotion to gods such as Krishna and Shiva is at the heart of Hindu religious practice, and it is expressed through offerings made in a temple service (*pūjā*).

Finally, this part will conclude, as the others have, with a discussion of Hinduism in the contemporary world (Chapter 18).

The *Bhagavad Gita*

The organization of the Hindu tradition into three aspects, the Trimarga, is based on a Hindu scripture entitled the *Bhagavad Gita*. The *Gita* is among the most important and the most widely read, recited, and translated of all Hindu scriptures, though it is not a "holy book" in the Western sense of the term – not a "timeless" or "revealed" scripture, as we think of the Hebrew Bible, the New Testament, or the Qur'an. The honor of being "eternal" or revealed is reserved for the Vedas and the Upaniṣads, the closest Hindu equivalents of the Abrahamic scriptures.

The *Gita*, itself divided into 18 chapters, is actually part of a much longer work called the *Mahābhārata*, an epic novel akin to the *Odyssey* or the *Iliad*. It recounts a great war that divided a single clan into two warring factions. The story tells of many heroes, but the one featured in the *Bhagavad Gita* is an archer named Arjuna. Arjuna's exploits, especially with the bow and arrow, are legendary, and he was regarded as the greatest warrior of his time. But, when faced with a final battle that will pit members of a single family against one another, Arjuna is overcome with grief and doubt. On the night before the great battle, he asks his charioteer to take him for one last look at the armies arrayed on either side of a temporary divide, soon to be filled with the blood and cries of mortal combat. Looking across to the "enemy," Arjuna sees nothing but family and friends – the cousins he played with as a child, the uncles he grew up to respect and admire, even his own archery master. Having a well-earned confidence in his own abilities as a warrior, he knows that he will be the agent of their deaths. Conscience-stricken, he sets down his bow and scabbard and announces to his charioteer: "I will not fight."

The remainder of the *Gita* is a discussion between the warrior Arjuna and his charioteer about Arjuna's duties as a warrior and about the tragic nature of life itself. The charioteer persuades Arjuna that he must go to war, and his message is based upon three arguments that correspond to the three margas of duty (*karma*), wisdom (*jñāna*), and devotion (*bhakti*). At the conclusion of their discussion, the charioteer reveals his true identity to Arjuna: he is none other than the great god Krishna (Figure 14.1). Krishna's sermon, seemingly about a warrior's ultimate destiny, is in fact a lesson about life itself, which is always and for everyone a struggle between wrong and right, between ignorance and understanding, between fatalism and self-determination. We will look at the specific forms of Krishna's advice in the ensuing chapters.

It is notable that the *Bhagavad Gita* is set within a context of war and that Krishna's literal advice to Arjuna is that he should go into battle. Comparatively, we may note that many of the world's religions are seemingly focused on conflict, even on bloodshed, in their foundational scriptures; this theme ranges from the many battles of the Hebrew Bible to the jihadist exhortations of the Qur'an; and even Jesus, the "Prince of Peace," bears a sword (Matthew 10:

Figure 14.1   Mural painting depicting Lord Krishna with Arjuna. Patora, Orissa, India. © Frederic Soltan / Corbis.

34–39). These coincidences have led some critics to conclude that religion is, by and large, steeped in blood and not only condones but advocates violence.

This issue deserves a larger and more focused discussion, but it may be instructive to look briefly at how Mahatma Gandhi (1869–1948) approached the *Gita*. In spite of fierce resistance from British colonial forces in the 1920s and 1930s, Gandhi and his Satyāgraha Movement ("holding on to truth" through peaceful non-cooperation) appealed to the conscience of the world and attained India's independence from British rule.

In a talk he gave in 1926, Gandhi described the *Bhagavad Gita* as the most inspiring of all the Hindu scriptures. "Even in 1888–1889," he said,

> when I first became acquainted with the Gita, I felt that it was not a historical work, but that, under the guise of physical warfare, it described the duel that perpetually went on in the hearts of mankind, and that physical warfare was brought in merely to make the description of the internal duel more alluring . . . I find a solace in the Bhagavad Gita that I miss even in the Sermon on the Mount. When disappointment stares me in the face and all alone I see not one ray of light, I go back to the Bhagavad Gita. I find a verse here and a verse there, and I immediately begin to smile in the midst of overwhelming tragedies – and my life has been full of external tragedies – and if they have left no visible or indelible scar on me, I owe it all to the teaching of Bhagavad Gita . . .[1]

The Three Margas as Religious Discipline (Yoga)

In the three chapters to follow we will examine the three paths (Trimarga) as three forms of discipline (*yoga*). The word *yoga* is the origin of the English words "yoke" (a harness or frame) and "to yoke" (to guide, harness, or control). One employs a yoke to tame an animal and to channel its energy. Similarly, one practices yoga in order to tame the ego and to channel its energy. Here what is meant by "ego" includes the elements of an individual personality that we consider to mark a person's identity: one's body or physical appearance, thoughts, desires and motivations. Though we think we should be in control of these dimensions of ourselves, too often the reverse is true: instead of me controlling my body, it is my body that controls me (often because I am feeling physical pain or discomfort, or because I am overcome with sexual desires, hunger, and other needs that "take over" my mind). Instead of me controlling my thoughts, they "run away," they "wander," they are unfocused; instead of me controlling my desires, they control me (I am overwhelmed by disappointed wants, or distressed by failure in love). In the absence of yoga – that is, in the absence of spiritual discipline – it is the ego that controls the self, like oxen that go whichever way they choose. The purpose of yoga is to reverse this pattern of control, so that "I" am in control of my body, thoughts, and desires, rather than vice versa. An analogy employed in the Hindu tradition is that of a charioteer in control of the horses pulling the chariot. Clearly the Hindu tradition distinguishes between the "ego," which is associated with my individual personality, and some deeper "I," some deeper dimension of the self.

The English word "to yoke" also means to bring together, to join together (as in harnessing two oxen by the same frame, so that they can work together as a team). Yoga "yokes" by bringing together the "I," the true self, with something more eternal, a greater "I," a cosmic "I," a sacred reality. Just as the true self is not limited to my individual personality, the cosmic "self" is not limited to the vast assembly of physical things in the universe. In Sanskrit, the true self is called *Ātman* and the cosmic self is called *Brahman*. We will explore these spiritual concepts further in Chapter 16. The great problem addressed by Hindu spiritual self-cultivation is our tendency to identify ourselves purely with our bodies, thoughts, and unconscious desires and to be ignorant of the deeper self within. Similarly, we tend to see the world in purely material terms, as consisting of a great multitude of things and persons, and we fail to see their underlying interconnection or unity. This is ignorance – literally, in Sanskrit, "blindness" or "not-seeing" (*avidyā*). Yoga – that is, the three margas – gives us the spiritual tools to "see" ourselves as we truly are, to see reality as it truly is, and to harness physical, psychological, and emotional energies in a way that is constructive and spiritually ennobling. It allows us to take control of our lives. So, in the chapters that follow, we will examine the three margas as three forms of discipline and control: the disciplining of action, the disciplining of the mind, and the disciplining of the emotions.

Note

1   John Strohmeier, ed., *The Bhagavad Gita According to Gandhi* (Berkeley: North Atlantic Books, 2009), p. xvii.

15

Karma-marga

One of Krishna's first lessons when addressing Arjuna in the *Bhagavad Gita* is that his concern for others actually masks an even greater concern for himself, that is, for his ego, which is willful and self-centered. Arjuna's refusal to fight arises from his excessive concern for the "fruits of action." He is overly worried about the consequences of his actions as they will reflect on *himself*. He should focus his attention instead on his duty alone, without attachment to consequences. To "do his duty well" and fulfill the role that society expects of him is selfless (ego-less) action. This is *karma-yoga*, the discipline of action.

What is the Hindu conception of *karma*, of action and its consequences? How do the consequences of action impact oneself, as well as the world? What is duty, and how do duties vary from one person to another? What duties are appropriate for me, in my station and my stage of life? In this chapter we will examine Hindu ideas of *karma* and rebirth, and the law (*dharma*) of personal responsibility, which is based upon one's caste and stage in life. This is a moral system that Hindus refer to as *varna-āśrama-dharma*. Then we will return to Krishna's advice to Arjuna on selfless action as a path of spiritual discipline.

Action and Its Consequences

The Hindu concept of rebirth or "reincarnation" has impacted virtually every culture of South and East Asia. It is a belief not limited to Hinduism; it extends to Buddhism as well as to Chinese and Japanese religions, and it is part of an almost universal understanding of the consequences of action. The "law of *karma*" is simply a law of moral cause and effect, a pattern of action that impacts others but also reflects back upon oneself, both in this life and in lives to come.

Asian Religions: A Cultural Perspective, First Edition. Randall L. Nadeau.
© 2014 John Wiley & Sons, Ltd. Published 2014 by John Wiley & Sons, Ltd.

In itself, *karma* means nothing more than "action" and its consequences. It is certainly not "fate," though it is undoubtedly "inevitable" that actions have consequences and that these consequences are seen and felt both *transitively* (by others) and *reflexively* (by oneself). Not all action is karmic – only intentional action is; hence motivation is crucial. Notice that, in the *Bhagavad Gita*, Krishna is not concerned about Arjuna's acts themselves, but about his thinking about action and inaction – his motives. Similarly, when the Buddha spoke to his disciples about *karma*, he said: "It is intention, oh Monks, that I call *karma*; having willed, one acts through body, speech, or mind."[1] Actions motivated by greed, hatred, or delusion generate negative karmic consequences; actions motivated by non-attachment, benevolence, and understanding generate positive karmic consequences.

As long as there is *karma*, there is rebirth. *Karma* is the "energy" that spins the wheel of rebirth: this ever-turning cycle of rebirths is called in Sanskrit *saṃsāra*, the spinning wheel of existence. *Saṃsāra* is our world of everyday experience, fueled by *karma* and governed by moral laws of cause and effect. At the personal level, *saṃsāra* describes the individual's path of innumerable rebirths, through many lifetimes, in its spiritual journey. Cosmically, *saṃsāra* describes innumerable rebirths of "worlds" – that is, the cosmos itself, which goes through vast ages of existence, degeneration, eclipse, and regeneration over eons and eons of time. The world as we know it, the age in which we live (and have lived for millennia) is in the *kali-yuga* (the "rust age"), an age in which injustice often prevails over justice, in which the world is beset by warfare and violence, and in which greed is a primary motivation for individual action. In such an age the individual must struggle against a destructive, immoral, and competitive environment and must resist the temptation to lead an equally self-centered life. This is our primary ethical task as religious persons.

The idea of *saṃsāra* and the cyclical conception of time and existence contrast fundamentally with the Western conception of time, which is linear. Western religious traditions see history as progressing along a single line, as having a beginning (God's act of creation, as recounted in Genesis) and, perhaps, an apocalyptic end – a conception that, if shorn of its supernatural elements, parallels the scientific view that the cosmos began with a Big Bang and is likely to end in a cosmic collapse, some millions of years in the future. Within this context human life is also linear, resembling a mathematical vector, with a point of origin at conception or birth and one of two possible outcomes: eternal reward in Heaven, or eternal punishment in Hell. We might call this the "double destiny" conception of the soul.

How is this destiny determined? For purposes of comparison with the Hindu tradition, we can survey the Christian response. Christians have been divided doctrinally over two positions: that one's ultimate destiny is determined by

"works" – that is, the sum of one's moral and immoral acts – or that it is determined by "faith" (a doctrine of salvation by faith alone). While most Christians
today would emphasize the dimension of faith, the idea that good and evil
actions determine one's eternal fate is still widely held. In 1999, when a group
of United States soldiers admitted to having participated in a massacre of
defenseless refugees during the Korean War some fifty years before, one of the
vets expressed his remorse: "That old boy upstairs is going to do the judging
on it. And so if you've done wrong, you don't stand too good a chance of getting
up there . . . I ain't figuring on making it."[2] Regardless of whether one's destiny
is determined by acts or by faith, it is eternal, so the decisions that one takes
and the actions that one conducts in this finite life have infinite importance.
We have but one life to live, and how we live it has eternal consequences.

From a Hindu point of view, this double destiny conception of the soul is
morally repugnant. First, it is morally repugnant because it is immensely dis-
proportional: not only do finite acts determine an infinite future, but the relative weight of one's moral and immoral acts is lost in the infinitude of Hell.
Second, it is morally repugnant because it allows for no redemption or relief;
few Christians have asserted the possibility of the salvation of beings in Hell,
and those who have done so are associated with fringe religious groups. By
contrast, the Hindu solution to this problem affirms not only that reward and
punishment are proportional, but that they are also finite – one can learn from
one's moral errors in future lives and redeem oneself by acting in accordance
with duty in spite of one's earlier wrongs.

The doctrine of *karma* is not fatalistic. On the contrary, it proposes that I
am the author of my own destiny. It is I – not God, not fate, not some random
set of causes beyond my control – who has produced the set of circumstances
in which I now find myself: the conditions of my birth, my social status and
family identity, my gender, my physical appearance, my intelligence and physical capacity or incapacity, unconscious aspects of my character and personality,
fortunate or unfortunate events that might befall me, successes and failures,
and the conditions of my death. The questions that should govern my life are
these: Given the circumstances in which I have placed myself, how can I make
best use of this life? It is I who placed myself here: for what purpose? What is
it that I can learn from this particular embodiment, this life experience? How
should I behave in the roles that I have chosen? What are my duties and responsibilities? How can I best insure that my next rebirth will be a fortunate one?

Critics of this religious and moral system, both in India and outside it, have
argued that the doctrine of *karma* holds individuals to be solely responsible
for their conditions, no matter how unpleasant. It is a system, they say, in which
the larger society is absolved from the moral need or responsibility to address
conditions of poverty, to care for persons who are mentally or physically challenged, to address gender inequalities, to reform political institutions, and so

on. And there can be no doubt that this doctrine has had a conservative effect, maintaining social hierarchies for generations. Twentieth-century reformers have condemned the *karma* doctrine as the remnant of a feudalistic, socially oppressive past, and they have proposed a social ethics of responsibility and care for society's least fortunate individuals.

These are valid arguments and, partly in response to them, India has developed social welfare programs, affirmative action policies, and democratic political institutions in contrast to traditional patterns, which simply "blamed the victim." Still, the doctrine of *karma* remains fundamental to Hindu and Buddhist self-understanding. Why?

- Certainly one reason why the *karma* doctrine has survived is the sheer weight of tradition; it has worked as a deep-seated principle of moral cause and effect for centuries of cultural history.
- The *karma* doctrine affirms self-transformation: though I may not be able to change the conditions of my present life, I have ultimate control over the conditions of my future lives.
- The doctrine reinforces moral responsibility: the effort to do good and to fulfill one's social duties is rewarded – good accrues to the giver as well as the receiver.
- *Karma* inspires self-reflection and provides answers to questions of personal identity: Who am I? What is my purpose in life? Why do I think and act as I do? What unconscious motivations (which are thought to be derived from thoughts and behaviors in a prior lifetime) predispose me to think and act as I do in this life?
- The doctrine encourages the individual to seek moral and spiritual lessons from present circumstances, none of which are the result of random chance; life as a whole, in all its details, is packed with meaning and significance; in terms of my deeper self, the self that persists through innumerable lifetimes and transformations, what can I learn from this experience: as a woman, as a laborer, as one born into poverty, as one born into wealth? All of these experiences contribute to the deeper wisdom of the unfolding self.

Varna-āśrama-dharma

My duties and responsibilities in this life are based upon my caste or social position (*varna*) and my stage in life (*āśrama*). That is, ethical duty is situational and determined by one's specific identity. The phrase *varna-āśrama-dharma* means generally "duty" and, specifically, "duties determined by my caste and my stage in life" – duties determined, as we have seen, by karmic laws of moral cause and effect.

Traditionally, *varna* was associated with occupations. Today caste is related to social, ethnic, family, and community identity, though it can still be occupationally restrictive. In the Laws of Manu, an ancient collection of moral rules and social values, four major castes were identified. (Lower still was a group of casteless individuals, and later on these became known as "untouchables" because of the ritually unclean work they performed.) The four castes and their primary roles and responsibilities are listed below from low to high:

- Sūdra (laborers) – labor and service;
- Vaiśya (merchants and capitalists) – production of goods;
- Kṣatriya (government officials, traditionally "warriors") – protection of social order;
- Brahmin (priests and religious teachers) – spiritual guidance.

The other determinant of social responsibility is my stage in life, that is, my age and the "rites of passage" that introduce each phase – such as rites of childhood, of marriage, and of retirement. Though most persons complete only the first three of the four *āśramas*, these are listed below, going from youth to old age:

- the student phase: study and learning, including religious education;
- the householder phase: creating a family, pursuing one's chosen vocation, serving one's community;
- the retiree phase: retirement, study, and contemplation;
- the Sannyasa phase: renunciation, "wandering," spiritual self-cultivation.

Collectively, *varna-āśrama-dharma* are directly related to *karma*: if I perform my duties well, I produce positive karmic outcomes; if I fail to perform them, I produce negative karmic outcomes. Moreover, just as *karma* is the energy that fuels *saṃsāra*, *dharma* is the moral law that sustains the community and the social world.

As we noted in the discussion of the Confucian tradition, Hindu *dharma* assumes social hierarchy. In a system that makes morality situational rather than general or universal, I should be mindful of my role and status, as well as of the role and status of those whom I serve, or who serve me. Of course, this system is much more complex than we see here (the *varnas* are general designations for a significantly more layered social network, consisting of social groups called *jātis* – the word from which we derived the English word "caste"), and one's sense of social place is even more specifically defined.

Karma-marga

To perform one's own duty well, without concern for oneself, is the thrust of *karma-yoga*, the spiritual discipline of action. In short, this spiritual path is action without attachment, that is, action without concern for the fruits of action. To do what is right, to act selflessly – without regard for one's own ego – is the basic motivational principle behind *varna-āśrama-dharma*. In the short term, such action is socially beneficial: it serves the family and the community. In the long term it redoubles upon itself with the reward of a higher rebirth. And, in an ultimate sense, it promotes the greater spiritual goal of egolessness and the unity of the deeper self with "God" or the cosmos. We will explore this last point in Chapter 17.

Ultimately Arjuna goes into battle, to fulfill his social duty. So, too, should I embrace my dharma, first by understanding it – by knowing what is expected of me – then by fulfilling it – by carrying out my responsibilities with their intrinsic value foremost in my mind. In doing so, I am serving others and creating a better world; moreover, I am moving forward along a multi-lifetime path of spiritual development and self-realization.

Notes

1   *Anguttara Nikaya*, iii 415; from the Pali Buddhist canon.
2   The Associated Press, "U.S. Veterans Have Mixed Reactions about No Gun Ri." Associated Press, October 1, 1999. At http://news.google.com/newspapers?nid=86 1&dat=19991001&id=1N9HAAAAIBAJ&sjid=JIAMAAAAIBAJ&pg=1541, 6593683 (accessed March 11, 2013).

16

Jñāna-marga

One way of describing the Hindu tradition is in terms of three dimensions: moral, spiritual, and religious. *Karma-marga* addresses the moral dimension, *jñāna-marga* the spiritual, *bhakti-marga* the religious. Clearly these are artificial distinctions with vague boundaries, but it is meaningful to say that the realms of moral self-cultivation, spiritual self-understanding, and religious worship and devotion are not one and the same; and sometimes they can come into conflict. Yet all, from a Hindu point of view, lead to the ultimate transformation of the self and "liberation" from embodied existence.

Jñāna-marga is described as the path of knowledge; it is best suited for persons who are controlled by their minds, whose egos are caught up in intellectual solutions and the mastery of knowledge. *Jñāna-marga* challenges the mind-driven ego by presenting a radically new, in some ways "anti-intellectual" understanding of ultimate reality. It does so by saying that the world we know, "this" world of differentiated beings, of multiplicity, of perceptual experience – the world we see and touch and feel – is an illusory world. We think we "know" the truth, when in fact our understanding of reality is based on ignorance. How so?

The spiritual teachings of the Hindu tradition, as expressed in religious texts like the Upaniṣads, emphasize the oneness of self and spirit, of soul and Soul, and the unity of oneself with every other person, every other being in the universe. We do not ordinarily "see" this – in fact we live almost in abject denial of it, affirming instead the individual uniqueness of things, especially our own ego. We are so attached to this uniqueness that we even claim to "possess" it – this is "my" body, these are "my" thoughts and feelings, this is "my" life, "my" money and property, these are "my" rights and this is "my" happiness, even if it comes at the expense of others'. The ego, in other words, is highly individuated: it uniquely identifies "me" as the person I am, with my own, distinct "soul and substance" (the *ahaṃkāra*, as ego is designated in Sanskrit). But, from a spiritual

Asian Religions: A Cultural Perspective, First Edition. Randall L. Nadeau.
© 2014 John Wiley & Sons, Ltd. Published 2014 by John Wiley & Sons, Ltd.

point of view, the yogic discipline of wisdom (*jñāna-yoga*) teaches that this passion for uniqueness blinds us to our true selves and to the true nature of the universe: we are ignorant, un-seeing (*avidyā*). If we awake to truth, if we achieve cosmic consciousness, then we see the unity of all things.

Hindu scriptures describe the self as multilayered. The ego is conditioned by laws of cause and effect, and it is material in form. This aspect of self is *prakṛti*, the physical aspect. It consists of the physical body, conscious thoughts, even unconscious motivations and desires – the aspects of myself that individuate me, make me different from others, identify me. We are materialistic in the sense that we grasp these aspects of the self as essential – we fear death, fear loss of property or of loved ones, fear for our reputations because our egos are so tied up in these distinguishing marks of identity.

The ego is subject to the karmic laws of cause and effect, as we have seen in Chapter 15. In fact the particular characteristics of our egos (physical appearance, conscious thinking, unconscious predilections) were self-caused, coming as a consequence of actions in the past, including actions in previous lives. But there is a deeper dimension of the self that is beyond individuation and is "pure spirit" (*puruṣa*). This deeper self survives my death and takes on new forms (it is "reincarnated" – made physical again) as a consequence of karmic energy.

In its individuated hypostasis, the spiritual essence that underlies my ego is called *jīva*, "drop" or "spark." "My" *jīva* has experienced countless rebirths and has learned from them, has undergone innumerable forms and capacities, and has gained in wisdom as a result. This wisdom may not be conscious (consciousness is an aspect of *prakṛti*) – it is not intellectual knowledge, like that possessed by the ego – but these lessons are like "marks of learning" (in Sanskrit, *sanskaras*) that the deeper "I" has absorbed. The progression of lifetimes, and the lessons that the soul learns in each, propels the self forward. These lessons incline me to seek rebirth in higher and higher forms. In this sense, rebirth at a higher level of existence from one life to the next does not reflect only moral reward ("good *karma*"), but also spiritual progress. In fact Hindus make no claim that an upper caste Hindu is a morally better person than a lower caste Hindu, but that person *is* spiritually more mature. Why?

The *puruṣārthas*

At the level of the unconscious, the level that is closest to the true self or to the soul, we are motivated by wants and desires that are only vaguely known. These inclinations are classified in Hindu scriptures as *puruṣārthas*: wants, desires, preoccupations.[1] Three of the *puruṣārthas* are related to the individuated ego and to the productive phases of the student and householder *āśramas*. These three are the *trivarga* ("triple set"):

- *kāma* – pleasure, especially pleasant physical sensations such as sexual sensations;
- *artha* – acquisitiveness, the desire for material wealth;
- *dharma* – service, moral responsibility, a desire to contribute to the creation of a better world.

As long as they are pursued morally (according to the dictates of *dharma*), the goals or "preoccupations" of sensual pleasure and accumulation of wealth are appropriate for the material, embodied self of everyday life. In Hinduism (as opposed to the ascetic strains of Christianity and Buddhism, for example), sexual desire is not, in itself, morally problematic. Certainly there are moral ways and immoral ways to satisfy sexual desires, and these actions have karmic consequences. Some forms of sexual expression, such as incest and adultery, are morally condemned. But sex itself is natural and appropriate for most persons. There is even a religious scripture dedicated to its proper satisfaction: the *Kāma Sūtra* (a *sūtra* is a religious text). In this sense sex is celebrated in Hinduism, both as a sustainer of life and as a means of spiritual development.

Though celebrating sexual desire as a creator and sustainer of material reality, the scriptural tradition regards *kāma* and its fixation on the body and its sensual satisfaction as spiritually inferior, spiritually childish. It has its own emotional rewards, at a higher level of consciousness, but sex itself is limited to the body and its sensations. Moreover, it is highly individualistic: even though I may be having sex with another person, my physical sensations are mine alone, and cannot be shared with or experienced by another. They are limited to my body, my self. Sex is ego-centered, and cannot be ultimately fulfilling. No wonder that most people eventually give it up, if not in old age, then at least in later lives dedicated to a celibate lifestyle. Over time the deeper self, the soul, grows tired of sex and sees its limitations. Sex can satisfy physical desires, but it cannot satisfy one's deeper wants and needs.

The second of the *puruṣārthas* is *artha*, the desire for material wealth. *Artha* resembles *kāma* in that both are highly materialistic and both should be governed by the third of the *puruṣārthas*, *dharma*. Yet wealth, too, is limited and ultimately unsatisfying. Unlike sex, it can be shared, but if shared too much, it dissipates; I can only share it to a certain point before it is no longer "wealth." Moreover, though it is undeniable that wealth can buy a certain amount of comfort and security, even happiness, it cannot secure any of these things, and it can also cause misery and strife. The possessions that I enjoy because of wealth are themselves ultimately unsatisfying; they cannot meet the soul's drive for freedom and for something lasting and eternal.

The third *puruṣārtha* is *dharma*, here understood as social service or responsibility. *Dharma* governs both *kama* and *artha* but goes beyond them. Unlike sexual sensation and personal wealth, service can be shared with society as a whole, and *dharma* can be fulfilled in government, education, and charitable activities. As the third of the "triple set," *dharma* represents the highest and most noble of personal aspirations.

The fourth *puruṣārtha* is *mokṣa*: liberation, the impulse to overcome embodiment altogether.

Striving for satisfaction in a material sense, the soul comes to the ultimate realization that this world is one of unending and irredeemable imperfection – wherever there are people, there inevitably is suffering, conflict, disappointment, and loss. These pains are simply part of life and, as long as we are living as embodied beings, they are unavoidable. The mature soul recognizes that true perfection and spiritual contentment can come only when the self is no longer embodied. This is the fourth of the *puruṣārthas*, the desire for liberation from embodied existence, *mokṣa*. Traditionally this motivation was associated with the later stages of life, the *āśramas* of retirement and renunciation, dedicated to spiritual self-cultivation, and it is regarded as the highest goal of human life (*paramapuruṣārtha*).

Some modern-day scholars and teachers associate the four *puruṣārthas* explicitly with the four *varnas* or the four *āśramas*, but a direct sequence is not found in the *Dharmaśāstras* (scriptural texts of moral instruction). Still, it is clear that the first three of the *puruṣārthas* are most appropriate in the productive stages of life and are ultimately supplanted and replaced by the desire for *mokṣa* in the later stages. Some texts and schools also reserved the *paramapuruṣārtha* (highest goal) for the highest – Brahmin – caste, but most Hindus throughout history have seen *mokṣa* as an appropriate goal for all, regardless of caste.[2]

Within Hinduism, the three goals of life associated with this-worldly existence, *kāma, artha,* and *dharma* – known collectively as the *trivarga* – are ultimately found to be unsatisfying. They are inevitably constrained by the sheer fact of human limitation. More often than not we are frustrated in the achievement of our desires, whether for sex, for money, or for a better world. Moreover, even when we achieve them, they are not ultimately fulfilling; they are not as great as we thought they would be. To illustrate this point to my students, I cite an interview by Terry Gross on Public Broadcasting's "Fresh Air" program with the Olympic gold medal winner Florence Griffith Joyner. "Flo-Jo" still holds the world records in the 100-meter and 200-meter dashes, set in the Olympic trials prior to the Seoul Olympics in 1988. Sporting neon-colored full-body track suits, gold shoes, six-inch fingernails, a full head of hair, and a model's good looks, she is arguably not only "the fastest woman who ever lived," but also the most stunning. One week before the tenth anniversary of her three Olympic gold medals, she died, at the age of 38, of a grand mal seizure – an epileptic condition that she had suffered from since age 30. In her interview with Terry Gross, Joyner commented that the moment when she became most aware of the limitations of the human body and experienced the frustration of being embodied was not during her epileptic episodes – which must have been terrifying, painful, and humiliating – but rather at the peak of her training as an Olympic athlete. It was at that time, when she had pushed her body to its limits and had attained perhaps the most "perfect body" that any human has ever attained, that she wished she could be free of it, and that the greatest attainments of this life and this world could not meet her ultimate desire and ultimate goal: to be free of embodiment altogether.

Moksha as Unity with Brahman

In spite of its morally sophisticated system of *karma* and rebirth, of duties according to caste and stage of life – which would seem to divide and classify human beings – Hinduism affirms that all beings are on the same path and are ultimately destined for spiritual awakening in the form of liberation from embodied existence. Religiously speaking, then, we are all equal. In essence, the Brahmin is no different from the Sūdra – the laborer. The Brahmin was once a Sūdra; the Sūdra will some day be a Brahmin. Hence the religiously perceptive individual recognizes no real difference between them.

When I was a graduate student, my advisor, Dr. Ashok Aklujkar, a world-renowned professor of Sanskrit literature, expressed this sentiment in an extraordinarily humble way. When I commented that I felt I was far below him in scholarship and ability, he said: "Randall, I am no better than you are; I simply started earlier." Now myself a teacher for some twenty years, I often think of these words: the teacher is simply one who has learned and passed on to others what he or she has gained; later on the student will do the same. My advisor was not making a religious claim, simply a point about the process of education and scholarly transmission – but Hinduism teaches this lesson in a spiritual sense: the Brahmin is no better than the Sūdra, simply further along on a common path.

What "happens" with *mokṣa*? What is the experience of "disembodiment," of pure spirit? Hindu scriptures describe *mokṣa* as the realization of the unity of soul and God. It is explained philosophically with the help of two senses of "realization":

1   First, "to realize" means to "make real," to achieve an objective, as in "realizing a goal." The scriptures describe the long course of the soul's individuated existence over innumerable lifetimes, as it finally ends when the goal of the soul's reabsorption in pure spirit, Brahman, is accomplished: this is a returning to God. As the individual soul, the *jīva* is likened to a drop of water or a spark of fire; *mokṣa* represents the immersion of the drop into

the "sea" of Brahman or the immersion of the spark in the "fire" of Brahman. The soul does not cease to exist, but it is liberated from its individuated form and absorbed into a greater reality.

2   Second, "to realize" means to "understand," to have an awakening. A major theme of the Upaniṣads, the most "mystical" of the Hindu scriptures, is that the individual is "already" liberated and always has been, but has simply not yet become conscious of this truth. Living in ignorance and failing to see reality as it truly is, the self exists under the illusion of difference, mul-tiplicity, and individuation. *Mokṣa* is the realization that the true essence of the self is *Ātman* (the soul essence, shared with all living beings) and that *Ātman* is Brahman – that Soul is God. Why, then, does this world of everyday experience seem to exist? It is but the "play" (*līlā*) of Brahman, an illusion (*māyā*). One who penetrates this illusion attains wisdom, the realization of ultimate unity, expressed in Sanskrit as *Advaita Vedānta*, "the non-duality of *Ātman* and Brahman, self and God, highest teaching of the Vedas." In Hindu mystical philosophy, what we see is not truly real; what is truly real is unseen.

The realization of *mokṣa* is the ultimate goal expressed by the god Krishna in the *Bhagavad Gita*. This realization can be accomplished by the discipline of wisdom and insight, *jñāna-yoga*. Quoting from the *Gita*:

> The truly wise mourn neither for the living nor for the dead. There was never a time when I did not exist, nor you, nor any of these kings. Nor is there any future in which we shall cease to be . . . Bodies are said to die but that which possesses the body is eternal.[3]

Notes

1   V. C. George, in his "Purusharthas: Dharma Artha Kama Moksha" (Mahatma Gandhi University doctoral thesis, 1995, p. 39), defines *puruṣārtha* as "meaning of life"; etymologically, it is "that which is desired" (p. 39).

2   For a discussion, see Patrick Olivelle, *The Asrama System: The History and Hermeneutics of a Religious Institution* (New York: Oxford University Press, 1993), pp. 216–218.

3   Translation adapted from Swami Prabhavananda and Christopher Isherwood, *Bhagavad-Gita: The Song of God* (New York: Signet Classics, 2002), p. 36.

17

Bhakti-marga

The third of the three paths to liberation is often described as the "easiest": trusting God in whatever form God may take, through ego-denying acts of worship and devotion. This is *bhakti-yoga*, the discipline of love, and it is expressed by Krishna to Arjuna in the *Bhagavad Gita* in these words:

> Offer up everything to me. If your heart is united with me, you will be set free from *karma* even in this life and come to me at last . . . Though a man be soiled with the sins of a lifetime, let him but love me, rightly resolved, in utter devotion: I see no sinner. That man is holy . . . Even those who belong to the lower castes – women, Vaishyas and Shudras, too – can reach the highest spiritual realization, if they will take refuge in me . . . Fill your heart and mind with me, adore me, make all your acts an offering to me, bow down to me in self-surrender, and you will come into my being.[1]

Offerings to the Hindu gods are made in a worship service (*pūja*) conducted in a temple (Figure 17.1) and presided over by trained priests. Devotees participate in these offerings with single-minded devotion. Thousands of Hindu temples can be found in India and throughout the world, including some 1,000 Hindu temples in North America.[2]

Theologically, Hindus explain that Krishna – or any of the other deities worshipped in Hindu temples – is a divine manifestation of the one great soul, Brahman. In fact, if you were to interview any of the devotees at the Hindu Temple of San Antonio (or any other temple situated in the English-speaking world), they would explain that Hinduism is a monotheistic religion, in spite of the presence of several deity images arrayed at the front of the temple, for instance the elephant-headed god Gaṇeśa, the goddess Lakṣmī, the kingly lord Rāma, the dancing god Shiva (Śiva), the shape-shifting monkey god Hanuman, and so on.

Asian Religions: A Cultural Perspective, First Edition. Randall L. Nadeau.

Figure 17.1   Hindu temple featuring images of the Lord Krishna. © Sunsetman / Shutterstock.

It is common among Hindus to choose one god as especially "cherished" or "favored," a personal *iṣṭa-devatā*. This choice may be conditioned by one's place of birth or family, but the devotee is free to choose the god who is most meaningful to him or her. Although the *iṣṭa-devatā* – the "cherished one" – is but one god among many, he is treated as "one alone without a second" (as Brahman is described in the Upaniṣads), an object of love and devotion that is all-encompassing and – in Western terms – monotheistic. *Bhakti* inspires this kind of single-minded focus on the divine object of love. The one god of worship is given one's full attention, affirming the unity of God: the unity of all gods, the unity of all souls, and the unity of self and God.

On different occasions or in different temples, other Hindu devotees direct their undivided attention to a different god or to a different manifestation of the one God (Brahman). In this light the worshipper can appreciate the greatness of God in all of God's forms and experience the love of God in all aspects.[3] As one devotee explained to me:

> In my life I experience many kinds of love – parental love for my child, sexual love for my lover, adoring love for my parent, tender love for a pet, grateful love for a teacher, and so on; if I imagine God in all forms, I experience love of God in all of these aspects.[4]

As one worships each of the gods in turn (some dedicate one day of the week to each of six or seven temple deities), one's concentration is so focused on a single god of worship and on that god alone. One is "seeing God" through one of God's particular manifestations.

Another way in which this multiplicity within unity is expressed is through the *pūja* or worship service itself. A key element of the ritual is the chanting of the "108 names" of the god. This is performed for a number of gods, and the number 108 is constant, but the particular names differ from one god to another. Among the 108 names of Krishna, for example, are *murali manohara* ("flute-playing god"), *shyam* ("dark-complexioned"), and *gopalpriya* ("lover of cow-heards"), distinctive characteristics that are described in Krishna's mythology. The 108 names of Gaṇeśa include *gajānana* ("elephant-headed"), *vighneśvara* ("remover of obstacles"), *eshanputra* ("son of Shiva"), and so on. By chanting the 108 names, the devotee is able to visualize the deity's form and functions as a multifaceted object of devotion.

Taken together, all of these forms create an experience of complete and total love, and at least an approximation of the limitless nature of Brahman and of the soul in union with Brahman. This is the multidimensional nature of *bhakti*.

Brahman is difficult to comprehend at a conceptual level. Brahman is described in the Hindu scriptures as being (paradoxically) "beyond description": "neither this nor that," neither male nor female, limitless, all-encompassing, indistinguishable from any other thing and yet not contained in any one thing, "one without a second." From a comparative point of view, Brahman is theologically parallel to the God of the Abrahamic traditions. But how far can this comparison take us, if we, being Westerners, wish to understand Hindu divinity? This is a theological and philosophical question that goes beyond the scope of this book; but, descriptively at least, it is a meaningful question. In his *Summa theologica*, Thomas Aquinas (1225–1274), who is often regarded as Christianity's most comprehensive theologian, describes eight attributes of God. Hindu theology regards Brahman as having parallel characteristics:

1   Incorporeality: the Abrahamic God and Hindu Brahman share the characteristic of being beyond any single form; in fact, both are described as immaterial, pure spirit.
2   Ineffability: God is inexpressible in words; Brahman is "*neti . . . neti . . .*," "not this . . . not that . . ."
3   Unity: though Christians have their notion of a "triune" God or "Trinity," God's oneness is always affirmed; in the Muslim prayer, too, "there is no god but Allah"; in the Upaniṣads, Brahman is described as "one alone without a second."
4   Eternity: the Abrahamic God existed before time began and is eternal; Brahman transcends all cycles and all rebirths.
5   Immutability: God's being is perfect and indestructible; Brahman is *sat-chit-ānanda*, perfect being, perfect consciousness, perfect bliss.

6   Omnipotence: God is all-powerful; Brahman is creator, sustainer, and destroyer of worlds.
7   Omniscience: God is all-knowing; union with Brahman produces a "cosmic consciousness."
8   Goodness: God is benevolent, though His ways may be incomprehensible; Brahman represents the fulfillment of the highest spiritual goal.

Aquinas insists that God cannot be fully comprehended; He is "ineffable." Brahman, too, is beyond description. If this is so, how can God/Brahman be known? The Abrahamic traditions propose two types of solution to this problem: either God can be known by virtue of God's appearances or manifestations within the world (Christians, for example, say that God was made "incarnate" in Christ), or God can be known through mystical union. The Hindu tradition shows similar approaches, and we will look here at two illustrations: "knowing Brahman" in the god Krishna (an avatar or physical manifestation of Brahman) and in the god Shiva (a god who evokes mystical union). Krishna and Shiva are among the most widely worshipped of all the Hindu gods, and so we are justified, in a short introduction such as this one, to limit ourselves to them as representative examples of Hindu divinity.

Krishna: Knowing Brahman in Human Form

The first sense in which Brahman can be known is through incarnation in worldly manifestations, that is, in physical forms that make Brahman approachable and accessible. In Sanskrit, this is *Saguna Brahman*, Brahman "with characteristics," in contrast with the "formless" nature of Brahman as "pure spirit," *Nirguna Brahman* (Brahman "without characteristics").[5]

As Krishna (Kṛṣṇa), Brahman loves the world and asks for love in return. Krishna is the most widely venerated object of *bhakti*. This love is total: in the *Bhagavad Gita*, Krishna enjoins the devotee to "keep the name of the Lord spinning in your mind in every instant."

When we think of love, we think of two kinds of love – or two of the most intense forms of love: the love of a parent, especially a mother, for her child, and the love of a lover for his or her beloved. Krishna satisfies both of these deeply emotional needs, in a way that is spiritually fulfilling thanks to his eternal nature.

Many stories about Krishna revolve around his childhood: he appeared to his parents as a blue-skinned infant who inspired their undying devotion (as portrayed in Figure 17.2, for example). The best known image of the infant Krishna is "Krishna the butter thief." After hours of toil over the butter urn, Krishna's milk mother discovers that the boy has helped himself to the sweet butter: the evidence is all over his face! Ready to spank the naughty child, she

Figure 17.2   Krishna the Butter Thief: a portrait of Krishna painted on a truck in Jodhpur. © Floris Leeuwenberg / Corbis.

is so overwhelmed by love for her darling boy that she stays her hand, smothering his cheeks with kisses instead. Such is the love that the mischievous god inspires. This well-known story is the subject of a classical Indian dance, learned by many teenage Indian girls, both in India and around the world, especially in the dance form called *Bharata natyam*.

In adolescence Krishna is even more mischievous – and even more alluring in his seduction of the goat-herding girls (gopis) of a pastoral forest (see Figure 17.3). There he engages in *rāsa-līlā*, the "relish of play," hiding the gopis' clothes, demanding that they raise their hands in worship of him, and seducing them with the intoxicating sounds of his flute. Krishna's favorite object of love is a gopi named Rādhā. Their love is consummated in a role reversal where it is the god who serves the mortal, and their sexual union represents the union of human and divine, soul and Soul, *Ātman* and Brahman. In his discussion of the love affair between Rādhā and Krishna, David Kinsley writes: "In the worship of Krishna, the earthly passions of love are refined, idealized, and endlessly embellished so that they may become the vehicles through which humans transcend their earthly limitations."[6]

Figure 17.3   Krishna and Radha, surrounded by the gopis of Vrindavana. Painting miniature. Rajasthan, India. © appujee – Fotolia.com.

Shiva: Knowing Brahman through Mystical Union

The second way in which Brahman can be known is through mystical union, in experiences that transcend material limitation. This mystical sense of God is illustrated by another of the major Hindu deities, the god Shiva (Śiva).

   Like the other gods, Shiva is also represented in form; but his forms are highly abstracted, possessing opposite and paradoxical aspects, and thus compelling the viewer to recognize Brahman as ultimately featureless, beyond representation or conceptualization. In one popular image, Shiva is *nataraja*, the "lord of dance" (Figure 17.4), where he manifests all the characteristics of Brahman in one image: in one hand he holds a drum, symbolizing the creation of worlds; a second hand is raised in a symbolic gesture (a *mudrā*) of fearlessness, which also represents Shiva sustaining the universe; a third hand holds fire, symbolizing the destruction of worlds at the end of a cosmic cycle;

Figure 17.4   *Shiva-nataraja*, "Lord of the Dance." © Bouzou / Shutterstock.

a fourth hand points downward, at that which is most important – the upraised foot – in a symbol of freedom from embodiment. The other foot is stamping on a demon, who represents the ignorance that ties us to the world: this gesture symbolizes overcoming illusion. Since the world as we know it – material, differentiated, bound by death and rebirth – is ultimately illusory, Shiva is known as the "destroyer of worlds," which is symbolized in the *Shiva-nataraja* by the ring of fire encompassing the dancing image.

Other images of Shiva demonstrate his capacity to hold opposite characteristics within one form. One example is *Ardha-nārīśvara*, the Lord who is "half-male, half-female" (see Figure 17.5). In this form Shiva demonstrates his capacity to overcome all dualities.

The most abstract forms of Shiva are the *Shiva-lingam* (the "mark" of Shiva, resembling the phallus) and the *yoni* (the vagina); the two are depicted sometimes separately, sometimes together (see Figure 17.6). In India Shiva is most frequently represented as the *Shiva-lingam*. The *lingam* is an aniconic, abstract image of Shiva: Shiva as *Nirguṇa Brahman* (in this case, Brahman without a fully anthropomorphized or human form). The *yoni* is the aniconic image of the Goddess (*devi*) – or of the Feminine Principle (*shakti*) – in union with the *Shiva-lingam*.[7]

Figure 17.5 Lord Shiva as *Ardha-nārīśvara*, "half-male, half-female." Chola Period. Bronze Gallery, Chennai, India. © Hal Beral / Corbis.

Figure 17.6 Aniconic image of Shiva as the unity of *lingam* and *yoni*. © rajidrc – Fotolia.com.

These physical symbols illustrate that manifestations of God (Brahman) in the form of Shiva bring opposite qualities together in one being. As creator, renunciant, and destroyer of illusion, Shiva is a composite figure in five aspects:

1 his name: etymologically, the name "Shiva" means "kindness, benevolence," but Lord Shiva is the "Destroyer" of worlds: in his male iconic form, Shiva has a third eye with which he burns desire (*kāma*) to ashes;

2 his aniconic form: Shiva is represented in aniconic form as the *lingam* – the phallus; and yet Shiva is the patron god of *sannyasi*, renunciants who have given up all forms of sexual desire;

3 his iconic forms, both male and female: Shiva is represented as *Ardha-nārīśvara*, "half-male, half-female";

4 his activity: as male, Shiva is quiescent; but in union with the divine feminine principle (*shakti*), in the form of Pārvatī, Kālī or of other deities, he is active;

5 his aniconic forms, both male and female: Shiva is represented as the *lingam* in union with the *yoni*, symbol of the feminine principle.

In all of these images, Shiva represents the overcoming of opposites and the non-duality of *Ātman* and Brahman, male and female, self and God.

Survey 3 Religious Attitudes Based on Hindu Worldviews

The link for this survey is http://goo.gl/NQKBFa. It asks you to choose statements that reflect your theological understanding in relation to Hindu conceptions of divinity.

Notes

1 Swami Prabhavananda and Christopher Isherwood, *Bhagavad-Gita: The Song of God* (New York: Signet Classics, 2002), p. 81.
2 Website of the Pluralism Project at Harvard University (pluralism.org), consulted on March 28, 2012.
3 "Each god is exalted in turn. Each is praised as creator, source, and sustainer of the universe when one stands in the presence of that deity. There are many gods, but their multiplicity does not diminish the significance or power of any of them. Each of the great gods may serve as a lens through which the whole of reality is clearly

seen." Diana Eck, *Darsan: Seeing the Divine Image in India* (New York: Columbia University Press, 1998), p. 22.

4   Conversation with Kedar Chintapalli, Hindu Temple of San Antonio, November 2011.

5   On the distinction between *Saguṇa Brahman* (Brahman "with characteristics") and *Nirguṇa Brahman* (Brahman "without characteristics"), see Eck, *Darsan*, p. 10.

6   David Kinsley, *Hinduism* (Prentice Hall: 1982), p. 79.

7   The "phallic" character of the *Shiva-lingam* is contested. Some Hindus, especially in response to Westerners who take offense that Hindus would "worship a phallus," argue that the *Shiva-lingam* is nothing more than the pillar-shaped "mark of Shiva" (the literal meaning of *lingam*). On the other hand, many scriptural sources clearly identify the *lingam* and the *yoni* with the sexual organs. In either case, the *lingam* is hardly limited to sexual associations. As is written in a commentary on the image, "when one looks at the *lingam*, one's mind is elevated and thinks of the Lord" (*Shiva-lingam sadhana*).

18

Hinduism in the Modern World

Enter a Hindu temple anywhere in the world, and you are met by colorful images of gods and goddesses. Appearing both within history and outside of it, both in "this world" and in other cosmic times and places, their stories are recited and reenacted in sermons, at the theater, in music and dance. Hindu cosmology describes vast cycles of time, traversing tens of thousands of years, in patterns of cosmic decline and regeneration. Yet an entire cycle, a *mahā-yuga*, is "but a single blink in the eye of Brahman." Myths of ageless gods and cosmological conceptions of eternal life, death, and rebirth give Hinduism the feel of something quite ancient, even timeless. Not surprisingly, in books such as this one, Hinduism usually comes "first," no doubt due in large measure to this almost primordial appeal.

Today Hindu influence extends far beyond India. Hindu gods, Hindu rites, and Hindu philosophy can be found all over the world: certainly in Buddhism, which many Hindus regard simply as a particular expression of Hinduism, but also in deity cults, temple architecture, conceptions of *karma* and rebirth, and other cultural symbols, from Indonesia to Japan. In fact it would not be a stretch to make the claim that Chinese religion and culture cannot be fully understood without reference to the Hindu tradition. Just to give one example, the fire offerings and talismanic writing that feature prominently in Taoist temple rituals resemble their Hindu counterparts too much for the similarity to be merely coincidental; an historical liturgical transmission is much more likely. Moreover, many Chinese temples also host Hindu gods, which stand out through their fierce expressions and what Chinese call their "Western" (that is, Indian) characteristics.

The Indian diaspora has also contributed to the globalization of Hindu traditions. Hindus have emigrated to every part of the world and, in England and

Asian Religions: A Cultural Perspective, First Edition. Randall L. Nadeau.
© 2014 John Wiley & Sons, Ltd. Published 2014 by John Wiley & Sons, Ltd.

the United States in particular, most Indian immigrants are highly educated. Many have sought to preserve their cultural and religious traditions by constructing temples and community centers in their new homes. Every semester, my students in Texas visit a local Hindu temple, built to resemble temples in India. The temple is maintained by recent immigrants from India as well as by the descendants of immigrants. Temple devotees hire Hindu priests from India to conduct periodic rites and use the temple for social and cultural events – such as dance classes for teenagers, service projects, and lectures on Hindu theology. My assignment entails participant observation and a reflection paper based upon a close reading of Diana Eck's *Darśan*.[1] Years after students have taken the course, they remember the Hindu Temple Project as the high point of the semester. They observe the *pūja* and are encouraged to ask questions of the temple devotees. These conversations contribute more than anything that students have read in textbooks or heard in lectures to a sympathetic understanding of Hinduism as it is practiced in the modern world.

Hinduism left its modern legacy in intellectual currents in Europe and America, beginning with eighteenth- and nineteenth-century American transcendentalism and its successors – theosophy, Christian Science, and self-help movements like the "mind-cure" movement, the "mind science" movement, the "new thought" movement, and so on. Both Henry David Thoreau (1817– 1862) and Ralph Waldo Emerson (1803–1882) were inspired by Hindu *advaita* (non-dualism) and the idea that all gods and all things are manifestations of a single, abstract spiritual force. Thoreau's transcendentalist reading of the Hindu scriptures was based on the first English translation of the *Bhagavad Gita*, by Charles Wilkins (1749–1836).[2] Thoreau wrote:

> In the morning I bathe my intellect in the stupendous and cosmogonal philoso-
> phy of the Bhagavat Geeta, since whose composition years of the gods have
> elapsed, and in comparison with which our modern world and its literature seem
> puny and trivial . . . I lay down the book and go to my well for water, and lo!
> there I meet the servant of the Brahmin, priest of Brahma, and Vishnu and Indra,
> who still sits in his temple on the River Ganga reading the Vedas, or dwells at
> the root of a tree with his crust and waterjug. I meet his servant come to draw
> water for his master, and our buckets as it were grate together in the same well.
> The pure Walden water is mingled with the sacred water of the Ganga.[3]

In his seminal work *The Varieties of Religious Experience*, which was based on lectures he gave in Edinburgh, Scotland in 1901 and 1902, the American pragmatist William James devoted much attention to American and European converts to Hinduism and to its Western forms.[4] One hundred years later there is no doubt that ideas of "positive thinking," of "spirituality without religion," and of personal disciplines like yoga and vegetarianism owe their existence in America and Europe to Hinduism in its modern, "mystical" forms.

In the 1960s and 1970s modern Hinduism erupted on the American and European scene, first with the worldwide popularity of "TM" – transcendental meditation – and, second. with the globalizing enterprise of the International Society for Krishna Consciousness (ISKCON).

The TM movement was founded by Maharishi Mahesh Yogi (1917–2008) in the 1950s. TM is indebted to the yogic tradition of meditation upon sounds or internal mantra recitation, but, in spite of its focus on the "deeper self," it describes itself as a "non-religious" mental discipline. The Transcendental Meditation Program website presents scientific and psychological arguments for its effectiveness, rather than religious ones, though it cites "500 years of Vedic tradition" for its inspiration. The website claims that more than 5 million people worldwide have taken the TM course of study.

> The Transcendental Meditation technique allows your mind to settle inward beyond thought to experience the source of thought – pure awareness, also known as transcendental consciousness. This is the most silent and peaceful level of consciousness – your innermost Self. In this state of restful alertness, your brain functions with significantly greater coherence and your body gains deep rest."[5]

ISKCON (the International Society for Krishna Consciousness) was founded in 1966 by A. C. Bhaktivedanta Prabhupada (1896–1977). Known colloquially as the "Hare Krishna movement," ISKCON was branded a "cult" in the 1970s, when new religions gained widespread attention – from the People's Temple at Jonestown to Eckankar, scientology, Jews for Jesus, and the Rajneesh movement (to name some of the best known ones at the time). Lumped together with these other religions, ISKCON was targeted by the anti-cult movement of the 1980s. Today ISKCON has more than 80 centers around the world.[6] It is a *bhakti* (devotional movement) dedicated to the worship of Lord Krishna and promoting vegetarianism, purity of lifestyle, and salvation through communal chanting of the Lord's name.

Perhaps the most visible form of Hindu practice outside of India is in neighborhood health clubs and local yoga franchises. The yoga industry is one of the fastest growing in the world, with revenues approaching $6 billion a year and projected to grow above $8 billion by 2016.[7] While the health benefits of recreational yoga have recently come under attack[8] and its connection to Indian yoga is questioned (especially in India),[9] schools of yoga are growing in number at an exponential rate, embracing a wide spectrum – from Ashtanga Vinyasa Yoga to Iyengar Yoga, Integral Yoga, Kripalu Yoga, Sivananda Yoga, Bikram Yoga, Power Yoga, Satyananda Yoga, and innumerable others. Are these practices "Hindu"? Are they "religious"? My own experience, I suspect, is typical: an hour-long series of stretches and bends begins and ends with "affirmations" and reminders to "connect with my innermost self and the innermost self of others," to "find the balance between body and spirit," and to "acknowledge the supreme spirit of the universe, whatever it may be called." "*Namaste!*" All of these phrases echo the non-dualistic philosophy of *jñāna-yoga* in its modern guise.

It was a German scholar, Max Müller, who first catalogued Hindu scriptures, had them transcribed from the oral tradition, and translated them into English. From this point in the late nineteenth century and up until the twentieth, religious pundits and yoga masters – both Indian and European – have spread traditional Hindu teachings and practices throughout the world, adapting nativist traditions to the needs and interests of spiritual seekers from every culture. In addition, over the past century and into the twenty-first, thousands of Euro-Americans have journeyed to religious centers in India for instruction in yoga and *advaita* philosophy. Though the label suggests the religion of a particular place, India, "Hinduism" is now most certainly a world religion, with followers of every culture and ethnicity.

Hinduism and Modern India

To be self-consciously Hindu in modern India is a statement of choice. It was not always so. For most of India's history, "being Hindu" was simply a function of cultural belonging: it was not a matter of individual preference, but simply of communal identity. In fact, as we have seen, the English word "Hinduism" was a relatively late European invention. Nevertheless, since the partition of Pakistan and the establishment of two independent states in 1947, "Hinduism" has become a social and political designation, a self-referential term chosen especially by nationalistic Hindus to contrast themselves with Muslims of Indian descent. A recent manifestation of this deepening sense of religious–nationalist identity has been the development of a movement called *Hindū rāṣṭravāda*, "Hindu state" or "Hindu nationalism." It was a Hindu nationalist who assassinated Mahatma Gandhi in 1948, and in the subsequent years the movement has evolved into a political party, a fundamentalist religious sect, and groups who affirm Vedic teachings as the essence of Indian identity. These groups insist that there is a Hindu "essence" (*Hindutva*) that is no more or less than the "essence of India."

Hindū rāṣṭravāda emphasizes nationalistic elements of *Hindutva* over religious ones; in fact major leaders of the movement such as Madhav Sadashiv Golwalkar (1906–1973) described Hindu nationalism in explicitly non-religious and non-theological terms. Today the Bharatiya Janata Party (BJP; the Indian People's Party), which has won major victories in Indian elections since its founding in 1980, claims that "Indianness" is not restricted to Hinduism or to a religious "litmus test." Nevertheless, the BJP adopts language and terms from the Hindu tradition throughout its virulently nationalist and ethnically purist party platforms and political literature. In this sense, modern-day Hindu nationalism resembles the "Confucian fundamentalism" of the national studies movement in the People's Republic of China, drawing upon explicitly religious language while affirming a decidedly secular agenda.

One especially troubling element of the Hindu nationalist movement is a high-pitched and increasingly confrontational repudiation of Western academic research on the Hindu tradition, which nativistic Hindus accuse of being sensationalist, liberal, and anti-Hindu. Some Western scholars have reported threats on their lives, coming from extremist elements within the *Hindū rāṣṭravāda* movement. To what extent these fanatical voices are representative of modern Hinduism is difficult to say, but clearly the divide between "fundamentalist" Hinduism and "liberal" Hinduism is as pronounced in the Indian context as it is in Islam, Christianity, Confucianism, and other religions. Conflicts regarding what it means to be "Hindu" or to be "Indian" are shaped by parallel debates in all of the world's major religious traditions, from the Americas to Europe, the Middle East, and Asia. We live in a world that struggles with forces of globalization and intercultural pluralism on the one hand, and the equally powerful response of ethnic purity, ultra nationalism, and religious fundamentalism on the other. The ongoing debate about Indian identity in relation to Hinduism is representative of this worldwide trend.

Notes

1　Diana Eck, *Darśan: Seeing the Divine Image in India* (New York: Columbia University Press, 1998).

2　*The Bhagvat-Geeta, or Dialogues of Kreeshna and Arjoon; in Eighteen Lectures; with Notes. Translated from the Original, in the Sanskreet, or Ancient Language of the Brahmans, by Charles Wilkins, Senior Merchant in the service of the Honorable The East India Company, on their Bengal Establishment* (London: C. Nourse, 1785).

3　James L. Shanley, ed., *The Writings of Henry D. Thoreau: Walden* (Princeton, NJ: Princeton University Press, 1971), p. 298.

4　William James, *The Varieties of Religious Experience: A Study in Human Nature* (New York: Random House 1929; originally published in 1902).

5　At http://orgmeditationwww.tm./-techniques (accessed July 17, 2012).

6　See http://directory.krishna.com/temples (accessed July 17, 2012).

7　IBISWorld, cited in CNNMoney, at http://money.cnn.com/2011/10/18/small business/yoga_pilates/index.htm (accessed July 17, 2012).

8　William J. Broad, *The Science of Yoga: The Risks and the Rewards* (New York: Simon & Schuster, 2012).

9　Heather Timmons, "The Great Yoga Divide." *New York Times*, January 17, 2012. At http://india.blogs.nytimes.com/2012/01/17/the-great-yoga-divide/ (accessed July 17, 2012).

Part V

The Theravāda Buddhist Tradition

19

Buddhism and the Buddha

When a young man or woman elects to leave home to become a monk or nun in a Buddhist monastery, they declare a vow: "I take refuge in the Buddha, I take refuge in the *dharma*, I take refuge in the Sangha" – that is, they place their faith in and commit their lives to the Buddha, the Enlightened One; the *dharma*, his teaching; and the Sangha, the community of monastics who have dedicated their lives to religious cultivation. In the following chapters we will examine the life of the Buddha (Chapter 19); the basic teachings of the Buddha and their ethical consequences (Chapters 20–21); and Buddhist practice, both monastic and lay (Chapters 22–23). In Part VI we will examine later currents of Buddhism, especially the Mahāyāna tradition of East Asia, as well as con-temporary forms of Buddhism as a global religion.

Who was the Buddha? Was he a man or a god? Did he actually live in north-ern India, attain enlightenment and preach the *dharma* there, and die peace-fully at a time that he himself determined? Was he born a Hindu, and did he then critique and reform his tradition through a new revelation?

Christians ask similar questions about their founder, and many Christians would say that such questions are crucial to judging the truth of the religion itself. Modeling themselves on the quest for the historical Jesus, the first Western scholars to encounter Buddhism sought to authenticate the historical reality of the Buddha, and they often characterized him in familiar terms: like Christ, they said, the Buddha brought a new teaching of personal liberation, in contrast to what they described as the caste-based taboos and arcane laws of Hinduism. Or they contrasted the "Protestant emancipation" of Buddhism over against the "papal," priest-bound ritualism of Hinduism. This parallelism inspired a romanticized view of Buddhism that, under different guises and in different terms, has remained strong in the West to the present day. The orien-talist fantasy of a peace-loving, calm, and centered people, which values and

Asian Religions: A Cultural Perspective, First Edition. Randall L. Nadeau.
© 2014 John Wiley & Sons, Ltd. Published 2014 by John Wiley & Sons, Ltd.

supports highly individualized, spiritual cultivation, is an image of Buddhism that most observers in the West have assumed for generations – an imagined tradition that has also inspired some Westerners to become Buddhists themselves, though usually in a form that would be only partly recognizable at the place where Buddhism originated and had its early development, which is also where most practicing Buddhists still live today. In this book we will focus primarily upon the Buddhism of Asia.

In contrast to the search for the historical Jesus, the "search for the historical Buddha" raises significant problems.

1 *First, the source problem* The life and teachings of the Buddha are recounted in the Buddhist canon, a three-part collection of sacred books: texts that appear to record the sayings of the Buddha directly, called *sūtras*; commentaries on his teachings, composed over several centuries; and the monastic code, a collection of rules for monastic living and ritual instructions. Some of the *sūtras* were written in Pali, a language spoken in the general part of India where the Buddha lived. Still, even the earliest of these texts only appeared some 400–500 years after the lifetime of the Buddha and had already passed through several generations of oral transmission. Even though each *sūtra* begins with the formula "Thus have I heard" (suggesting that the author was present at the Buddha's assembly), it is doubtful that the "hearing" came directly from the Buddha himself.

2 *Second, the problem of objectivity* The Buddhist canon is the product of the Buddhist tradition, which was already well established by the time the texts were first written and collected. This does not make them any less important to Buddhists today, but there is no possibility of independent corroboration from other written sources: we cannot see the Buddha except through the eyes of the early Buddhist community.

3 *Third, the problem of historicity* "Historicity" here refers to the philosophy of history: attitudes and values surrounding the nature of history itself. Western and Hindu/Buddhist views of history are quite different. First, the Western, linear view of time sees history as "unfolding" and gives greater emphasis to unique, transformative, or unparalleled events. In fact, in the Abrahamic traditions, the commemoration of these historical events (Passover, Easter, Ramadan) is central to religious practice. Even outside of religious contexts, we seem to place greater store by things that happened only once; our history books often repeat the phrase "this was the only time in history that . . ." – and these events are seen as having greater significance than the recurrent ones. Second, the West tends to take history literally: we emphasize "factuality," the sense that things recorded in history actually happened. When he was asked how he knew that Jesus Christ was truly the Son of God, the Reverend Billy Graham replied, "because *only once* in

human history did a man die, was buried in a cave, and after three days rose from the dead."

Buddhists are less concerned with either of these ideas of history. Historical events are recounted, and the Buddhist tradition teaches that rebirth "at a time when the Buddha can be known and his teachings can be heard" is considered to be a "fortunate rebirth." Yet the factuality of particular events in the Buddha's life is less important than their mythological and symbolic significance. Why?

First, the Indian cyclical conception of history emphasizes timeless truths over particular persons and events. In fact, the tradition teaches, the historical Buddha was but one of many Buddhas, existing both sequentially (the Buddha experienced innumerable prior lifetimes, and in all these lifetimes he displayed his enlightened nature) and synchronically (particularly in Mahāyāna Buddhism, there are many Buddhas existing simultaneously). The historical Buddha of "this" world is neither unique nor comparatively more important. Second, the Buddha himself – if we read the *sūtras* recounting his teachings – denied the importance of his own life, and even predicted that he would eventually be forgotten. When he died, he is purported to have said: "Life and all things in life are fleeting and will one day disappear: work out your own enlightenment with diligence." Many Buddhists say that the Buddha was not a savior; they would deny that one can achieve enlightenment only through him. He simply pointed out the way, which others can follow and test for themselves. The ultimate authority for enlightenment is the practitioner him- or herself.

These two points should dampen our enthusiasm for trying to *prove* that the Buddha actually lived and taught. Still, a rich tradition has been passed down that describes the life of the Buddha in highly mythicized terms. Thinking of "myth" as a narrative with symbolic importance and generalizable teachings, the religious myth of the Buddha is much more important to Buddhists than any effort to uncover an "accurate" history.

The Mythical Buddha

Although at the time of his birth the Buddha declared that this would be the last of his rebirths (he predicted his enlightenment immediately upon emerging from his mother's womb), he had enjoyed many prior lifetimes. Stories of these prior rebirths expanded during the centuries and were eventually assembled in collections called *Jātaka* (*Lives*), numbering well over 500. The Buddha appeared in diverse forms – as a human being in every station of life, from king to pauper; as a spirit; and as an animal of various kinds, large or small. All of these stories illustrate the two salient characteristics of one who would one day become fully enlightened: his wisdom and his compassion. Reborn as

a jackal, the Buddha saves the life of a lion; reborn as a deer, the Buddha persuades a hunter to give up hunting; reborn as a monkey, the Buddha cares for
his blind mother; reborn as a prince, the Buddha feeds a starving tigress and
her cubs with his own flesh; reborn as a merchant, he pays a fair price for a
gold plate that its seller thought was made of clay; and so on. Today these
stories are told to children as moral fables. They demonstrate that every being
is potentially a Buddha, which he or she becomes by performing acts of kindness and justice.

In his latest rebirth, the Buddha was said to have been born to a king. He
was thus a Kṣhatriya, a member of the governing or warrior caste. He was
named Siddhārtha Gautama. The tradition often refers to the Buddha as
Śākyamuni (his father was the leader of the Śākya clan, and Siddhārtha became
known as the "sage of the Śākyas"); thus Śākyamuni, Siddhārtha, or Gautama
all are names referring to the Buddha. When Siddhartha was born, his father
noticed that the infant had strange physical features; these are known as the
"32 major marks and 80 minor marks of the Buddha" and included elongated
earlobes, webbed fingers, a large skull, a "male organ like that of an elephant
or royal stallion," curly hair, and a wheel-shaped design on his palms and on
the soles of his feet (see Figure 19.1).

Seeing these features, the king knew that his son was destined for greatness,
as these were the mythical characteristics of a "great being" (a *mahāsattva*).
But when the king consulted his seers, they predicted that the marks indicated
one of two possible outcomes: either the prince would become the greatest
conqueror the world has ever known (a *Cakravartin*, "wheel-turner" – leading
chariots into battle), or he would become the greatest renunciant the world has
ever known (a *sannyasin* – one who renounces all material needs and desires).
Hoping that the prince would become a military leader, the king did everything
in his power to encourage his son to embrace the world, to cultivate his desires
and to see that they were fulfilled. He gave him three palaces: a warm palace for
the winter months, a cool palace for the summer months, and a dry palace
for the monsoon season. He trained him in martial skills, from wrestling to
archery and horseback-riding. He surrounded him with dancing girls, one of
whom he chose to be Siddhartha's wife. When the prince stepped out, the king
swept the parks of any offensive scenes, such as beggars or old folks, so that his
son would see only beauty, youth, and vitality wherever he looked.

It is often argued that religion arises out of hardship, as a response to sickness, death, poverty, and want. Especially in the case of the Asian subcontinent,
the claim is made that conditions are so bad there that people naturally turn
to religion as an escape from this world of suffering. What is remarkable
about the Buddha is that he actually experienced quite the opposite: a life of
luxury, comfort, and sexual fulfillment. And yet, eventually, he taught that
these things are fleeting and unsatisfying and that the world is indeed replete

Figure 19.1 Hand of the Buddha. © Jun Mu / Shutterstock.

with suffering, even in the most ideal circumstances. We will turn to these teachings in Chapter 20.

Destined as Siddhartha was to become enlightened, the course of his life up to this point was hardly conducive to religious awakening. And so the gods (actually minor spirits called *devas*, whose function is simply to ensure that events unfold as they should) fashioned four encounters during the prince's excursions from his father's palace. These are called the Four Passing Sights – "passing" in the sense that they were transient, or even perhaps projections of the future Buddha's growing awareness of the true nature of the world.

On the first excursion he came upon an old man, supported by a cane, his back bent with age, his eyes failing, his muscles sagging and weak. "Does this follow inevitably from youth?" the future Buddha asked.

On the second excursion he came upon a sick man, with suppurating sores and labored breath, unable to stand or walk, wracked with pain and distress. "Must it be that birth leads to this?" the prince lamented.

On the third excursion he came upon a corpse covered with flies and maggots, skin grey and peeling, a ghostly look in his eyes. "Woe to birth that it must lead to death!" cried Siddhartha.

On the fourth excursion he came upon a *sannyasin*, his vision clear and posture straight, a look of calm and contentment on his face. The thought of renouncing the world of pleasures and pains was immensely pleasing to the future Buddha.

Having learned from these experiences that there is suffering and that there is a way out of it, the prince decided to leave his sheltered life. Again aided by the *devas*, who gently cushioned the hooves of his horse so that they would not clatter on the cobblestones and awaken the royal family, Siddhartha left his father's palace. This is described in the tradition as the *pravrajya* (the Great Going Forth), and the same term is used today of a young man or woman when they become initiates in a Buddhist monastery. Going out into homelessness, the prince subjected himself to the traditional practices of yogic renunciation, including self-deprivation, fasting, and exposure to the sun and rain. Ultimately these practices merely enfeebled him and, after receiving sustenance in the form of the aroma of flowers and the dew of grass, he became strong enough to pursue his spiritual reflections with a healthy body. The path of moderation is known in the tradition as the "middle way" between the two extremes of hedonism (indulgence in pleasure) and asceticism (rejection of pleasure), and it is a fundamental principle of Buddhist practice: physical health is a basic prerequisite for mental and spiritual health.

In this more productive state of mind and body, the Buddha contemplated the true nature of life in all its aspects, beneath a banyan tree, and he attained enlightenment – the substance of which will be discussed in the next chapter.

The Buddha shared what he had learned in a teaching career that spanned some 30 years. He continued to practice homelessness, travelling from place to place and never spending more than one night under the same tree. He was extraordinarily egalitarian in his acceptance of followers, and the crowds of listeners became greater and greater. He collected disciples as well as patronage from the land-holding class, which indicates that early Buddhism may have appealed primarily to members of the Vaiśya caste. These land-owners provided temporary resting places called *vihāras* for the Buddha and his disciples. Though the name refers to temporary quarters or "rain retreats," Buddhist monasteries retained this name even after becoming permanent structures in the first centuries of Buddhist history.

At a time said to have been determined by the Buddha himself, he lay down in peaceful repose (Figure 19.2) and gave his last teaching. Preparing his followers for his departure, he cautioned them against relying upon any external authority, even that of the Buddha himself: "Do not take on faith anything taught to you by your parents, by your teachers, by your priests, or by your

Figure 19.2 Reclining Buddha. Wat Than wall mural. Phnom Penh, Cambodia. ©
Philippe Lissac / Corbis.

tradition; believe only what you have experienced for yourself to be true."[1] This
is one of the most fundamental principles of Buddhist teaching and practice.

The Life of the Buddha as a Model for Spiritual Self-Cultivation

What do Buddhists take from this story?

- Though the details of the Buddha's life are undeniably mythicized, it is
  important to Buddhists that there was once a man who lived in this world
  and attained enlightenment; moreover, we are fortunate to have been born
  in a time when his teachings can be known.
- In his every appearance in the world, the Buddha taught timeless, universal
  values of kindness, compassion, wisdom, and justice.
- Offered everything that a man could want, the Buddha chose material
  simplicity and a religious life, and he invited us to do the same.
- Though suffering exists – in sickness, old age, and death, and even in the
  midst of pleasure – it can be overcome through religious practice.
- The best way to live is in moderation, between the extremes of self-
  indulgence and self-denial.

- The most effective way to practice spiritual self-cultivation is within a community of like-minded persons dedicated to the same goal.
- The only true knowledge comes from one's own experience, and religious practice is more meaningful and fruitful than dogma or belief.
- Death is not to be feared, and it can be accepted calmly and peacefully; ultimately all things pass away.

Note

1   Adapted from the *Kālāma Sutta*. For a complete translation, see *Kalama Sutta: To the Kalamas* translated from the Pali by Thanissaro Bhikkhu. At http://www.accesstoinsight.org/tipitaka/an/an03/an03.065.than.html (accessed July 25, 2013).

20

Suffering and Its Causes

The core of Buddhist teachings is expressed in the Four Noble Truths:

1　All of existence is suffering (*duḥkha*).
2　The cause of *duḥkha* is desire (*taṇhā*).
3　To end *duḥkha*, eliminate *taṇhā*.
4　To end *taṇhā*, follow the Eightfold Path.

The Four Noble Truths are purported to have been spoken by the Buddha in his first sermon in a deer park near Benares, India. In commemoration of this sermon, Tibetan temple roof ornaments feature images of deer flanking the symbol of the *dharmacakra* ("wheel of the *dharma*"), and the picturesque eighth-century Tōdaiji Temple in Nara in Japan allows deer to roam freely on the temple grounds (see Figure 20.1).

The sermon in which the Buddha expounded the Four Noble Truths is recounted in a *sūtra* entitled *Dharmacakra-pravartana sūtra* (*The Sūtra Setting in Motion the Wheel of the Dharma*). Recall that Śākyamuni's father hoped that his son would become a *cakravartin*, a great military leader. Instead his wheel was that of the *dharma*, and the *dharmacakra* is the primary symbol of the Buddhist tradition. The Buddha set forth his teachings almost as a doctor would prescribe treatment for an illness. Indeed the Buddha is known in the tradition as "the Great Physician," and his Four Noble Truths can be read as diagnosis ("there is *duḥkha*"), analysis ("its cause is *taṇhā*"), description of a healthy state ("there is relief from *duḥkha* by eliminating *taṇhā*"), and prescription ("follow the Eightfold Path through ethical practice and meditation"). In this chapter we will examine the first two of the Four Noble Truths, with an

Asian Religions: A Cultural Perspective, First Edition. Randall L. Nadeau.
© 2014 John Wiley & Sons, Ltd. Published 2014 by John Wiley & Sons, Ltd.

Figure 20.1   Feeding deer at Tōdaiji Temple, Nara, Japan. Photo by the author.

analysis of duḥkha and taṇhā; Chapter 21 explores ethical means for overcoming suffering, and Chapter 22 examines the goal of enlightenment as a fruit of meditation.

Duḥkha

Just as the Christian tradition predicates the promise of salvation upon the prior condition of *sin*, Buddhist practice begins by calling attention to *suffering*. Buddhism teaches that suffering is endemic: it is everywhere and in every experience. To paraphrase the Buddha, life is suffering, death is suffering, youth is suffering, old age is suffering, health is suffering, disease is suffering, pleasure is suffering, pain is suffering. Many of my students, when first confronted with the bald statement "Life is suffering," cannot help but think of Buddhism as negative and pessimistic. But this would be true only if the tradition taught not only that there is suffering, but that suffering is inevitable and cannot be overcome, that the patient is "incurable." In other words, Buddhism would be a pessimistic religion if it stopped at the first of the Four Noble Truths. Clearly this is not the case. Nevertheless, the teaching begins with the dramatic, forceful, bold, and even counterintuitive statement that *life is suffering*, and if the "patient" refuses to accept this diagnosis – if we live in denial of the ubiquity of suffering – then Buddhism has nothing to teach us.

What is meant by *duḥkha*? "Suffering" is the most common translation, but this English word may draw too much attention to physical pain and discomfort. *Duḥkha* is both a physical and an emotional state: it certainly includes physical pain and suffering, but also anxiety, disappointment, despair, sadness, imbalance, and worry. One good translation of the *Dharmacakra-pravartana sūtra* renders *duḥkha* as "stress."[1] So the first Noble Truth states: "Life is stressful."

In the *sūtra*, the Buddha provides examples of what he means by *duḥkha*:

- the trauma of birth;
- illness and physical decline;
- death and the fear of death;
- being tied to what one hates;
- being separated from what one loves.

Some of these things are self-evident, and we have all experienced them to greater or lesser extent. They are certainly painful. At the same time they seem to be simply episodes in the course of life. They happen, but then they are gone. Why would the tradition conclude from these experiences that life *itself* is suffering?

Moreover, aren't some of these experiences *pleasurable* as well? Certainly we could cite *birth* in particular, which – if all goes well – many parents would describe as the happiest event of their lives. Elsewhere the Buddha explains: the ubiquity of suffering does not mean that pleasure does not exist. It does not mean that there is no happiness in life. However, *even* the happiest and most pleasurable experiences in life are tinged with suffering. The birth of a healthy child is certainly a happy occasion, but it is hardly "pleasurable": neither for the mother nor for the newborn infant, whose cries of anguish are simply met with cold air, pricks, probes, and laughter! The pain of childbirth for the mother is especially emphasized in Buddhism, and one of the major stages of a Chinese or Japanese funeral for a mother is a ritual expression of gratitude, thanking her for suffering so that her children could have life.

In fact every kind of pleasure involves suffering. Like most people, I derive a significant amount of pleasure from money – that is, from things that money can buy: my air-conditioned home, my car, food (especially when it is prepared by others in a nice restaurant), fashionable clothes, travel, and recreation. But all of these pleasures come at a cost: not only to me (over-indulgence, inevitable disappointments, wishing for an even better car or a more luxurious trip), but, more importantly, to others. The world simply cannot sustain the kind of lifestyle that I enjoy. Of course, there are many people who are much more affluent than a university professor – and many more who are much less affluent. For those less well off, a lot of my pleasure creates direct or indirect hardships: it's not "fun" to make my shirts, butcher the animals I eat, power the plants for my central heat and air, or stand at a sales counter from morning till night. One could argue that my consumption patterns contribute to a global economy that benefits laborers and the service industry; they are earning a wage, but whatever benefit those workers may gain, they are also suffering for my pleasure.

Even seemingly non-harmful activities cause others to suffer. I derive great pleasure and satisfaction from my job as a professor and I believe that it does the world good to have broadly educated citizens, with a deeper appreciation for Asian cultures. I'm proud of my work and I try to do it well. But I also know that there are others, perhaps many others, who could fill my job ably and would love to have it. At least indirectly, my pleasure as a teacher is coming at their expense.

When my father died, my wife graciously insisted that my mother, who was diabetic, come live with us. She did so for over 12 years and was fortunate to see my two children grow up. As good as my wife was, as good a son as you might say I was, there was something my mother used to say that I will always remember. Every day after I visited her in her room, whether I stayed with her for five minutes or for an hour, she would say the same thing: "Leaving so soon?" No matter how much time I spent with her, she wished for more. Of course, we could say that her expectations were unreasonable, that she should have been satisfied with our occasional visits, but there is no doubt that she felt lonely when her family was not with her. The ordinary activities of our busy lives caused her to suffer.

Such examples could be multiplied infinitely. Yes, pleasure exists and, on balance, life may be more pleasurable than painful, but the fact is that suffering is found in every aspect of life.

Acknowledging this fact is one of the first steps, and arguably the most important one, in following the way of the Buddha. If I am aware of suffering and of the unintended consequences of my own enjoyment of life, I will naturally want to lessen that suffering, and I will begin to take concrete steps to alleviate suffering when I can.

Taṇhā

The second Noble Truth states that the cause of *duḥkha* is *taṇhā*. The word *taṇhā* is etymologically related to "thirst" or "grasping" and is usually translated as "desire" or "attachment," that is, "desire for things that I do not have" and "attachment to things that I do." I grasp the things that I want to keep and I grasp for things that I want to attain. More often than not, my grasping is met with frustration. In other words, a lot of suffering arises from unrealistic expectations. The things I am attached to decay and disappear; they change in unexpected ways; or they fail to satisfy me fully. The things I wish I could have fill me with longing, disappointment, and self-doubt: my wishes are never completely fulfilled, and I am disappointed with myself for not attaining my dreams. Moreover, my desires have negative consequences for others. They make me think about myself above others, they occupy my attention, and they are competitive. The Buddhist tradition identifies five objects of desire and attachment:

1 things (material objects/wealth);
2 sensations (especially sexual);
3 ideas/opinions/thoughts;
4 traditions/conventions/habits/lifestyles;
5 self/ego/I (especially as a permanent entity).

If I can, deliberately and progressively, lessen my desires and my attachments to these things and qualities, I will find that suffering is lessened as well: both my own suffering and the suffering of others.

Let's look briefly at each of these objects of desire and attachment. The list progresses from the most concrete and material to the most abstract and spiritual or psychological, and thus from the desires that are easiest to overcome to the desires that are the most difficult to overcome.

1 *Things (material objects/wealth)*   Buddhism teaches that the attachment to "things" and the desire for more "things" is a fundamental cause of suffering in the world. The most basic characteristic of monastic life is material simplicity. Traditionally, monks and nuns do not own anything but the so-called "six possessions": a begging bowl, a razor for shaving the head, a pair of homespun robes, a pair of sandals, a needle, and a strainer (to remove impurities from drinking water and to avoid causing injury to any insects that might be living there). Today most monks and nuns have personal possessions that they have brought from home. However, the principle remains the same as it has always been: the monastery will provide the basic necessities of food and shelter and will allow the monk or nun to cultivate a religious life through the practice of the "middle way" between the extremes of self-indulgence and self-denial. The monastery is a refuge from the rat race of the working world, where I "live to work," conditioned by the world to want the newest gadgets, a bigger house, a higher salary, a more pleasing appearance, and the highest status that money can bring. Consumerism is competitive, insatiable, and ecologically irresponsible.

2 *Sensations (especially sexual)*   The second most obvious characteristic of monastic life is celibacy. We will survey this practice more thoroughly

in Chapter 23, but for now we can simply observe that sexual sensations are a primary source of suffering. This is an odd statement, especially since sex is usually associated with pleasure. In fact, for most people, the very word "pleasure" has sexual connotations. But, just as all pleasures cause pain, so too – and so especially – do sexual pleasures. Whatever pleasure sex may bring, I can guarantee that there is no reader of this book who has not suffered because of sexual attachment and desire. However pleasurable it may be, sex also produces pain, frustration, yearning, loss, loneliness, and disappointment. Of course, sex is not simply an act, it is also a mindset: we long for physical and emotional contact and we often go to great lengths to get it, only to be frustrated when we cannot or disappointed when we can. Desire for sex is not only obsessive, but it is also ultimately unfulfilling.

3   *Ideas/opinions/thoughts*   "Attachment to ideas" is another deep fixation. In fact, we are so attached to our ideas that we claim to *own* them, to have a "right" to them. We feel challenged and upset if our ideas are not accepted by others, and arguments about ideas – opinions, statements about feelings, beliefs about the way things "should be" – can be socially divisive and even violent. In the Buddhist tradition the practice associated with this "craving" is meditation: Buddhist meditation does not entail a trance-like, deadened mind in which ideas are eliminated, but rather a calm, non-discriminating mind in which ideas are simply observed and then released. Buddhists try not to dwell on ideas but to let them come to mind and then be freed, like flotsam floating on a stream.

4   *Traditions/conventions/habits/lifestyles*   The Buddha is said to have predicted that, like all things, even his teachings would one day pass away and be forgotten. And he taught further that attachment to his teachings, like all attachments, could be a cause of suffering. Perhaps he meant that "religion" (whether or not he thought of the *dharma* as "religion") can be an object of attachment if its followers are too doctrinaire, exclusivistic, or intolerant of others. Insofar as a religion is not simply a set of ideas or beliefs, but a kind of lifestyle – a moral, behavioral, social, and institutional system – it is certainly true that people can cling to religion in a way that is potentially damaging to themselves and to others. Many of us are guilty of cultural chauvinism: the "other" lives strangely, is ill-mannered, eats strange foods, practices barbarian rites, and cannot speak our language or adapt to our ways. Even in a world that has become globalized to an extent that the Buddha never could have imagined, cultural bias and religious exclusivism create suffering in the form of prejudice, ostracism, and war.

5   *Self/ego/I (especially as a permanent entity)*   The fifth and most difficult of the objects of attachment to overcome is the attachment to the very idea of the self. Self-absorption in the form of an enlarged ego, an inability to see

the world as others see it, self-protection, and self-indulgence, is, in the Buddhist tradition, a physical, mental, and psychological condition that goes to the heart of suffering in all its aspects. In fact my idea of myself is so grand that I cannot help but want to live forever, to be a permanent and unchanging being. But, as we will see in Chapter 22, there is nothing in the world that is permanent and unchanging, so this kind of attachment is especially fruitless and frustrating. This may be the most radical teaching of the Buddha, and what sets Buddhism apart from all the great religions of the world. As the great Buddhological scholar Edward Conze wrote:

> The doctrine of the Buddha, conceived in its full breadth, width, majesty and grandeur, comprises all those teachings which are linked to the original teaching by historical continuity, and which work out methods leading to *the extinction of individuality* by eliminating the belief in it.[2]

This elegantly phrased statement can be summarized in one word: *anattā*, "no *Ātman*," the Buddha's teaching of non-attachment with regard to an undying and unchanging self. We will explore the ramifications of this teaching and its application to the Buddhist idea of enlightenment in Chapter 22.

Notes

1   "Dhammacakkappavattana Sutta: Setting the Wheel of Dhamma in Motion" (SN 56.11), translated from the Pali by Thanissaro Bhikkhu. *Access to Insight*, February 12, 2012. At http://www.accesstoinsight.org/tipitaka/sn/sn56/sn56.011.than.html (accessed April15, 2012).
2   Edward Conze, *Buddhism: Its Essence and Development* (New York: Dover Books, 2004), p. 28. (Original publication 1951.)

21

Buddhist Ethics

The first two of the Four Noble Truths, as spoken by the Buddha in his first sermon after attaining enlightenment and as recorded in *The Sūtra Setting in Motion the Wheel of the Dharma* (*Dharmacakra-pravartana sūtra*), describe the true nature of life – the ubiquity of *duḥkha* – and the causes of *duḥkha*: desire and attachment. The third and fourth of the Four Noble Truths affirm that suffering can be overcome, and they explain how. Like a physician, the Buddha prescribes a cure to suffering, namely the holy Eightfold Path.

The Eightfold Path

The Eightfold Path can be summarized as follows:

A Wisdom (*prajñā*):
   1 right views: acceptance of the Four Noble Truths and of "things as they are";
   2 right intention: thoughts of compassion for others, non-violence, and selfless detachment.

B Ethical conduct (*śila*):
   3 right speaking: abstaining from the "four vocal wrong deeds" (lies, slander, abuse, gossip);
   4 right action: abstaining from the "three bodily wrong deeds" (killing, stealing, and sexual misconduct);
   5 right livelihood: avoiding any occupation that does harm to another living thing.

Asian Religions: A Cultural Perspective, First Edition. Randall L. Nadeau.
© 2014 John Wiley & Sons, Ltd. Published 2014 by John Wiley & Sons, Ltd.

C   Mental discipline (*samadhi*):
  6   right effort: avoiding "unwholesome states of mind"; mental preparation;
  7   right mindfulness: developing self-conscious meditative awareness of the body, sensations, and thoughts;
  8   right concentration: "pure equanimity" of mind, detached from the illusion of self.

The notion of a "path" is slightly misleading, in that the word suggests a sequence of steps or stages. Rather the holy Eightfold Path is a simultaneous practice with eight aspects, all of which mutually inform and inspire one another. This is the reason why the path, the *dharma*, and the Buddhist tradition itself are conventionally represented by a wheel with eight spokes (see Figure 21.1).

The two aspects listed first (right views and right intention), which encapsulate the wisdom (*prajñā*) of the Buddha's teachings, are both the *foundation* and the *fruit* of Buddhist practice. Buddhist practice, incorporating ethical conduct (*śila*) and mental discipline or meditation (*samadhi*), is certainly based upon the teachings of the tradition – that is its foundation; but it also yields a deeper awareness of life and an alleviation of suffering in oneself and in others – which are its fruits. As one engages in ethical conduct and the practice of meditation, one deepens one's wisdom and compassion. Thus the path comes full circle.

Figure 21.1   The wheel of the *dharma* (*dharma-cakra*). © Momo5287 / Shutterstock.

In this chapter we will examine the first of these two pillars of Buddhist practice: ethical conduct. In Chapter 22 we will turn to the practice of meditation and its fruit, Buddhist enlightenment.

Ethical Practice

The three dimensions of ethical practice (*śila*) listed in the Eightfold Path are "right speaking, right action, and right livelihood." These are non-harmful behaviors and, of course, by eliminating "harm" they reduce suffering.

The ethical dimension of Buddhism is considered by most Asian Buddhists to be its most important element. Traditionally meditation was a practice limited to monasteries, although, as we will note in Chapter 26, there is now greater interest in meditation among lay Buddhists around the world. Ethical conduct, by contrast, is fundamental, and for most Asian Buddhists – who live the "householder's" life, working and raising families and only visiting monasteries on special occasions such as the birthday celebrations of the Buddha, temple festivals, funerals, and rituals for deceased ancestors – to be "Buddhist" means to live a moral life to the extent that one can do so. In Asia, recognizing another person as a Buddhist does not relate to some abstract "pursuit of enlightenment," but rather to an ethically disciplined life, something like what we might call being "socially conservative" with regard to one's moral commitments and behaviors.[1]

Though monasticism is highly regarded, especially in Southeast Asia, most Buddhists will never be ordained as a monk or nun. Their goal is to integrate their religious commitments with everyday life, in the context of work, family life, relationships, and community.[2] In Thailand and other Asian countries religious commitment is expressed on a daily basis, in the recitation of the Five Precepts (*pañca-śila*) of ethical practice, both by monastics and by laypersons.

1   I resolve to avoid harming sentient beings.
2   I resolve to avoid taking that which is not freely given.
3   I resolve to avoid sexual misconduct.
4   I resolve to avoid harmful speech.
5   I resolve to avoid intoxicants.

Before examining each of the five precepts and how they are put into practice in Buddhism, notice two characteristics that all of the precepts have in common. First, they each begin with the words "I resolve." They are self-directed, and ultimately the Buddhist practitioner is responsible for his or her own behavior. As ethical practice, this differs in form from the Ten Commandments of the

Judeo-Christian tradition, which begin with the words "Thou shalt not." The Ten Commandments are part of the "Covenant with Israel," that is, a kind of contract between the God of Abraham and His followers; in return for their obedience, God promises to guide and protect them. The Buddhist Five Precepts are self-motivated and, although "taught by the Buddha," they are not viewed in terms of obedience and sin.

Second, the precepts are phrased as vows to "avoid" certain behaviors. Again, if we think of the Ten Commandments as prohibitions invested with the force of a contractual relationship, the word "avoid" suggests a grey area between success and failure. In other words, I can "resolve to avoid" an action even though I may not be able to excise it completely from my everyday life. Even if I do not intentionally hurt others, my every pleasure comes at the expense of another being's pain. Still, I can make every effort to *reduce* the suffering I cause, and hence a commitment to the Five Precepts is still a worthy and noble undertaking. The Vietnamese Buddhist monk and author Thich Nhat Hanh suggests that the sincere person should think of ethical practice like following the North Star: one can set a course and move in a positive direction even if one cannot actually "reach" the destination, or attain "perfect" virtue. The idea here is to reduce the harm that one causes to others: Thich Nhat Hanh makes the point that even an army general can practice the first precept, if he makes a sincere effort to reduce the suffering of his enemy – though ideally, of course, he should reject the "wrong livelihood" of killing altogether.

The application of the Five Precepts is both self-directed and incremental, as opposed to the other-directed and oppositional phrasing of the Ten Commandments. What does this mean in practice? We can look at examples of how the Five Precepts are applied in the Buddhist tradition.

The vow to avoid harming sentient beings

What is a "sentient being"? "Sentience" could refer to "the ability to think"; but, for the tradition as a whole, "sentience" has meant the capacity to feel, or physical sensation. Obviously people are sentient beings by both definitions, but more broadly animals, large and small, regardless of their relative intelligence, as well as insects and other creatures having a central nervous system are all capable of feeling pain.

In the Buddhist tradition there is a broad continuum of practice related to the goal of non-injury. In Chinese Buddhism, this practice takes the form of vegetarianism: monasteries do not serve meat, and many lay Buddhists practice vegetarianism as the primary outward sign of their faith. (In Chinese, to say that one "eats vegetables" – *chi su* (吃素) – is a kind of shorthand for saying that one is a Buddhist.) In Japan, by contrast, even monastics eat meat: according to tradition, a debate was held in the ninth century about the sentience of trees and, by extension, of plants in general. The decision was reached that "even a tree has Buddha-nature," that is, even a tree has the capacity for enlightenment and for ending suffering. Since people must eat, there is little point in distinguishing between one sentient being and another, so Japanese monks eat meat. Tibetan Buddhists eat some kinds of meat but not others: since it is better to kill one animal rather than many, it is preferable to eat beef over fish. One cow can feed a great many monks. In Theravāda Buddhist countries, a monk is permitted to eat meat as long as the animal was not killed especially for him.

Buddhists have been inspired in recent years to apply the first precept quite broadly. Buddhist organizations are involved in anti-war movements and in protest against colonialist occupations – both Vietnamese monks in the 1960s and Tibetan monks in the 2010s have practiced self-immolation, a traditional form of Buddhist monastic protest. They also participate in environmentalist and animal protection movements, in volunteerism and the establishment of social services (from major hospitals in Taiwan and Japan to safe houses for child prostitutes in Thailand), and in other forms of peace making, compassionate interventions, and disaster relief.

The vow to avoid taking that which is not freely given

In lay society, "not taking that which is not freely given" means taking only things that one has either earned or paid for – that is, not stealing. But, on a more strict interpretation, even paying for something is coercive: the merchant will not give up his goods *unless* he is paid. As a result, the monastic application of this precept is the traditional begging round of Buddhist monks, which is still practiced daily in some countries and on holidays in others. The word "beg" is unhelpful if we wish to understand the practice, because the monks do not beg in an aggressive way and never approach the householders who provide them with food. They do not solicit contributions. Rather the monks walk down the street at a slow pace and simply receive what is offered by the householders who come out to greet them. Traditionally, in observance of this precept, monks do not handle money.

Since most of us participate in commercial activities on a daily basis, should we be content simply not to rob or steal? Or does this precept inspire more thoughtful forms of consumption? In the modern world, some Buddhists have taken this precept to mean that one should be mindful of one's use of money and should work for economic justice. Just paying for something does not absolve me of the responsibility related to how it was produced; this includes the working and living conditions of the laborers who assembled it, transported, and sold it. To the extent that the goal of Buddhist practice is to reduce suffering in all of its forms, modern-day Buddhists promote awareness of the potential suffering caused by conspicuous consumption. In addition, the Buddha's directive to practice the "middle way," neither wallowing in poverty nor indulging in wealth, corresponds to a lifestyle that is ultimately more sustainable – both for the individual and for the planet.

The vow to avoid sexual misconduct

In Asia, Buddhists are socially conservative when it comes to sexual practice. For most, this means that sexuality should be expressed only within the context of marriage or of a committed relationship. Attitudes toward homosexuality are determined by culture as much as by religion, and some Buddhist countries are more tolerant of homosexual practices than others; in Japan and Thailand homosexuality and other forms of sexual expression are not seen to be inconsistent with the *dharma* and homosexual traditions are centuries old.

Attitudes toward abortion are, again, cultural as much as they are religious, but one of the main reasons why Buddhism in Asian countries discourages sex outside of marriage is that it can result in unwanted pregnancies. Abortion is legal in some Buddhist countries and not in others, but is readily available. Still, it is seen to be regrettable, and in Buddhist scriptures an unborn child is regarded as a sentient being. In Japan women who have elected to terminate a pregnancy can sponsor a Buddhist temple to conduct a "water-baby rite" (水子供養, *mizuko-kuyō*), which comforts and pacifies the spirit of the aborted fetus.

Monks and nuns, by definition, do not have sex, and a major portion of the Vinaya (the monastic code) enumerates sexual practices that are prohibited. We will look at the code in depth in Chapter 23. Sexual intercourse is one of four reasons why a monk or nun would be expelled from a monastery; and sex in general is seen to be harmful to religious self-cultivation. Why? First, sex impedes spiritual progress by arousing desire, the cause of suffering. Second, sex entails responsibilities that monks and nuns, living a communal life, cannot fulfill (buying or renting a house, caring for children and raising them, managing the family income, and so on). From a monastic point of view, any kind of sexual behavior constitutes "sexual misconduct." Monks and nuns are encouraged to "desexualize" the body by wearing loose-fitting, non-gender-specific robes and by shaving the head; they are trained to regard the body as undesirable, a "sack of blood and pus" that ties us to the world of suffering from which we ultimately hope to escape. The main issue here, for both lay and monastic Buddhists, is to reduce our infatuation with sex and the inevitable suffering it causes, and – for laypersons – to practice sex in a way that is responsible, caring, considerate, and unharmful.

The vow to avoid harmful speech

Buddhist ethical conduct includes "right speech": abstaining from the "four vocal wrong deeds," namely lies, slander, abuse, and gossip. "Speech acts" such as these can be psychologically harmful, and so this precept is in some ways an extension of the first one, related to non-injury. But there is a reason why this precept is listed separately: lies, slander, abuse, and gossip not only cause harm but also distort the truth. In other words, they promote non-awareness, when the primary goal of Buddhism is enlightenment and awakening. Awareness of the self and of the world is the goal of meditation and ultimately leads to enlightened insight, as we will see in Chapter 22.

Avoidance of the "vocal wrongs" can also be placed on a continuum, from less strict to more strict observance. For example, think about the difference between these two expressions:

- "speaking what one knows not to be true" (related to lying and slander);
- "speaking what one does not know to be true" (related to abuse and gossip).

If I say something that I know not to be true, then I am lying: I am saying or repeating something that I know to be false. These are the first and second of the four vocal wrong deeds: lying and slander. ("Slander" entails not simply lying, but spreading lies as well.) Most lay Buddhists interpret the fourth precept as an injunction to avoid lying whenever possible.

The second phrase, "speaking what one does not know to be true," describes a more demanding awareness of my speech. Gossip, for example, is not a deliberate form of lying, but it does involve spreading rumors, that is, saying things that I know only by hearsay. Is such speech harmful? Perhaps not directly, but gossip certainly does not enhance the pursuit of truth or the cultivation of awareness.

What would be the most extreme practice of "avoiding speaking what one does not know to be true"? Since we can never be absolutely sure about anything we know, strict observance of this precept confines one to silence. Indeed there is in Buddhism a tradition of forest monks who make a vow of silence, either temporarily or for many years, in observance of this precept.

The vow to avoid intoxicants

To the chagrin of many Euro-American Buddhists, the fifth of the Five Precepts discourages the consumption of alcohol and mind-altering drugs. Since clarity of mind is the goal of meditation, we should not subject ourselves deliberately to distortions and illusions. In addition to causing lack of awareness, intoxicants should be avoided because they loosen one's inhibitions and make it difficult to follow the other four precepts. The daily news certainly make us aware of the injurious effects of alcohol and other drugs: they cause harm to self and others, contribute to crimes against persons and property, incite to sexual behaviors that one may later come to regret, and reduce one's ability to control one's speech. In a monastic setting, this precept is extended to entertainments such as novels and movies, which are also "intoxicating" and promote "illusory" thinking – though I have visited monasteries that feature an occasional movie night for the entertainment of the monks.

Survey 4   The Five Precepts Survey

The weblink for this survey is http://goo.gl/JpYuyR. The survey allows you to apply Buddhist ethics to your own behaviors, as well as to your ideals for ethical living.

Notes

1   The primary way in which Asian Buddhists differ from American social conservatives is that they see ethical self-cultivation as a personal commitment rather than as a political position or as promotion of traditional public policies.

2   As we will see in Chapter 26, more and more Western Buddhists are also recognizing Buddhism as an ethical tradition. Whereas Western Buddhism once focused almost exclusively on the practice of meditation – and in fact saw Buddhism as ethically neutral, or even permissive – today ethics is a core dimension of Buddhist practice in the West.

22

The Fruits of Meditation

Buddhist enlightenment is a state of mind that is exceedingly difficult to describe. Unlike the Judeo-Christian tradition, Buddhism does not represent the goal of religious practice as a heaven or paradise, or indeed as any kind of "place" at all. It is rather a state of awakened consciousness. The Eightfold Path outlines three stages of meditation leading to this realization: mental preparation, focused concentration, and enlightened consciousness.

Meditation

Not all Buddhists meditate. However, what was once a tradition limited to monks and nuns is now widely practiced by lay Buddhists, both in Asia and in the West. Meditation entails the quieting of the body and mind, focused attention on physical and mental activities (such as breathing and thinking), disciplined "non-attachment" to thoughts and sensations, and a state of insight and contentment that arises from meditative practice (see Figure 22.1). Meditation teachers warn against either deadening the mind or "blissing out" on a euphoric high. Meditation is not trance, and it is not ecstasy. Rather it is keen awareness of one's range of experience (thoughts, sensations, emotions, feelings, and perceptions), without assuming their permanence or continuity over time. Ultimately, meditation leads to the consciousness of "no self" or "no mind." This is not "self-annihilation" – Buddhism is not nihilistic in this sense – but the overturning of the idea of the self as a permanent, unchanging thing. Meditation helps us to overcome our attachment to that idea and to recognize all aspects of the self – thoughts and sensations, emotions and desires, and the very sense of "I" – as impermanent and in a constant state of flux, coming and going.

Asian Religions: A Cultural Perspective, First Edition. Randall L. Nadeau.
© 2014 John Wiley & Sons, Ltd. Published 2014 by John Wiley & Sons, Ltd.

Figure 22.1 Seated meditation. © Qingqing / Shutterstock.

If there is no permanent and unchanging center of the ego – if this idea is "illusory" – then what is there? What constitutes personal identity? The Buddha described five *skandhas* or aggregates of personal identity: the body, perceptions, emotions, karmic dispositions (what Western psychological interpreters have called "unconscious motivations"), and consciousness. In meditation, one observes these elements and finds them all to have a number of common characteristics:

- First, they are mutually interactive, with relations of cause and effect upon one another – not having had enough sleep, I feel cranky; smelling a fragrant scent, I am reminded of a scene from my childhood; thinking of a parent's imminent death, I feel shortness of breath and a knot in my stomach; and so on.
- Second, they are "event-like" as much as they are "object-like": that is, the processes of thinking and sensing are constantly moving and changing; nothing stays the same from one moment to the next.

- Third, none of these "object-events" are permanent; dispassionate observation of my "self" yields nothing that is eternal – the objects of observation disappear before my very eyes.

On the basis of these meditative observations, the Buddha abandoned the traditional idea of any permanent thing in the universe, including *Ātman* and Brahman. This is why many Western interpreters of Buddhism – and now some Asian Buddhist intellectuals as well (especially those who are familiar with Western religions) – describe Buddhism as a religion that promotes "atheism" – or even go so far as to say that Buddhism is not a "religion" at all. As we will see in Chapter 24, however, there is plenty of supernaturalism within the Buddhist tradition, and the Buddha himself never argued for the *non*-existence of *Ātman* and Brahman. Rather, his teaching of *anattā* (non-*Ātman*) should be understood as avoidance of all "clinging ideas," including ideas of permanent existence *or* non-existence. In fact the Buddha denied all of four statements, a set of denials that has been described as the "negative tetralemma of the Buddha":

- denying that *self exists*;
- denying that *self does not exist*;
- denying that *self both exists and does not exist*;
- denying that *self neither exists nor does not exist*.

That is to say, Buddhism avoids both eternalism and nihilism. When asked to explain this difficult philosophical point, the Buddha resorted to an analogy. One of his followers could not stop peppering the Buddha with questions about the soul, one's state of existence before birth and after death, the nature of *nirvāṇa*, and so on.

> The Buddha said, "You are like a man who has been shot by an arrow. As the man is rushed to the field hospital, the doctor says to him, 'If the arrow is not removed, you will die.' Just as the doctor begins to extract the arrow, the warrior stops him, saying, 'Before you remove the arrow, tell me, who shot it? What is his name and where is he from? What tree made up the arrow's shaft, and what stone its point? From what bird's plume were its feathers made to guide its flight?'
>
> And before the warrior could exhaust his questions, he died. I have come to suggest a way to end suffering, not to engage in philosophical speculation."[1]

Meditation is the tool by which the practitioner overcomes the illusion of self and the most fundamental of all the attachments; in this way, meditation is a path to enlightened consciousness and to *nirvāṇa*.

Nirvāṇa

Why is the state of existence that is described by the English word "enlightenment" called in Sanskrit *nirvāṇa*, literally "annihilation"? And how is this state attained?

Nirvāṇa is the "annihilation" of the false idea of a permanent and undying self. But if this idea is rejected, what new understanding arises? What, in other words, are the fruits of meditation, the insight that arises from practice? The Buddhist tradition has developed answers to these questions over centuries of its historical evolution, in various social, cultural, and sectarian environments. We can examine the idea of enlightened consciousness in three major historical, social-cultural, and sectarian contexts: the three *yānas* or "turnings of the *dharma* wheel" – Theravāda, Mahāyāna , and Vajrayāna – as well as in the major philosophical schools associated with each (see Table 22.1).[2]

The First Turning of the *dharma* wheel is a scholastic tradition corresponding to the Theravāda branch of Buddhism – the "school of the elders." Its canonical texts were first composed in Pali before the Common Era, some 100–200 years after the life of the Buddha. The word "elders" here refers to monks: Theravāda Buddhism reveres the monastic life and sees monastic renunciation as the highest form of Buddhist practice. Today Theravāda Buddhism is centered in Southeast Asia, and its most vibrant monastic communities can be found in Sri Lanka, Burma, Thailand, Laos, Cambodia, and Vietnam. Philosophically it is centered on Abhidharma thought and on a tradition of commentary based on the *sūtras* (sayings of the Buddha) attributed to Siddhārtha Gautama.

In reaction against the body–soul dualism of the ancient Indian (Hindu) sages, Abhidharma thought emphasizes *anattā* (no soul) and non-attachment to self. Non-attachment of every kind is best attained through self-denial (though not to the point of asceticism) and rejection of mental and physical attachments – attachments to ideas, to ego, to pride, to the body, to money, and to material possessions. On the basis of the suffering nature of the world, its constant fluctuation, and its impermanence, Buddhist monks are encouraged to cultivate an attitude of *aśubha*, "revulsion," toward the things of this world.

Table 22.1 Three turnings of the *dharma* wheel.

	First appearance	*Geographic center*	*Philosophical school*	*Focus of meditation*
Theravāda	500 years BCE	Southeast Asia	Abhidharma	aśubha
Mahāyāna	0 years BCE	East Asia	Madhyamaka	śūnyatā
Vajrayāna	500 years CE	Tibet	Yogācāra	tathāgata-garbha

The word *aśubha* means loathesomeness, inauspiciousness, something impure or unpleasant. An example is the practice of "meditation on corpses" – that is, observing a dead body in the process of decay in order to contemplate the fleeting nature of life. In the Theravāda tradition, *nirvāṇa* is a state of existence that is far removed from the suffering and stress of everyday life; it stands in contrast to the world, an escape from the wheel of *saṃsāra*.

The Second Turning of the *dharma* wheel involves an internal critique, reflected in the philosophical tradition called Madhyamaka, the school of the "middle way" and conceptual non-dualism. The texts of this school were composed in Sanskrit and include *sūtras* that were reputed to have been hidden away for some 500 years after the time of the Buddha. This tradition arose, then, in the first years of the Common Era and spread north and east; it originated in India but is now centered in China, Korea, and Japan. This is the Mahāyāna ("Great Vehicle") tradition. In Mahāyāna Buddhism the dualism between *saṃsāra* and *nirvāṇa* is rejected. *Nirvāṇa* is found within *saṃsāra* – within this world of everyday experience. When one looks deeply into the true nature of reality, as the Buddha taught, all things are found to be enmeshed in a universal web of cause and effect, such that no one thing or being can stand alone, independently of the rest. In Madhyamaka thought, things are said to be "empty of own-being," "empty of essence," or "empty of self-existence": this is known in the tradition as the "doctrine of emptiness" (*śūnyatā*).

- Philosophically, all things are interconnected and interpenetrating; this is termed *pratītya-samutpāda*, the interdependence of all things. This condition extends to the very notion of *nirvāṇa* itself – which is why *nirvāṇa* should not be conceptually separated from everyday life. As the great second-century ce Indian philosopher Nāgārjuna wrote in his *Mūlamadhyamaka-kārikā* (*Fundamental Verses of the Middle Way*): "There is nothing whatsoever to distinguish *nirvāṇa* and *saṃsāra*. They are both empty of essence."
- Ontologically (that is, in relation to the fundamental nature of things), all "being" is seen to be "becoming." Since nothing has an innate, fixed, unchanging essence or core, things are rather in constant flux, appearing and disappearing like bubbles on a stream. All things are embedded in a web of existence: a slight change in one element of the whole sparks a system-wide, universal transformation. This is analogous to the popular idea of the "butterfly effect," so named from a Zen Buddhist expression: "the track of a butterfly in the sky changes the entire universe." A person, a tree, an egg, a house, a brick, a flower, a mountain is not so much a "thing" as it is an "event," and part of the "event system" of a dynamic universe.
- Religiously, the Buddha also exists in interdependence and cannot stand alone as an independent being or as just "one" enlightened being. So Mahāyāna Buddhism affirms the belief in many Buddhas existing simulta-

neously and in direct interaction with sentient beings in the world. This is the *bodhisattva* doctrine of Mahāyāna Buddhism: the belief in innumerable enlightened beings (*bodhisattvas*) who delay their own enlightenment until all other beings can be enlightened as well. In other words, the idea of *pratītya-samutpāda* (interdependence) makes "private" enlightenment inconceivable and affirms a doctrine of universal salvation, sometimes projected into the future as an eschatological ideal. We will look at this theme in more detail in Chapter 24, on faith.

- Socially and institutionally, monks and nuns should not isolate themselves or hold themselves above others. Mahāyāna emphasizes the spiritual accomplishments of insightful laypersons and does not insist upon monasticism as a religious requirement, though the monastic tradition remains strong in East Asia. Mahāyāna monks and nuns are often self-deprecating, seeing their monastic lifestyle as a function of their own weakness, of their inability to deal with the troubles of the world. While certainly respected, monastics are not held in the same reverential esteem as they are in Southeast Asian Buddhism, and lay practice is encouraged and respected. Moreover, the non-essentialism and non-dualism of Madhyamaka encourages non-hierarchal modes of institutional organization, including gender equality. Indeed, today the order of nuns is vibrant in East Asian Buddhist countries, whereas in the Theravāda cultures of Southeast Asia it died out some centuries ago, for various historical reasons.

Perhaps the most fully developed expression of Mahāyāna belief and practice can be found in Zen Buddhism, which arose in China in the seventh and eighth centuries CE and then spread to Korea, Japan, and Vietnam. Zen takes the theory of emptiness and puts it into practice. Zen elaborates upon Madhyamaka philosophy in its practice of *ippitsu-no-Zen* (一筆の禅, as expressed in Japanese – literally "one-stroke" or "one-pointed" Zen), "doing one thing at a time" – that is, finding enlightenment in the course of everyday life. Chapter 25 contains a separate discussion of Zen.

The Third Turning of the *dharma* wheel is a further elaboration on emptiness – paradoxically, as the *fullness* of consciousness. If emptiness means "lacking independence," then all things, including all "minds" or "mental formulations," are interdependent. This web of interdependent minds is the *tathāgata-garbha*, the "womb of suchness," a womb generating the cosmos. As part of this interconnected web, each of us participates in the mental projection of all things, expressing in our own mind the "storehouse consciousness" of enlightenment. This projection penetrates the cosmos like a thunderbolt; and the name of this school is Vajrayāna, "the Vehicle of the Thunderbolt." A further extension of Madhyamaka philosophy, Vajrayāna thought arose about 1,000 years after the time of the Buddha and is today associated with Tibetan

Buddhism, Chinese Esoteric Buddhism, and the Shingon school in Japan. Teaching that all existence is a projection of the universal mind, the philosophical position of Vajrayāna Buddhism is Yogācāra, "consciousness only" or "mind only" – not the individual mind of one person (not solipsism or idealism, to use Western philosophical terms), but the collective mind of all beings. This mind is pure and sparkling, like gold or a diamond, and reality is affirmed for its "suchness" rather than being dismissed for its "emptiness." Thus Vajrayāna meditation consists of complex, layered mental images or "visualizations," often employing a circle or sphere (a *maṇḍala*) in which numerous Buddhas and other enlightened beings appear. The universe is a rich, stunning, and wondrous realm of saviors and spiritual companions, and we too are godlike enlightened beings participating in the creation and elaboration of this marvelous cosmos.

Meditation Practices and Experience of *nirvāṇa*

It is not difficult to understand the Buddhist teaching of interdependence from an intellectual point of view. Today "non-essentialism" – the idea that things have no fixed, permanent, hidden, and isolated core – is a basic assumption of postmodern thought, and it is even more widely accepted in popular culture. In our modern world of constant and accelerating change – where peoples from all over the world interact with one another on a daily basis, where innumerable forms of media and communication shape our thoughts and perceptions, where the very idea of "I" has become protean and multifaceted – these centuries-old Buddhist conceptions seem remarkably contemporary.

But it is one thing to understand Buddhist "emptiness" intellectually, and quite another to internalize this understanding through personal experience, as described in Buddhist meditation and visualization practices. The experiential encounter with the universe as an interconnected web of existence is the heart of Buddhist enlightenment. It generates both compassion for all beings and a sense of personal identity that is cosmically embedded.

Notes

1 Adapted from the *Majjhima Nikaya*. For a full translation of the sutra, see *Cula-Malunkyovada Sutta: The Shorter Instructions to Malunkya*, translated from the Pali by Thanissaro Bhikkhu. At http://www.accesstoinsight.org/tipitaka/mn/mn.063 .than.html (accessed July 25, 2013).
2 The organization of the discussion that follows is based upon Roger Corless, *The Vision of Buddhism: The Space under the Tree* (New York: Paragon House, 1998).

23

Monastic Practice

Life in the monastery should be ethically pure and spiritually focused. The simple lifestyle of monks and nuns, where all basic needs are met, is less harmful to self and others than the life of a householder, whose every moment of waking life is dedicated to the satisfaction of wants and needs in a noisy, competitive environment. In the monastery one need not be concerned with money, with keeping up appearances, with being attractive to the opposite sex, or with outperforming one's enemies in the commercial, political, or military battlefields of worldly existence. Instead, one can dedicate one's life to cultivating awareness through meditation and to overcoming suffering through service and ethical living.

Despite how austere it may appear to lay persons – especially in our modern world of affluence and material comforts – the monastic life is not ascetic. It is not a life of material deprivation, but rather of material simplicity. Monks and nuns are adequately clothed and adequately fed, and their monastic quarters are solidly built, clean, and comfortable. Moreover, the rules of the monastery are so detailed and comprehensive that one need not be burdened with the petty concerns of lay life: what to buy at the grocery store, how and when to pay the bills, what to wear and how to wear it, keeping up with news or gossip, affording the newest gadgets, balancing rest and exercise, even deciding when to wake and when to sleep. Having all of these things already decided for oneself, and therefore outside one's control, is tremendously liberating, and all kinds of time and mental energy are released for the pursuit of more fulfilling and more interesting work: the work of spiritual self-cultivation.

Unlike in the tradition of the Hindu *sannyasin* (renunciant), Buddhist monastic practice is not confined to the late stages of an individual's life in solitary pursuit of transcendent goals. Rather it is a career recommended to all (even if not suitable for all), begun, ideally, in youth. In some Buddhist countries young men are initiated as novices for a short period – perhaps a year or two – before

Asian Religions: A Cultural Perspective, First Edition. Randall L. Nadeau.
© 2014 John Wiley & Sons, Ltd. Published 2014 by John Wiley & Sons, Ltd.

undertaking military service and entering a commercial profession; but in most Buddhist countries one takes the monastic vows for an indefinite period. With rare exceptions – such as the *yamabushi* (山伏) tradition of solo practice in Japan, or the forest or "rhinocerous" monks of Southeast Asia – monastic life is thoroughly communal, and the monastery resembles a religiously based university no less than a center of ritual practice. Quite apart from whether the "grand goals" of liberation or enlightenment are reached, life in the monastery is intrinsically rewarding. Monastics enjoy a disciplined life of worship and study, enhanced by ritual performance, by teaching and community service, and by a healthy balance of work and leisure, in a peaceful setting. Far from being places of deprivation or austerity, monasteries are healthful, ecological, and often beautiful. They are also repositories of cultural and aesthetic traditions, with libraries of rare books and manuscripts, magnificent creations of artistic and architectural grandeur, peaceful parks and gardens, protected areas for rare plants and animals, and thoughtfully designed centers of worship and repose. It is no wonder that many lay persons idealize the monastic life and that Buddhist monasteries in Southeast Asia, China, Korea, and Japan are major sites of tourism and cultural preservation.

Lay persons participate significantly in the life of the monastery. Primarily they support it through financial contributions, and the relationship between monastics and lay persons is a symbiotic one. Lay persons are also welcome to worship in the monastery temples, they have funerary rites performed for loved ones there, and (in some monasteries) they are invited to go into retreat for extended periods of practice. Many monasteries also support lay initiation, where individuals are able to declare modified vows and work closely with the ordained monks and nuns. This option is often taken by women who have passed child-bearing age and are seeking an environment for religious practice in their later years. In other words, the divide between monastics and lay persons, especially in Mahāyāna Buddhist countries, is not as sharp as it might appear.

Nor do monks isolate themselves from lay society, especially in the modern era. They not only conduct funerary rites (both within the temple and in their patrons' homes), but also give "*dharma* talks" in the community, operate medical clinics, and participate actively in social and political movements. Since 2000, monks in Tibet, Burma, Thailand, and Sri Lanka have been especially visible, putting their lives on the line in support of peace work, liberation movements, and social and economic justice (see Figure 23.1).

The Vinaya

Life in the monastery is governed by the Monastic Code, the Vinaya. With its greater emphasis on practice over doctrine, the Buddhist tradition in fact

Figure 23.1 Burmese monks protesting against the military government crackdown of 2007, Rangoon. © Mizzima News / epa /Corbis.

places the Vinaya ahead of the *sūtras* and the commentaries in the "three baskets" (Tripiṭaka) of the Buddhist Canon. This is consistent with the Buddha's own teaching that one's own experience, through practice, has greater meaning and importance than strict adherence to his words.

Depending on which version of the Monastic Code one reads – each of the major Buddhist traditions has adapted the code to local conditions – there are well over 300 rules addressing institutional organization and personal comportment. Hierarchy is emphasized, and rules of subordination and service are applied to younger members of the community.

Pārājika

Only four rule violations are so serious that they would result in expulsion from the monastery. These are called *pārājika*, "defeat":

- If any monk who has taken upon himself the monks' system of self-training and rule of life has *sexual intercourse* with anyone, down even to an animal, he shall be expelled.
- If any monk takes, from village or forest, *anything not given*, he shall be expelled.

- If any monk knowingly deprives a human being of *life* or incites another to *self-destruction*, he shall be expelled.
- If any monk, without being clearly aware of possessing extraordinary qualities, *pretends* that he has gained insight into the teachings of the Buddha, he shall be expelled.

There is nothing very surprising here, as we would expect celibacy and non-injury (avoiding killing or stealing) to be definitive of monastic practice. But what about the fourth rule, the prohibition on "pretending" to be enlightened? Why would this be taken so seriously – and, in any case, how could it ever be substantiated? How would the community know that a monk was "pretending to be enlightened" or "pretending to have become a Buddha"? Functionally, this rule has had two effects. First, it has kept the institution intact and has contributed to the remarkable resilience and conservatism of the tradition: the rule limits schisms by discouraging individuals from claiming a "new" insight or doctrine. Second, it has made individual monastics reluctant ever to claim "enlightenment" at all, for fear of being branded "pretenders" – in other words, it has had a humbling effect on Buddhist practitioners. In fact claims to enlightenment are extraordinarily rare in the history of the tradition. The question "Are you enlightened?" would never be asked of a Buddhist monk or nun, as "Are you saved?" is asked in some Christian contexts.

Sangha-disesa

The second set of rule violations require a "meeting of the community" (*sangha-disesa*) and a period of penance, usually in isolation from others. Most are elaborations on the first of the four *pārājika* (prohibiting sexual activity) or on the fourth (prohibiting false claims and sectarian schism). For example, although such activity would not result in expulsion, monks are forbidden from engaging in the following sexual acts:

- emitting semen ("except while sleeping");
- intentionally touching a woman's hand, hair, or "any part of her body";
- addressing a woman with lewd or suggestive words;
- serving as a romantic go-between for a layman and a laywoman . . . and so on.

In order to preserve the integrity of the monastic institution, a monk is forbidden from:

- constructing a non-approved abode or meditation hut;
- making false charges against another monk;

- "calling attention" to dissension within the community or taking sides in doctrinal disputes;
- "refusing to listen to what is said to him";
- failing to uphold the moral and ethical principles of the tradition, "so that his evil deeds are seen and heard" . . . and so on.

Rules of comportment

The largest set of rules, numbering in the hundreds, is concerned with the minutiae of everyday life and individual comportment. These rules are remarkably detailed, covering standards of dress, bedtime and waking routines, eating, bathing, using the toilet, and almost every imaginable personal behavior. A small sample gives a sense of the Vinaya's reach:

- "Put on the robe correctly."
- "When putting away a robe, take it with one hand, stroke the other hand along the rod or cord [to check for any rough spots or splinters on the cord or rod that will rip the cloth], and place the robe over the cord or rod with the edges away from you and the fold toward you."
- "Do not make noise with your mouth when eating."
- "Do not lick your fingers when eating."
- "Wash your bowl without splashing or scraping."
- "Whoever goes first to the sauna, if ashes have accumulated, that person should throw out the ashes. If the sauna is dirty, sweep it. If the outer corridor . . . the yard . . . the porch . . . the sauna hall is dirty, sweep it."
- "Defecate in order of arrival" (= at the latrine; not in order of seniority).
- "Walk in the village without laughing."
- "With one's begging bowl, walk in the middle of the street [without demanding or soliciting alms]" . . . and so on.[1]

For my American students, many of these rules seem invasive or petty. But, once they are learned and internalized, they become automatic – and one's attention can be devoted to the immensely more important tasks of religious work.

Female Monasticism and the Treatment of Women in the Vinaya

In the Theravāda countries of Southeast Asia women are permitted only the lay vows; the order of nuns died out centuries ago. Though efforts have been

Figure 23.2   Buddhist nun, Tibet. © Dhoxax/ Shutterstock.com.

made to restore the order of nuns, the very rules and standards that have preserved the monastic order for two millennia also make it difficult to reestablish
a tradition that has been lost. In the Mahāyāna countries, however, the nuns'
order remains strong, particularly in Tibet (see Figure 23.2) and in Chinese-
speaking communities. Thanks for example to the efforts of an influential
abbess – Cheng Yen (證嚴, Zheng Yan, b. 1937), founder of the Buddhist
Compassion Relief Foundation (慈濟, *ciji*) in Taiwan – the Chinese order of
nuns has become a model for the world, promoting monastic reforms as well
as joint volunteer efforts and social services shared by lay and monastic communities. Buddhist monasticism in the West has also promoted gender equality, and women have been at the forefront of the meteoric rise of Buddhism in
America and Europe.

   To be sure, attitudes toward women as expressed in the Monastic Code are
conflicted. The very existence of a nuns' order has meant that women as well
as men were encouraged to dedicate their lives to religious self-cultivation, the
fruits of which were seen in the high educational levels attained by Buddhist
nuns throughout the centuries. But monks themselves were taught to "loathe
a woman's body," to regard it as "a sack of blood and pus," to think of a woman's
vagina as "the mouth of a cobra," to think of attractive women as "snares and
nets." If a man is unfortunate enough to be caught in a woman's net, she will

"slice him up and serve his entrails on a platter." The easiest way to prevent such a fate is to avoid women altogether.[2]

> If a monk sees a beautiful woman and says he does not like her, he is telling a lie. He is still a human being and a human being is an animal that has desires. So in monasteries there are no women to be seen. But if a monk does see a beautiful woman, he can suppress the train of thought that arises, and he can do so by reflecting: "I must not think about her. I am a person who has left lay-life. I want to become a buddha. If I think about her, I will not become a buddha."[3]

Clearly the purpose of such language is to inspire non-attachment and to help monks overcome their own sexual desires. Put in the most positive terms, these injunctions are designed to help men with their own spiritual advancement and to encourage them not to regard women as sexual objects. The Buddha taught that there is nothing that intoxicates a man more than the look, touch, sound, smell, and taste of a woman. So, in order to avoid the sexual objectification of women, a monk is encouraged to regard every woman as if she were his own mother, sister, or daughter.

Despite this more positive reading of the treatment of women in the Monastic Code, it goes further still, describing women as especially prone to sexual attachment. The code implies that women are by nature more preoccupied with sex than men. Women are more closely tied to the earth, to reproduction, and to their need for sexual fulfillment. Compared to the monks' code, the rules for nuns are far more numerous and violations have more serious consequences. Instead of four *pārājika*, for example, there are eight reasons why a nun can be expelled from the order: not just sexual intercourse but any sexual contact, flirtation, or "immodest behavior" with a man – as well as the protection of errant nuns or discipleship under "heretical monks." Rules governing personal comportment are much more specific in the nuns' code; they prohibit a number of sexual activities described in quite explicit detail, ranging from various methods of masturbation to flirtatious behavior and subtle methods of enhancing one's personal attractiveness.[4]

My American students are shocked and amused to read about the restrictive rules of the monastic code and about its underlying assumption that women are more "sex-starved" than men. Perhaps the authors of the monks' code were unable to differentiate the *problem* of desire and attachment from the *objects* of desire and attachment. It is understandable that monks would be taught to regard objects of desire as undesirable, even "loathesome" (*aśubha*), whether those objects be material (money, objects of wealth) or sexual (a woman's body). And it may be understandable that women's sexuality, expressed variously in the reproductive functions – pregnancy, birth, lactation, and menstruation – is seen to be more "difficult to overcome" than the parallel reproductive functions in men. Still, the confusion of gender and sexuality is an unfortunate legacy of the Buddhist monastic tradition.

Survey 5   Religious Dimensions of Gender and Sexuality

The weblink for this survey is http://goo.gl/mT8UVM. The survey is inspired by Buddhist monastic values and assumptions. It measures attitudes concerning the relationship between gender and sexuality as well as between gender and religious practice.

Notes

1   Quoted or summarized from "Vatta Khandhaka: Collection of Duties," translated by Thanissaro Bhikkhu. *Access to Insight*, June 30, 2010. At http://www .accesstoinsight.org/tipitaka/vin/cv/cv.08x.than.html (accessed on April 25, 2012).

2   All these passages come ftom "The Celibate Life," from *Awareness Itself by Ajaan Fuang Jotiko*, compiled and translated by Thanissaro Bhikkhu (Geoffrey DeGraff). At http://www.accesstoinsight.org/lib/thai/fuang/itself.html (accessed July 25, 2013).

3   Holmes Welch, *The Practice of Chinese Buddhism* (Cambridge, MA: Harvard University Press, 1967), p. 117.

4   Karma Lekshe Tsomo, *Sisters in Solitude: Two Traditions of Buddhist Monastic Ethics for Women* (Albany: State University of New York Press, 1996), pp. 28, 81–82.

Part VI
The Mahāyāna Buddhist Tradition

24

Faith

Most Buddhists have no intention of becoming monks or nuns. They integrate their religious practice into the social and economic patterns of the householder's life. They make every effort to live a good, moral life and to follow the Five Precepts of lay Buddhist practice, and they express their faith in prayer and offerings. While in the West lay Buddhists focus on meditation, in Asia lay Buddhism is primarily faith-oriented. For most Buddhists over many centuries, Buddhism has consisted of worship and offering, hope for better circumstances in this life and the next, and prayer for family fortune and good health.

The Mahāyāna tradition developed a great cosmic system of multiple realms featuring mythical mountains, parallel worlds, layered destinies of richly described heavens and hells, and powerful *mahāsattvas* ("great beings") with magical powers harnessed for the salvation of living beings. The compassion of these god-like celestial beings is so great that, simply by "calling upon their names," one can evoke their miraculous response. Philosophically, this idea of universal salvation is based upon the doctrine of interdependence (*pratītya-samutpāda*), which asserts that individual salvation is both ethically and conceptually impossible. Religiously, this is expressed in the *bodhisattva* vow – the vow of the "enlightened being" (which is the literal meaning of *bodhisattva*) – to delay his or her own "complete disappearance" (*pari-nirvāṇa*) and to remain in this world of *samsāra*, in this world of rebirth and suffering, until all beings in the universe are saved as well. These *bodhisattvas* employ infinite means to bring about universal salvation, and their enlightened natures are made manifest in their display of *upāya* – a capacity to use whatever means are needed (including supernormal powers and physical self-transformation) to ease suffering wherever it is found. The term *upāya* is often translated as "skillful means" or "efficient means," which suggests the *bodhisattvas'* marvelous responsiveness and

Asian Religions: A Cultural Perspective, First Edition. Randall L. Nadeau.
© 2014 John Wiley & Sons, Ltd. Published 2014 by John Wiley & Sons, Ltd.

supernatural power to ease suffering, especially the simple pains and anxieties of everyday life: they can bring about a healthy pregnancy and birth, success in a middle school exam, recovery from an illness, financial prosperity, protection from traffic mishaps, or give one the strength to overcome a drinking problem, to cope with an abusive spouse, to mourn the death of a loved one, or to face financial difficulties. Given the inevitability of everyday – but still formidable – concerns of this kind, *bodhisattvas* are invoked often and everywhere, and their grace extends to every place in every moment.

Cosmic Buddhas and *Bodhisattvas*

The buddhas and *bodhisattvas* are too numerous to count, much less to name, so we will look at a small sampling of the most widely worshipped *mahāsattvas*.

Amitābha (Radiant Light)

The most widely worshipped of all the buddhas is Amitābha Buddha, also named Amitāyus (Radiant Light) in the Sanskrit Mahāyāna scriptures (see Figure 24.1). The name Amitābha is transliterated in Chinese characters *O-mi-tuo-fo* (阿彌陀佛), and the same characters are pronounced *Amida-butsu* in Japanese. Just as Śākyamuni Buddha is the wheel-turning monarch of this

Figure 24.1 The Buddha Amitābha, Kamakura. © tiger_barb / iStockphoto.

world, Amitābha Buddha sits on his kingly throne in a heavenly paradise called the Pure Land. On the strength of either good works or faith, those who believe in the saving grace of the Buddha Amitābha hope for rebirth in his Pure Land, a heavenly realm described in scriptures like *Sukhāvatī-vyūha* (*The Pure Land Sūtra*). In the Pure Land all cares fade away, one's lifespan is extended indefinitely, one is surrounded by loved ones, and all this takes place in a beautiful and serene environment of verdant hills, songbirds, tender animals, and sparkling waters.

Pure Land Buddhism developed first in China, where it was eventually integrated into Zen (Chinese "Chan") as the "dual practice" of Zen meditation and Pure Land faith, and later in Japan, where it became the most widely practiced form of lay Buddhism in Japanese culture. Taking as its foundation the "doctrine of pure grace" of the great Japanese theologians Hōnen (法然, 1133–1212) and Shinran (親鸞, 1173–1263), the New School of Pure Land Faith (Jōdo Shinshū, 淨土真宗) describes rebirth in Amida's paradise, based on "faith alone" and on Amida's universal grace. Today Jōdo Shinshū has a congregational structure: local parishes, ministers, choirs, and regular worship services similar to Protestant Christianity.

Devotional practice directed toward Amitābha Buddha has a meditative aspect. The scriptures of the Pure Land tradition, with their rich descriptions of the heavenly paradise, are employed as visualization manuals. The devotee reads and recites the scripture, then practices a discipline of focused visualization of the various elements of the Pure Land. As the devotee is picturing this heavenly realm, his or her mind becomes calm, filled with the positive energy of a perfect world. The visualizer creates a personal Pure Land in conceptual space.

Another type of worship consists in repeating or reciting the name "Amitābha" in chanting sessions that can last for an hour or more and generate hundreds, even thousands of repetitions. These repetitions are recorded by the devotee in a small booklet; every filled circle represents 100 repetitions of the Buddha's name. As the devotee chants the name of the Buddha, he or she counts on a rosary bracelet of sandalwood or jade beads, which is worn on the left wrist. This worship practice is called 念佛: *nian-fo* in Chinese, *nembutsu* in Japanese. It is perhaps the most common form of Buddhist devotional practice in Asia.

Maitreya (The Kindly One)

Maitreya is an "advanced *bodhisattva*" – that is, an enlightened being who has tremendous supernormal powers he extends to the world in order to bring beings to salvation. In the case of Maitreya, salvation takes the form of this-worldly transformation, expressed in concrete terms. Maitreya rewards those who worship him in the process of their own efforts to better themselves and the world, both materially and socially. In its simplest form, this *bodhisattva* is represented as the fat, jolly Buddha that one often sees in Chinese businesses: a bearer of mirth, wealth, and blessings, both spiritual and material. As the "future Buddha," Maitreya promises "future reward" – including financial prosperity.

Maitreya is also venerated in the context of social and political reform movements, especially movements of liberation from colonial rule. The Nobel Peace Prize winner Aung San Suu Kyi has invoked the name of Maitreya when addressing political oppression in Burma (Myanmar). In Qing Dynasty China, Maitreya was called upon to protect laborers seeking a more just and equitable distribution of land and wealth, and in other parts of Southeast Asia Maitreya is a divine protector in the face of state-supported violence against disenfranchised populations.

Avalokiteśvara (The Perfect Companion)

The *bodhisattva* Avalokiteśvara is the most immediate, most present, and most accessible of the cosmic buddhas and *bodhisattvas*. Though male in Sanskrit scriptures dedicated to him such as *The Lotus Sūtra*, in China and Japan Avalokiteśvara is portrayed in feminine form, as a kind and powerful goddess known as 觀音 – Guanyin or Kannon. One especially illustrative form of this *bodhisattva* is her representation as "Kannon of a thousand eyes and a thousand hands" (see Figure 24.2), symbolizing her sensitivity to the suffering of the world (her thousand eyes) and her power to bring suffering beings to salvation (her thousand hands). In one famous temple in Kyōto, Japan, a thousand such images were constructed, each 5–6 feet in height, gilded and jeweled. These marvelous religious statues constitute one of the greatest displays of religious material culture in the world.

Guanyin/Kannon appears in numerous other forms as well – "fish-basket Guanyin," the "white robed Guanyin," the great aide to Amitābha Buddha, and so on – being named after the various, in fact theoretically infinite forms in which the goddess can appear. Guanyin is a "shape-shifter," demonstrating her marvelous powers of self-transformation – that is, her *upāya* ("skillful means"). According to *The Lotus Sūtra*, for example, Avalokiteśvara is capable of appearing in any of 32 forms, depending on her devotees' particular needs, including a king, queen, monastic elder, householder, priest, peasant, man, woman, boy, girl, or non-human spirit. In the Chinese and Japanese tradition, Guanyin/Kannon also appears as a child prodigy who cures her cruel father's mortal illness with flesh from her own body (even her own liver and eyes). She also appears as a prostitute who employs sexual seduction to heal a man

Figure 24.2   Statues of Thousand-Armed Kannon at Sanjūsangendō (三十三間堂), Kyoto. © Christophe Boisvieux / Corbis.

from sexual addiction, and as a fishing girl who saves sailors from shipwrecks at sea.

How does one receive these rewards? By single-mindedly calling upon the name of the *bodhisattva*, by offering food and incense to her images, and by practicing charitable giving and compassionate acts of kindness and caring to those in need.

Kṣitigarbha (Earth Matrix)

The realm in which Kṣitigarbha aids those in need is the realm of the various hells and purgatories of the Buddhist cosmological system. Because the law of *karma* is so exact and, one might say, so just, punishment for wrong-doing is finely calibrated and fits exactly the "crime": there is a mechanical distribution of karmic cause and effect. In fact there is no "divine judge" in Buddhism, no cosmic law-giver, only the law (the *dharma*) itself, which works impersonally, like the natural laws that govern action and reaction in the physical universe. The only god-like beings who participate in this process are *bodhisattvas*, who work to ameliorate the suffering of "guilty parties" and to lessen their pain. One of the most powerful of these hell-relievers is Kṣitigarbha.

Figure 24.3   Line of stone statues of the *bodhisattva* Jizō, carved by the disciples of archbishop Tenkai (1536–1643). Nikko, Japan. © Albert Mendelewski / iStockphoto.

Kṣitigarbha is best known in Japan, where he is called Jizō (地藏, Earth Matrix, a reference to something like the underworld of the Western tradition). Jizō enjoys the worship of persons who believe that they are wrong-doers and fear a hellish destiny. Jizō temples come alive late at night, when they are visited by underworld figures (criminals, gang members, prostitutes and call girls). Even more commonly, Jizō temples are visited by women who have miscarried or have elected to abort an unborn child, and a Jizō temple will conduct a funerary rite for the fetus and a rite of forgiveness for the mother. The aborted fetus is called in Japanese a "water baby" (水子, *mizuko*), as represented in Figure 24.3, and the rite is called a "propitiation of the water baby" (水子供養, *mizuko-kuyō*).

Kṣitigarbha also protects other children who have died prematurely. A few years ago, when I was living in Taiwan, I was curious about a small shrine to Kṣitigarbha (Dizang in Chinese) placed near a railroad crossing. I was informed that the shrine had been erected in propitiation of the spirits of two small boys who had been struck and killed by a train several decades ago. The spirits of the boys who died prematurely are calmed by the *bodhisattva*, so as not to harm other children. Children at play are now protected by the *bodhisattva* from suffering the same fate.

We can notice several unique characteristics of a religious system that has populated the cosmos with saviors – beings such as Amitābha, Maitreya, Avalokiteśvara, and Kṣitigarbha. For those many millions of people, past and present, who have preserved their faith in these *mahāsattvas*, the following statements are true:

- No matter how dire one's present circumstances, belief in the existence of powerful, compassionate saviors instills confidence, optimism, and hope.
- The marvelous power of self-transformation exhibited by Avalokiteśvara and other cosmic *bodhisattvas* means that anyone one encounters in life could be a *bodhisattva* in human form; believing this, one treats all beings with reverence and appreciation.
- Persons who believe they have done wrong are confident that there are divine beings whose grace extends even to them; in the case of women who have chosen to abort a child, Buddhism offers a ritual means to care for their spirits.
- Faith and devotional acts are accompanied by good works, such that anyone is capable of rebirth in heaven.
- In the face of unjust social and economic conditions, buddhas and *bodhisattvas* (such as the Future Buddha Maitreya) are cosmic defenders of righteous protest and rebellion.

The *Bodhisattva* Path

Though the cosmic buddhas and *bodhisattvas* described above are certainly extraordinary, if not supernatural, the Buddhist tradition insists that anyone can become a buddha by following the path of the Buddha, the *Buddha-dharma*. We have already explored the Eightfold Path of the monastic tradition. This path was expanded in the Mahayāna tradition, which places emphasis on universal salvation – a form of salvation extending to monastics and lay-persons alike. It is a linear 10-step path beginning with lay practice, advancing to monastic practice, and finally reaching the four supernormal skills of the *bodhisattva*:

A lay practice:
1 *dāna* (giving, generosity, cultivation of merit);
2 *śīla* (moral virtue, responsibility for one's actions);
3 *kṣānti* (patience, forbearance in adversity, avoidance of anger, perseverance in the path);

B monastic practice:
4 *vīrya* (energy, vigor, mindful alertness as cultivated by a monk or nun);
5 *dhyāna* (meditation, comprehension of the "four noble truths," mastery over concentration/*samadhi*, skills in math, medicine, poetry);
6 *prajñā* (wisdom, full insight into conditioned arising/*pratītya-samutpāda* and emptiness/*śūnyatā*);

C   *bodhisattva* practice:
   7   *upāya* (skillful means, a heavenly savior/*mahāsattva* who magically
       projects him-/herself into many worlds in order to teach and help
       others according to their needs);
   8   *praṇidhāna* (non-relapse, certainty about attaining Buddhahood,
       mastery over the transfer of merit and of the gift of grace);
   9   *bala* (power, perfecting the use of *upāya* for any nature of being);
   10 *jñāna* (knowledge – a tenth-stage *bodhisattva* like Maitreya resides
       in the Tuṣita Heaven, aided by lesser *bodhisattvas*, all-knowing and
       all-seeing).

Rather than describing each of these stages in detail, we can make several
observations:

First, anyone – not just monks and nuns – can be on the path to enlightenment, to becoming a tenth-stage *bodhisattva*, and eventually a Buddha. Monks
and nuns – even *bodhisattvas* and buddhas – are not qualitatively different from
the rest of us, not a "different order of being." We are all on the path together.

Second, the path begins with charity, for instance the sharing and the basic
acts of kindness that we encourage in our children and that soon come naturally to them. It is easy – appropriate even for children – to be on the path to
enlightenment.

Third, the path to enlightenment is not private but universal, and always
involves others. The focus of Mahāyāna practice is kindness and compassion.

Fourth, "supernatural powers" are merely an extension of the "natural" acts
of kindness and religious self-cultivation of "this-worldly" practice – not something beyond or outside the world of everyday experience.

Finally, we can see that the early Western representation of Buddhism as
an "atheistic non-religious" practice of self-effort in emulation of the Buddha
is an incomplete picture at best. Buddhism as practiced in East Asia and elsewhere contains a rich cosmology of multiple worlds governed by multiple
divine beings, all of whom can be present to us in our daily lives. Buddhism
is not simply a meditative tradition, but a "religion" in every sense of the
word. Even "Buddha" is not simply "a man," but rather an abstract idea in
many forms. In the Mahāyāna tradition Śākyamuni Buddha is merely one
form, the *nirmāna-kāya*, or "transformation body" of Buddha. In addition,
there is the *sambhoga-kāya* (the "bliss" or "cosmic" body), multiple in form and
including all the buddhas and *bodhisattvas*, and the *dharma-kāya*, the "formless" body of Buddha that is beyond any concrete description – a conception
that ultimately inspired the Mahāyāna tradition known in the West as "Zen."

25

Principles of Zen Buddhism

"Zen" is the Japanese pronunciation of the Chinese character 禪 (Chan). The school first arose in China in the Tang and Song Dynasties, in response to the growing wealth and power of the great state-supported monasteries of the Chinese Empire. The first Chan cloisters were established in mountain retreats far from these recognized centers and, fortuitously, survived a major government persecution from 842 to 845 CE during which monastic wealth and properties were seized by the state and many monks and nuns were forcibly returned to lay life. At the same time Buddhist monks from Korea and Japan were carrying the tradition to their respective countries, inspired by Chan monastic reforms and meditation practices, in addition to the cosmological systems of Vajrayāna (Tibetan) Buddhism and Pure Land devotionalism. Institutionally, Chan took root in Korea (as Seon) and Japan (as Zen) and became the primary monastic tradition of those countries, while Pure Land Buddhism is now associated with congregational lay practice.

As a reform movement within the Buddhist tradition, Zen has distinct characteristics, which are expressed in rhetorical opposition to much that preceded it. A Chinese couplet is often cited as a summary description of Zen:

A special transmission beyond tradition	*Jiao-wai bie-chuan*	教 外 別 傳
With no dependence on words and letters	*Bu-li wen-zi*	不 立 文 字
Pointing directly to the human mind	*Zhi-zhi ren-xin*	直 至 人 心
Seeing into one's nature and becoming Buddha.	*Jian-xing cheng-fo*	見 性 成 佛

"Beyond words and letters," Zen takes the Mahāyāna doctrine of emptiness (*śūnyatā*), depicted in Zen as an empty circle (see Figure 25.1), and puts it into practice. We can think of the "practice of emptiness" in two ways:

Asian Religions: A Cultural Perspective, First Edition. Randall L. Nadeau.
© 2014 John Wiley & Sons, Ltd. Published 2014 by John Wiley & Sons, Ltd.

Figure 25.1 The "empty circle" of Zen. © andylin / iStockphoto.

First, Zen affirms emptiness in a literal sense, symbolized by the "empty circle." Zen undermines the traditional forms of Buddhism (institutional authority, the images and symbols of religious faith, the buddhas and *bodhisattvas*, the scriptures and their contents) through the affirmation of "formlessness" and "wordless teaching."

Second, Zen promotes the idea of "interdependence" (*pratītya-samutpāda*) by affirming Buddhist practice in the context of everyday life and by cultivating a meditative attitude toward all activities. This focused attention (which is the primary meaning of the word *chan*) is described in Japanese as *ippitsu-no-zen* (一筆の禪), "one-stroke Zen." Enlightenment can be experienced not only through the traditional practice of the holy Eightfold Path, which consists of ethics and formal meditation, but also through simple, mundane activities, from sweeping a courtyard to washing one's bowl after a meal, and through disciplines such as flower arranging (生け花, *ikebana*), the preparation of tea (茶の湯, *chanoyu*), and archery (弓道, *kyudō*).

Legends of the Patriarchs

The history of Zen Buddhism is steeped in myth. Its fantastical elements are central to the history of Zen in East Asia and have also captured the attention of Western orientalists since the mid-twentieth century to the present day. Modern scholars have made great strides in distinguishing historical reality from mythical imagination and have placed Zen in the context of Buddhist monastic and scholastic traditions. Yet the lyrical and inventive parables of Zen history and practice are central to its self-understanding, both in Asia and in the West. Within institutional settings based upon strict discipline, detailed rules of practice and daily life, and the ritual veneration of tradition, Zen mythology is, paradoxically, anti-authoritarian and iconoclastic. In this section we will examine the projected image of Zen as the "tradition beyond tradition."

According to legend, the First Patriarch of Zen was a purely legendary figure with the Sanskrit name Bodhidharma ("Way of Enlightenment," represented in Chinese as Pu-ti-da-mo 菩提達磨 and in Japanese as Daruma 達磨). Bodhidharma was said to have surfed from India to China on a rush-leaf, and then sat in a cave practicing meditation for years on end – to the point where his arms and legs fell off (a Japanese "Daruma doll" is a limbless piggy bank in the shape of Bodhidharma's head). In homage to his Indian roots, he is portrayed as a hirsute figure with a swarthy complexion. He is nicknamed "the wall-gazer," in honor of his years of meditation on the cave wall.

When Bodhidharma was approached for instruction by a Chinese monk named Huike 慧可, he merely rolled his eyes – a form of instruction that came to be known as "transmission from mind to mind" (以心傳心, *yi xin chuan xin*). Subsequently this phrase refers to teaching based upon imitation and practice rather than verbal instruction – in martial arts, calligraphy, ink painting, archery, or any of the other Zen skills.

Another set of legends surrounds the Chinese monk Huineng (惠能, c. 638–713 CE), an illiterate wood-cutter whose insightful embrace of "wordlessness" was recorded (ironically) in *The Platform Sūtra of the Sixth Patriarch* – an elusive and aphoristic text affirming concepts such as "no mind," the "interruption of all thought," and "direct practice." Portraits of Huineng show him tearing traditional *sūtras* to shreds and cutting bamboo with "the knife that penetrates ignorance."

Initially rebuffed when he attempted to enter a Chan cloister for instruction, Huineng returned three times before gaining admittance. (This episode is now routinized in Zen monasteries in East Asia: before being admitted, one must attempt three times, on three consecutive days, and be "refused" twice – one is only admitted on the third effort.) Finally permitted to enter the monastery, Huineng then served as the wood-cutter responsible for keeping the kitchen fires aflame.

The illiterate Huineng gained the "transmission of the lamp" of enlightenment in a poetry-writing contest. When a new patriarch was to be appointed by the Fifth Patriarch of Chan, all the monks assumed that a senior monk named Shenxiu (神秀) would be so honored. Indeed his poem was so profound that none of the other monks dared to make an entry of their own. Here is Shenxiu's poem:

The body is the *bodhi* tree	Shen shi pu-ti shu	身是菩提術
The mind is like a clear mirror	Xin ru ming-jing tai	心如明鏡台
At all times we must strive to polish it	Shi-shi jin ti-shi	時時進涕視
And must not let the dust collect	Mo shi you chen-ai	末使有塵埃

When the poem was read to him, Huineng remarked: "A marvelous poem indeed. But I have another one":

Originally there is no *bodhi* tree	Pu-ti ben wu shu	菩提本無術
The mirror has no stand	Ming-jing yi wu tai	明鏡益無台
The Buddha nature is basically clean and pure	Fo-xing chang qing-jing	佛性常清淨
Where is there room for dust?	He chu you chen-ai?	和處有塵埃

Of course Huineng's poem, with its emphasis on the idea of "original enlightenment" and the "emptiness" of all conceptions, won the day and Huineng was given the robe of Chan authority.

Characteristics of Zen

What do these legends mean? What is distinctive about Zen? We will examine Zen from the perspective of four kinds of "emptiness": the emptiness of authority, the emptiness of mind, the emptiness of activity, and the emptiness of enlightenment.

Emptiness of authority

The traditional aspects of Buddhism – scriptures, images, and monastic authority – are viewed with contempt.

- *Emptiness of Buddha*   Zen stories abound in enlightened figures mocking the symbols that the tradition held in highest regard, including the buddhas and *bodhisattvas*. Empty of substance or significance, the Buddha is deemed unnecessary for individual self-cultivation, his own enlightenment being accessible to all. As the modern Zen master Yamada Mumon (山田 無文, 1900–1988) remarked: "The Buddha exists for those who need the Buddha; the Buddha does not exist for those who do not need the Buddha" (quoted from the film *Buddhism: Land of the Disappearing Buddha*, from *The Long Search* television series, Episode 9, BBC 1977).

Chan master Danxia Tianran (丹霞天然, 739–824) was stopping by the great monastery at Luoyang. Chilled by the winter frost, he took a wooden image of the Buddha Amitābha and set it aflame. Shocked, the monks at the temple asked how Danxia could destroy an image sacred to the Great Vehicle. Danxia replied: "I'm burning the image to get to the essence!" The monks asked: "What is the essence of the Buddha?" To which Danxia replied: "There is no essence! Bring me another to warm my ass!"[1]

- *Emptiness of dharma*   The teaching of emptiness requires no verbal instruction; it is "beyond words and letters." Not only is the Sixth Patriarch portrayed tearing up *sūtras*; others are seen trying to read in the dark or to write on air (which signifies the futility of reading and writing). The traditional teachings are of no use to us now, and the verbalized *dharma* of scripture is replaced with direct, immediate experience.
- *Emptiness of Sangha*   Though Zen certainly established its own highly authoritarian system, it did so while reforming centuries of monastic practice. "A day without work is a day without food" (一日不做一日不食)[2] reflects not only the value of physical labor, but also the self-sufficiency of the Zen monasteries. A new code was established, attributed to Baizhang (百丈, 720–814) and celebrating the value of physical labor. One of the reforms was the institution of the "medicine meal" in the evening, so named because the original monastic code prohibits any food after noon, "except for medicine." When emphasis is placed upon physical labor, it would be unreasonable to expect monks to go all day without food! The phrase "medicine meal" is still used in Zen monasteries today as the name of the evening meal.

Emptiness of mind

Logical thought is viewed with hostility, as a hindrance to true understanding.

- *The "stick-and-shout method" of the School of Rinzai*   The Rinzai (臨濟) School, with Sōtō (曹洞), is one of two major Zen schools in Japan. It is named after the Chinese master Linji Yixuan (臨濟義玄), a ninth-century figure famous for "shouts and blows of his staff" in lieu of verbal instruction. Stories abound of his "direct method," exercised for instance when he threw a monk into a river as the latter remarked "The river of Zen is very deep," or when he choked a student to silence him when the latter attempted "to speak a word of Zen." A "warning stick" (*keisaku*) is still employed in Zen monasteries to slap meditators who are drifting off to sleep, in three swift blows to one's back, between the neck and shoulder. The School of Rinzai repudiates all forms of verbal instruction in favor of personal experience.

- *Meditation on the kōan* (公案)   A *kōan* is a nonsensical statement or conversation between a Zen master and his student; it is designed to frustrate the logical processes of the mind. Said to have been created spontaneously by Chinese and Japanese Zen masters in the ninth to thirteenth centuries, *kōans* were eventually set down in collections such as the *Wumenguan* (無門關, *The Gateless Gate*). In Zen monasteries disciples are assigned a *kōan* by their masters and are instructed to "solve the unsolvable" as a way to penetrate, and ultimately transcend, all dependence on language and logic.

The Gateless Gate, a collection of 48 *kōans*, can be assigned the following typology:

The unanswerable question   Examples:

"What is the sound of one hand clapping?"
"What was the appearance of your original face before your parents were born?"
"Why does the Western Barbarian have no beard?"

The question and answer (問答, *mondō*), *or "encounter dialogue," where the response is logically unexpected or paradoxical. Examples:*

Q: "What is the path to no birth?"
A: "Last night I lost three coins by my bed."

Q: "What is 'Buddha'?"
A: "Dried shit-stick."

Q: "How can I cultivate the original mind?"
A: "I call this a staff. What would you call it?"

The response of silence, "deafening like thunder"   Examples:

In lieu of instruction, Master Juzhi (俱胝, ninth century) would simply hold a finger in the air. One day, observing a student doing the same, Master Juzhi sliced off the monk's finger with a dagger. "Why did you do that?" cried the student. Master Juzhi held up his finger in the air.

Master Baofu (保福, 860–928) was asked: "What is no mind?" After a long period of silence, Master Baofu asked: "What did you say?" The student repeated his question. "I'm not deaf!" the Master shouted.

Someone asked: "The patriarch Bodhidharma sat facing the wall. What was he trying to show?" The Master covered his ears with his hands.

I had the good fortune of "solving" the best known of all the *mondōs*, one frequently employed in Zen monasteries today:

Q: "Does a dog have Buddha nature?"
A: "*Mu!*" (無)

What does this *kōan* mean? The word *mu* (pronounced *wu* in Chinese) can mean simply "no" – so here it might mean no, a dog does not have Buddha nature (that is, the capacity for enlightenment). At a more abstract level, the character *mu* means "empty" or "emptiness" – so here it might mean "yes," a dog does have Buddha-nature, and that nature is equated with emptiness.

How did I penetrate the *kōan*? Once when traveling in Japan, I played a game with an 8-year-old child as I was staying with the boy's family at a *minshuku* (民俗, a people's guesthouse or bed and breakfast). We were naming animals and the sounds they make on the family farm. Seeing a cat, the boy said "*mi mi mi*"; seeing a duck, he said, "*weng weng*." When a dog crossed our path, the boy shouted, "*Mu! Mu!*" At that moment I achieved my own "Zen enlightenment": the "answer" to the famous *mu kōan* was, simply, "woof!"

Since they were collected in major compendia such as *The Blue Cliff Record* (*Biyanlu*, 碧巖錄) and *The Gateless Gate* (*Wumenguan*, 無門關) in the twelfth and thirteenth centuries, *kōans* have been employed as historical records, hagiographic parables, and objects of meditation. Hardly "spontaneous" in their present use, *kōans* are assigned by the master and repeated daily as a focus of concentration.

We can say that *kōans* "make no sense." This is, of course, their purpose. But the student must make every effort to understand and interpret them, in order to achieve a breakthrough. He (or she) must "hold the *kōan* in his belly, like an iron ball." Frustration leads ultimately to sudden awareness of the "suchness" of existence, beyond language and logic. Rinzai Zen Master Hakuin (白隠, 1686–1768) says:[3]

> If you take up one *kōan* and investigate it unceasingly, your mind will die and your will shall be destroyed. You face death and your gut feels as though it is on fire. Then suddenly you are one with the *kōan* . . . and you discover your true nature.

Figure 25.2 The *kare-sansui* (枯山水, dry landscape) rock garden at Ryōanji (龍安寺). © Theodore Scott / iStockphoto.

The "emptying of the mind" is also represented in the Zen tradition of the *kare-sansui* (枯山水, dry landscape) rock garden – such as the famous garden at Ryōanji (龍安寺), Kyōtō, a Rinzai Zen temple (see Figure 25.2).

Emptiness of activity

The emphasis here is on simplicity and spontaneity and on appreciation of the commonplace and ordinary:

- "Buddha-nature" in all things and all activities;
- the highest form of practice: "doing one thing at a time" (one-pointed Zen);
- Zen arts: *ikebana, cha-no-yu, haiku*, ink-painting, calligraphy, archery, swordsmanship;
- "transmission from mind to mind."

In practice, the Zen school does not limit meditation to *zazen* (坐禪, "seated zen") but applies the principles of meditation to all activities, through focused concentration. A number of Zen *kōans* and "encounter dialogues" illustrate this principle:[4]

"How wondrously profound this is: I draw water, I carry fuel."

A student asked his master: "Every day we must dress and eat. How can we go beyond this?" The master replied: "We dress. We eat." "I do not understand," said the monk. "If you do not understand, put on your clothes, eat your food."

A student asked his master: "I have studied with you these many years and have learned nothing." The master replied: "When you brought me food, I ate it, didn't I? When you brought me drink, I drank it, didn't I? Look directly into it. If you think about it, you miss it."

A Zen master tells this story: "The son of a thief wished to be instructed by his father in the arts of robbery. Taking him into the grandest house in the village, the father slapped the boy into a trunk and closed the heavy lid. Shouting 'thief thief,' he roused the village. The boy struggled out of the trunk, jumped from the second floor window, and ran for his life, only escaping by chucking a rock into the stream to throw his pursuers off his trail. When he returned home, he was furious with his father. 'Why did you do such a thing? I could have been killed by that mob!' 'There,' his father replied, 'I have taught you everything I know.'"

Emptiness of enlightenment

It is not the gradual accumulation of merit that achieves liberation, but a sudden act of recognition – a totally "free" event. This is the emptiness of enlightenment.

Zen enlightenment is not "once and for all," a one-time or life-ending event. In fact *satori* (悟り, the Japanese term meaning "awakening") is repeatable, episodic, and transitory. Moreover, even though it may be preceded by years of preparatory work in the form of Zen practice and meditation, the experience itself goes beyond anything that has been done to bring it about. Of course, no direct descriptions of *satori* have been attempted, as such descriptions would violate the basic Zen principle of "wordless understanding." But a few Zen *kōans* give a sense of its paradoxical nature:

- "the ripe fruit falls from the tree";
- "a baby's hand releases one object to grasp another";
- "the bamboo leaf slowly bends under the weight of the snow, and it falls";
- "the mountain is climbed, the vista appears."

What do these expressions mean? In each case, the end result – the consequence of the preparatory activity – is dependent upon what has come before, but at the same time it is *qualitatively different*, a radically new grasp of reality. The student meditates upon the *kōan* or focusses a "one-pointed" attention on a single activity for many years, but nothing can prepare her for the moment of enlightenment itself.

Principles of Zen Buddhism

In the summer after graduating from college, I took a road trip across the United States. Driving north from Flagstaff on Route 60, I made my way to the Grand Canyon, a place that is indeed beyond description, beyond what can be captured in words, or even in video or film. Counting the 120 miles from the city to the entrance, the preparatory work was done – I had endured the monotony of the flat and arid countryside, following the many signs that directed me on the route. And then, suddenly, the vista appeared: I saw in an instant a grandeur that I could never have imagined after camping in the desert the night before, or holding pedal to metal for the miles leading to the canyon. *Satori* demands rigorous, disciplined preparation, but its true nature cannot be anticipated. It is spontaneous and unpredictable.

Notes

1   For a full account of this legend, see John Kieschnick, *The Impact of Buddhism on Chinese Material Culture* (Princeton, NJ: Princeton University Press, 2003), p. 76. It should be pointed out that such behaviors would be inconceivable in a Chinese Chan or Japanese Zen monastery today. No one – not master, novice, or visitor – would desecrate images, violate monastic rules, or mock traditional practices that have been upheld for centuries. For a vivid account of a young Japanese businessman who spent a year in training at the famed Zen Eiheiji Temple, see Kaoru Nonomura, *Eat Sleep Sit: My Year at Japan's Most Rigorous Zen Temple*, translated by Juliet Winters Carpenter (New York: Kodansha USA, 2009).

2   This is a well-known Zen saying. Its origin is the *Pure Rules of Baizhang* (Chinese 百丈清規). A translation of the full text can be found at http://www.thezensite.com/ ZenTeachings/Translations/Baizhang_Monastic_Regulations.pdf (accessed July 25, 2013).

3   Adapted from Heinrich Dumoulin, *Zen Buddhism: A History*, vol. 2: *Japan* (New York: Macmillan, 1989), p. 382.

4   See William Barrett, ed., *Zen Buddhism: Selected Writings of D. T. Suzuki* (New York: Doubleday, 1996).

26

Buddhism as a Global Religion

For most Asians, Buddhism remains a tradition of moral living, devotion, and ritual practice. Buddhism provides ritual means – as it has done for many centuries – for coping with death and for remembering the dead: ritual practices associated with death and dying are the only interaction that lay persons may ever have with Buddhist monastics, who might be referred to as "priests" no less than as "monks" on account of the important role they play in Asian social life. "Priestly" or "liturgical" Buddhism is Buddhism in its most visible form in modern East Asia.

In Japan, some critics have argued that the "funeral industry" is now the defining characteristic of Japanese Buddhism, "all that is left" of it – reflecting the "decline" of Buddhist practice as a tradition of monastic self-cultivation.[1] In fact the same social functions are performed throughout the Buddhist world: Chinese readily associate Buddhism with death or with coping with death, and funerary rites are performed by Buddhist monks in Sri Lanka, Thailand, Burma, Cambodia, Vietnam, and Korea as well.

Although it is true that traditional Buddhist monasticism appeals to fewer and fewer young men and women in recent years and has had to adapt to cultural and technological change, it remains an option for religious seekers throughout East Asia and throughout the world.[2] It is hardly the case that monasticism is "dead." In the twentieth century significant reforms were carried out in Sri Lanka, Cambodia, Vietnam, China, Japan, and Korea, ensuring that monastic life is responsible to concerns of the modern age.

The Buddhist tradition has undergone profound changes within Asia, partly as a consequence of encounters with the West in social and economic terms, and partly due to its own dynamics and evolution. Before focusing our discussion on broader cultural trends, we can list some of the most evident transition points:

Asian Religions: A Cultural Perspective, First Edition. Randall L. Nadeau.
© 2014 John Wiley & Sons, Ltd. Published 2014 by John Wiley & Sons, Ltd.

- the weakening of state control and the institutionalization of Buddhism as a distinct "corporate entity" in administration, taxation, and economic activities;
- the influence of enlightenment thinking and modernist scientific rationalism, which is evident in Buddhist monastic reforms and in Buddhist publications for public consumption;
- a decline followed by a modest recovery of both monastic and lay Buddhism, in parallel with a growth in the enhanced status of women as nuns or lay practitioners in East and Southeast Asia;
- engagement with social and political causes in the form of Buddhist reform movements, hospitals, NGO's, and social services;
- the commercialization of ritual services, especially in the form of "funerary Buddhism";
- increasing lay interest in Buddhism as a "self-help" movement, accompanied by broader participation in activities once limited exclusively for monastics: meditation classes, retreats, study groups, and the like;
- expansion of Tibetan Buddhism throughout Asia and the world since 1959, as a consequence of the Tibetan exile.

Buddhist Modernism: From Scientific Rationalism to Depth Psychology

The Buddhist tradition is dynamic. Although some Buddhist institutions are committed to traditional forms and practices, and although the most visible dimensions of Buddhism in Asia (its temples and monasteries, its ritual performances) retain the grandeur and classical feel of the past, Buddhist thought and practice are as responsive to modern life and cultural changes as any other dimension of human social life. Some scholars consider the transmission of Buddhism to the West, together with the complementary phenomenon of Western influence on Asia, as a primary agent of change; but Buddhist modernity is not simply a process of "Westernization" – in fact some of the most interesting contemporary Buddhist movements and thinkers in both Asia and the West are highly critical of "Western" values and define themselves in contrast to Westernizing global trends. Still, the Buddhist encounter with the West is one of the most dramatic developments within the tradition in the past several centuries. It affects both the self-definition of Buddhism and its future course, and it is difficult to find any Buddhist institution in the modern world that does not relate itself some way or another to Western culture.

One example is the emergence, in the past few centuries, of "Protestant Buddhism" – a style of practice that incorporates formal elements from Protestant Christianity: a pastor, a regular service incorporating both ritual and instruction (a sermon), membership rolls, tithing to support the temple, volunteerism, and community service. Protestant Buddhism can be found in contemporary Sri Lanka and some Southeast Asian Theravāda communities, in Japanese Pure Land congregations and Buddhist-inspired new religious movements, and in congregational communities in the West.[3]

Another example is the increased interest, among young urban professionals – that is, educated persons usually from the upper middle class – in Buddhist meditation and Buddhist thought, which they pick up through reading, workshops and seminars, university courses, and short-term formal practice. This is especially true of Western Buddhists inspired by Western seekers in the 1960s and 1970s, who themselves were the heirs of the transcendentalists, theosophists, and free thinkers of the eighteenth century (one of the first English translations of *The Heart Sūtra* – a foundational scripture of Mahāyāna Buddhism – was done by Henry David Thoreau from a French translation by an eminent European scholar). However, Buddhist modernism – lay-based, individualistic, focused on meditation and psychological introspection, "self-help"-oriented – is developing all over the world, including Asia.[4]

Though lay Buddhists have constituted the great majority of practicing Buddhists throughout history, their role in traditional times was limited to worship, prayer, alms-giving, and ritual participation. Today lay Buddhists are more spiritually active and show a greater interest in meditation and philosophical expression. Part of this is a function of literacy: hundreds of Buddhist books are published every year, in every language, and are read by practitioners who may have no institutional affiliation at all, or by groups of individuals sharing common interests. Much of the Buddhist canon has now been translated into English, vernacular Chinese and Japanese, and other languages. Even more widely, books on Buddhism by both scholars and practitioners now reach a worldwide audience.

What do these books have to say? For better or worse, the image of Buddhism presented in "guidebooks" written for mass consumption – as well as by popular media such as television, pop music, and film – is a mixture of traditional Buddhism with modern psychology, counterculturalism, and aesthetic expression. Modern Buddhist spirituality is contrasted with "religion" (especially Western religions) and with "consumerism" or materialism.[5] Many of my own students, taking their first course on Buddhism in a university setting, come into the class with preconceived ideas of what Buddhism is: a spiritual practice that does not affirm a belief in God, that emphasizes freedom and self-expression, that requires no rules and makes no authoritarian demands, that promises a state of "enlightenment" largely self-actualized and self-defined, and that teaches peace, tolerance, and love. Even before knowing much about the history of Buddhism and its rich variety and cultural forms, most American university students think of it in highly romanticized terms.

Figure 26.1   The 14th Dalai Lama. © vipflash/ Shutterstock.com.

This view of Buddhism in the modern age was inspired by the countercultural movements of the 1960s and by a few cosmopolitan Asian intellectuals who have lectured and published in the West. Though they represent very different styles of thought and practice and are extremely diverse in their own right, these Asian intellectuals have responded to a chord of discontent in the West – discontent with religious institutions and with traditional Judeo-Christian teachings and practices. Increasingly, their messages of self-actualization and of relief from psychological pain and trouble are gaining popularity in Asia as well. Among the most influential of these public intellectuals are D. T. Suzuki, Shunryu Suzuki, Thich Nhat Hanh, Kelsang Gyatso, Chögyam Trungpa, and the fourteenth Dalai Lama (shown in Figure 26.1). Spanning a half-century and representing a broad spectrum of moral and ethical teachings, these teachers have transformed Buddhism into a truly global, truly modern phenomenon.[6]

Today American and European Buddhists are shaping the tradition's present form and future course. Some have taken the vows to become monks and nuns (often adapting the Vinaya to fit modern needs) and are themselves authorized to initiate disciples, creating *dharma* transmissions that are fully self-contained within the West. Western Buddhist teachers have established an authoritative presence by publishing regularly and by teaching seminars and workshops such as those associated with the San Francisco Zen Center established in 1962 (it recently celebrated its fiftieth birthday), the Massachusetts Barre Center for Buddhist Studies ("for the integration of scholarly understanding and meditative insight"), Boulder's Naropa University (the first degree-granting Buddhist institution of higher education in the United States), the University of the West (associated with Hsi lai Temple in Hacienda Heights, Los Angeles), and others. There are hundreds of Buddhist centers dedicated to Zen and Vipassana meditation in the United States, in England, and on the European continent; Pure Land, Sōka Gakkai and other devotional movements; and Tibetan-based organizations including Shambhala International and the Foundation for the Preservation of the Mahāyāna Tradition. The history and diversity of Western Buddhism is extraordinarily rich and has now been the subject of a number of detailed studies.[7]

One of the most significant social and institutional developments of contemporary Buddhism is the rising status of women, in both lay and monastic contexts. In Asia and in the West, Buddhist women have become empowered to be institutional leaders, teachers, and writers with a more powerful voice and more receptive audiences. In some countries the nuns' order has held steady while the monks' order has declined; in Southeast Asia lay nuns have seen an increase in numbers and status while continuing their calls for the restoration of the nuns' order; and in the West there is now no significant gender divide in either intellectual or institutional leadership – a significant change since American Buddhism first arose in the 1960s and 1970s. While some would argue against defining this trend as "feminist Buddhism," there is no doubt that women's roles have expanded within Buddhist communities in both Asia and the West to a level not seen in most of the world's great religions.[8] At the same time – and partly in a critical response to feminist Buddhism – persons of color and LGBT Buddhist practitioners have also found a voice in community and publication.[9]

Buddhism is one of the fastest growing of the world's religions, with estimates of several million adherents in Europe and America. We tend to think of this as a new phenomenon, but there has never been a time in its history when Buddhism was not inspiring new cultural forms and adaptations, from Sri Lanka to Southeast Asia, from Tibet to Mongolia, from China to Korea to Japan. The emergence of Buddhism in the West, now some 150 years in the making, is just the latest chapter in this story of growth and change.

Engaged Buddhism in Asia and the West

"Engaged Buddhism" is an activist, lay-centered movement with a goal of ethical transformation on personal, social, and global scales. It is non-institutional (there is no "church" of Engaged Buddhism and no particular branch of Buddhism that lays claim to it) and exists primarily in a wide community of writers and readers who attempt to put Buddhist ethical teachings into practice on a daily basis. It has generated a library of publications, especially since the mid-1990s, and it could be argued that Engaged Buddhism is the defining characteristic of Western Buddhism in the twenty-first century, both expanding upon and in some cases supplanting the more inward-looking "cult of meditation" that defined Western Buddhism a generation before.[10]

Figure 26.2   Exiled Tibetans chant slogans in front of mock coffins as they hold pictures of Tibetans who allegedly have either died by self-immolation or were killed in a Chinese police firing during a protest march in New Delhi, India, on Sunday, January 29, 2012. More than 100 Buddhist monks, nuns, and other Tibetans have set themselves on fire in protest since February 2009, mostly in traditionally Tibetan areas of southwestern Sichuan Province. © AP Photo / Kevin Frayer / Corbis.

Buddhist participation in the social and political life of Asian countries has also become increasingly more visible – the immolations of Tibetan monks since 2010 (see Figure 26.2), inspired by those of Zen monks during the Vietnam War, the construction of hospitals and orphanages from Taiwan to Sri Lanka, and anti-government activism in Burma, Cambodia, and beyond. It is rare now to find Buddhist monastic institutions that isolate themselves from the social issues of their communities –poverty, prostitution, political oppression, environmental pollution, health care, education, and so on.[11] Increasingly, the English publications of eminent Asian Buddhist leaders focus primarily on ethical practice and social concerns.[12]

Notes

1   For an excellent study of funerary Buddhism, see Mark Michael Rowe, *Bonds of the Dead: Temples, Burial, and the Transformation of Contemporary Japanese Buddhism* (Chicago, IL: The University of Chicago Press, 2011).

2   For a fascinating personal account, see Kaoru Nonomura, *Ku neru suwaru: Eiheiji shugyoki* (1996), translated into English by Juliet Carpenter as *Eat Sleep Sit: My Year at Japan's Most Rigorous Zen Temple* (Tokyo: Kodansha International, 2008).

3   For a perspective on "Protestant Buddhism" from those who created this category, see Richard Gombrich and Gananath Obeyesekere, *Buddhism Transformed: Religious Change in Sri Lanka* (Princeton, NJ: Princeton University Press, 2004).

4   See Donald S. Lopez, *A Modern Buddhist Bible* (Boston, MA: Beacon Press, 2002). On "Buddhist modernism" by the author who coined this phrase, see David McMahon, *The Making of Buddhist Modernism* (London: Oxford University Press, 2008). On Buddhist psychology, see Mark Epstein, *Psychotherapy without the Self: A Buddhist Perspective* (New Haven, CT: Yale University Press, 2007).

5   These books owe a debt to the colorful writings of the Beat Generation. See especially Alan Watts (1915–1973), *The Way of Zen* (New York: Vintage, 1999). Today a whole market of countercultural Buddhist books can be found reflecting similar themes. Some of the most popular of these books are by Brad Warner, beginning with *Hardcore Zen: Punk Rock, Monster Movies, and the Truth about Reality* (Boston, MA: Wisdom Publications, 2003). See also Stephen Batchelor, *Confession of a Buddhist Atheist* (New York: Spiegel & Grau, 2010).

6   These six writers have well over one hundred English-language publications or translations between them. Often mixing historical accuracy with orientalist-inspired imagination, Buddhist popularizers have shaped the Buddhist experience for a global audience. See, for example, D. T. Suzuki, *An Introduction to Zen Buddhism* (New York: Grove Press, 1999); Shunryu Suzuki, *Zen Mind Beginner's Mind: Fortieth Anniversary Edition* (Boston, MA: Shambhala, 2011); Thich Nhat Hanh, *Peace is Every Step: The Path of Mindfulness in Everyday Life* (New York: Bantam, 1992); Kelsang Gyatso, *Introduction to Buddhism: An Explanation of the Buddhist Way of Life* (Glen Spay, NY: Tharpa Publications, 2008); Chögyam Trungpa, *Cutting through Spiritual Materialism* (Boston, MA: Shambhala, 1973); and the 14th Dalai Lama, *The Art of Happiness: A Handbook for Living, 10th Anniversary Edition* (New York: Riverhead Books, 2009).

7   For an overview, see Charles Prebish and Kenneth Tanaka, eds., *The Faces of Buddhism in America* (Berkeley: University of California Press, 1998); Charles Prebish, *Luminous Passage: The Practice and Study of Buddhism in America* (Berkeley: University of California Press, 1999); and Robert Bluck, *British Buddhism: Teachings, Practice and Development* (London: Routledge, 2006).

8   Perhaps the most influential of the feminist critiques from within the Buddhist tradition can be found in the work of Rita Gross, a scholar-practitioner. See especially her *Buddhism after Patriarchy: A Feminist History, Analysis, and Reconstruction of Buddhism* (Albany: State University of New York Press, 1993). See also Karma Lekshe Tsomo, ed., *Buddhist Women across Cultures: Realizations* (Albany: State University of New York Press, 1999). For a contemporary response from an Asian Buddhist scholar, see Wei-yi Cheng, *Buddhist Nuns in Taiwan and Sri Lanka: A Critique of the Feminist Perspective* (London: Routledge, 2007).

9   See, for example, Hilda Gutierrez Baldoquin, ed., *Dharma, Color, and Culture: New Voices in Western Buddhism* (Berkeley, CA: Paralax Press, 2004).

10 There are many good recent books describing the practices and goals of Engaged Buddhism. Here are just two: Arnold Kotler, ed., *Engaged Buddhist Reader: Ten Years of Engaged Buddhist Publishing* (Berkeley, CA: Parallax Press, 1996); Stephanie Kaza, ed., *Hooked! Buddhist Writings on Greed, Desire, and the Urge to Consume* (Boston, MA: Shambhala, 2011).

11 For a background, see Peter Harvey, *An Introduction to Buddhist Ethics: Foundations, Values, and Issues* (Cambridge: Cambridge University Press, 2000).

12 See the English writings or translations of Thich Nhat Hanh, the fourteenth Dalai Lama, Maha Ghosananda, A. T. Ariyaratne, and Master Hsing Yun.

Part VII

Japanese Religions

27

Japanese Religion and Culture

In the eighteenth century, in response to foreign religion, culture, and trade, a nativistic movement developed among Japanese intellectuals to "restore" an indigenous, home-grown religious tradition, which they dated to a period in Japanese history prior to the importation of Chinese characters and cultural influence. This indigenous tradition was Shintō. Partly authentic and partly an invented tradition, Shintō came to represent the essence and core of Japanese culture. Claiming purely Japanese roots, Shintō can be said to be the native, indigenous, or autochthonous religion of Japan.

The name Shintō (神道) is derived from the Chinese "Way" (道, Dao) of the sacred (神, shen). Shintō is the so-called "Chinese pronunciation" of the characters 神道, which in purely Japanese pronunciation are rendered as kami-no-michi (神の道), "the Way of the Kami".[1] What is the meaning of the word kami? What is the Japanese understanding of its own native religious tradition? How is "the sacred" conceptionalized in Japanese culture?

Kami-no-michi is conventionally translated as "the Way of the Gods." So kami are the gods of Japan, and Shintō describes the traditional beliefs and practices associated with these gods. But kami has other meanings too – it is a more complex semantic entity. It can be understood as a concrete noun – in which case it relates to a polytheistic conception of "gods" – or as an abstract noun, meaning "the sacred" – in which capacity it names a sacred quality of existence. Based upon this continuum, we can identify four kinds of kami:

1 mythological creators;
2 exceptional persons;

Asian Religions: A Cultural Perspective, First Edition. Randall L. Nadeau.
© 2014 John Wiley & Sons, Ltd. Published 2014 by John Wiley & Sons, Ltd.

3   extraordinary things;
4   natural objects and implements.

Moving from top to bottom, from concrete to abstract, Shintō is both a *polytheistic* religion affirming the presence of many gods and an *animistic* religion affirming the sacred quality of all things Japanese. The present chapter will examine these various meanings of the word *kami*.

Mythological creators

A reconstructed history of Japan called the *Kojiki* (古事記, *The Record of Ancient Things*) describes the creation of the Oya-shima-no-kuni (大八洲国, Country of the Eight Great Islands) from the formless sea. The creators were the male god Izanagi (イザナギ) and the female god Izanami (イザナミ) (see Figure 27.1) who, performing a sacred dance in the clouds above the waves, grasped a spear with which they stirred the waters, then drew it up and formed the Japanese islands from the precipitate dripping from its point. The last drops shaped the highest place, Mt. Fuji – the *axis mundi*, central axis of the known world.

Among the many gods and goddesses to which the creator gods gave birth was a daughter, Amaterasu 天照 (Sun's Brilliance), who emerges from an east-facing cave every morning, holding a circular mirror with which she guides the sun along its course. Her daily greeting gives Japan its name: the word "Japan" is the English equivalent of a Portuguese mispronunciation of the Japanese *Nihon* (日本), "Land of the Rising Sun." Amaterasu is represented at the Grand Shrine at Ise simply by a large mirror, a material symbol of Shintō. She is an *ōmi-kami* (大神), a "great *kami*," one of many *ōmi-kami* associated with the natural environment of the Japanese islands. This is the first type of *kami*: gods and goddesses who confer upon Japan the status of a sanctified place.

Exceptional persons: imperial descent from Amaterasu

The second type of *kami* is that of exceptional persons such as personal ancestors (*mitama* み霊, the family dead), who are worshipped in a *kamidana* (神棚) – a small shrine within the home. The family dead are *kami*, and in the Japanese context "ancestors" are indistinguishable from "gods."

Stemming from the establishment of Shintō as the state religion in the eighteenth century, the emperors were themselves regarded as *kami*, "ancestors of the nation," and therefore as divine beings. So *kami* include the ancestral line of the imperial family, from the first emperor, Jinmu (神武, r. 660–585 BCE),

Figure 27.1 *Izanagi and Izanami*, by Kobayashi Eitaku, circa 1885. Museum of Fine Arts, Boston, Massachusetts, USA / William Sturgis Bigelow Collection / The Bridgeman Art Library.

to the 124th, Hirohito (裕仁), the longest reigning emperor in Japanese history (1926–1989). The divine status of the emperor is ritualized at his coronation, called the Daijosai (大嘗祭). In the course of this ceremony the new emperor enters a special chamber of the Grand Shrine at Ise and symbolically impregnates the goddess Amaterasu, who ultimately gives birth to the next emperor in the imperial line. Thus, symbolically at least, the emperor has sexual relations with the goddess, who is his own mother, and the imperial line passes from father to son. A succession crisis has occurred in recent years, as Crown

Prince Naruhito (德仁), grandson of Emperor Hirohito and son of the current Emperor Akihito (明仁), has only one child with his wife, Princess Masako (雅子) – namely a girl named Aiko (愛子). Suffering from stress and depression attributed to the lack of a male heir, Princess Masako has withdrawn from the public eye since 2003. Time will tell whether Aiko (born in 2001) or Prince Naruhito's younger brother's son (born in 2006) will succeed to the Chrysanthemum Throne.

This question is politically insignificant, however, as Japan was forced to repudiate the divine status of the emperor at the conclusion of the Pacific War and as a condition of Japan's surrender to the Allied Powers. The document that formalized the separation between Shintō and the state in 1945 is entitled "The Directive for the Disestablishment of State Shintō" and was signed by Corporal Allen on behalf of General Douglas MacArthur, Supreme Commander of the Allied Powers.[2] Two elements from this document should be emphasized: first, the separation between Shintō and the imperial state, modeled upon the Disestablishment Clause of the US Constitution; and, second, the preservation of religious freedom at the level of the individual and the community. That is, the post-war Japanese constitution prohibits State Shintō while protecting Shrine Shintō (Shrine Shintō will be the subject of Chapter 28). While Emperor Hirohito emphasized his divine right to wage war against Japan's enemies – defended at the end of the war by young pilots called *kamikaze* (神風, "wind of the kami") – his son Akihito, the current emperor, denies his divine status and is in fact a symbolic ruler with no political power.

Nevertheless, when Akihito ascended to the imperial throne in 1990, a Daijosai was performed, inciting protests both at home and abroad. A contemporary press release describes why:

> Japan's Emperor Akihito, in the role of a Shintō chief priest, performed a controversial religious rite Thursday night, sparking protests around the country.
>
> Prime Minister Toshiki Kaifu, American Vice President Dan Quayle, King Baudouin of Belgium, King Carl Gustav XVI of Sweden, President Suharto of Indonesia, and President Corazon Aquino of the Philippines observed Akihito's enthronement in gala public ceremonies last week. Last night, 900 Japanese dignitaries waited in darkness as Akihito, hidden from view, offered sacred rice to ancestral gods in an all-night communion ritual that critics say violates constitutional separation of state and religion.
>
> Several thousand people in Tokyo, Osaka, and other cities demonstrated against the ceremony in the emperor's Tokyo palace, which was guarded by 30,000 police.
>
> Despite security precautions, suspected leftist radicals set fire to four railway stations and three Shintō shrines around the country at about midnight Thursday.

In addition, suspected radicals launched six rockets at the Katsura imperial palace in Kyoto. No injuries were reported.

Palace aides said the *Daijosai* would cost a total of $20 million in taxes. More than half went toward constructing a temporary shrine in the style of a 7th century Japanese palace, to be torn down in the coming weeks.[3]

In violation of the constitutional separation of church and state, government officials still worship at Yasukuni Shrine (靖国神社), the Shintō shrine to war heroes. Whenever a prime minister visits the shrine – which houses the spirits of executed war criminals as well as the tens of thousands of soldiers who died in the Japanese war of aggression in China and Southeast Asia – cries of outrage are heard from the governments of China, Korea, and others. A museum adjacent to Yasukuni Shrine, the Yūshūkan (遊就館), is a fascinating example of revisionist history, as it attempts to persuade the viewer, through 18 rooms of emotional display, that the Pacific War was in fact a defensive response to Western colonialism and a last-ditch effort to avoid annihilation at the hands of the United States and its allies. While the sentiments expressed at Yasukuni Shrine represent a small minority of Japanese opinion, they symbolize a remnant of State Shintō and the religious support for state power. For the most part, however, State Shintō and the idea of the divine status of the emperor (the emperor as *kami*) represent a relatively brief period of Japan's imperial past.

Extraordinary things: the cult of Mt. Fuji

The third type of *kami* consists of extraordinary things, especially those extraordinary things in nature associated with the Japanese landscape. A large boulder in a flowing stream, a stand of bamboo within a deciduous forest, a fox or a deer appearing and disappearing through the trees, all are *kami* – less "gods" per se than objects of sacred power, animae ("spirits") of the mystical natural environment. Best known among these sacred things is Mt. Fuji (富士山, Figure 27.2), Japan's primary symbol, a sacred mountain rising mysteriously from the Kantō Plain. It is a visual "mystery," though geologically explicable: Fuji is a dormant volcano, part of the Ring of Fire of the western Pacific Rim. So sacred is Fuji that its very appearance inspires reverence and awe, and sightings of the mountain are eagerly anticipated on the Shinkansen (新幹線, "new trunk line" – a high-speed train) between Tokyo and Osaka. Once when I was travelling on the Tokyo–Osaka Express, the train announcer made a public apology to the passengers because Fuji was obscured from view by clouds and rain. Not only do most Japanese hope to have a glimpse of Fuji, but many also aspire to climb it, though these days most visitors take busses to the seventh stage of the

Figure 27.2   "South Wind Clear Sky" (凱風快晴). From *Thirty-Six Views of Mt. Fuji* (富嶽三十六景, *Fugaku Sanjūroku-kei*), by Katsushika Hokusai (葛飾 北斎), 1760–1849. Private Collection / The Stapleton Collection / The Bridgeman Art Library.

mountain and ascend in the early morning hours to the tenth – the summit. Once a year a *matsuri* (temple festival) is held at the foot of Mt. Fuji. It is a fire festival that marks the end of the climbing season and the beginning of fall, when ascent of the mountain is made impossibly dangerous by wind and cold. Even in fall and winter, however, Fuji Worship Societies conduct fire rites or stage ritual ascents of a miniature Fuji in Tokyo. As Japan's national symbol, Fuji's sacred status represents the sacred status of Japan as a whole.

Natural objects and implements

The final type of *kami* is represented by natural objects and implements, especially those associated uniquely with Japan. This category includes the most ordinary things:

o-mizu お水 (water, esp. spring water);
o-cha お茶 (tea);
o-sake お酒 (rice wine);
go-han ご飯 (cooked rice);
o-furo お風呂 (the communal bath);
o-genki お元気 (the body, personal health);
o-sumo お相撲 (sumo wrestling) . . . and so on.

The Japanese language marks grammatically the "sacred quality" of these things with the help of the "honorifics" *go* and *o* – as in the sequence *gohan o taberu* (ご飯を食べる, "to eat rice") or in the question *ogenki desu ka*? (お元気ですか, "how are you?" – or, more literally, "how is your honored body?"). As natural things originating in the sacred land of Japan, the life-sustaining foods and implements listed above are sanctified and sanctifying, bringing a sacred quality of existence to everyday life.

The sacred things associated with Japan are often personified. It is in this sense that Shintō can be described as an animistic religion: it gives anthropomorphic qualities to material things. In a book on the preparation of sushi, for example, notice the personification of the rice that forms the sushi base:

> The rice cannot be just squeezed. Instead it must be molded. Squeezing the rice into a wad ruins the sushi base. Instead, the grains are *invited* to cling with just the right amount of pressure. It takes years to learn how to do it right.[4]

Even chopsticks (*hashi*, 箸【はし】) have a sacred quality. A popular Japanese dietician and food writer has described children today as *hashi nashi zoku* (箸無し族【はし なし ぞく】), "chopstickless culture" – because of their preference for Western fast food, which is eaten with one's hands. While chopsticks encourage communal dining around a common meal, family unity and sharing, and a healthy diet, the diminished use of chopsticks has had numerous ill effects: "chopstickless" eating is individualized, fast-paced, and unhealthy. For the author, Asako Aramaki, a Japanese "chopstickless culture" is out of touch with its social–cultural roots and has created a desacralized environment.[5]

Characteristics of Kami

The word *kami* is often translated simply as "gods," and the word Shintō as "the Way of the Gods"; but *kami* includes more abstract conceptions of purity, mystery, sanctity, and sacrality. Shintō is both a polytheistic and an animistic, immanentalist religion – that is, it affirms a sacred quality of existence contained within the natural world of Japan and of the Japanese people. Shintō is, first and foremost, a "nature religion"; but, because Japanese culture is so closely associated with its natural environment, nature and culture are unified as one. As a result, even though the emperor has been divested of his divine status and State Shintō has been annulled constitutionally, it is still impossible to conceive of Shintō outside of Japan.

Unlike the Abrahamic God, who is a God of history overseeing the significant events of His people, the Shintō *kami* are immanent, present, resident.

Though they are associated with a mythical past – the creation of "the eight great islands" of Japan – that past is perennially re-created, with Amaterasu's daily greeting of the sun. As an animistic religion, Shintō recognizes a divine quality in the most ordinary things; this is a religious conception that rejects the Western "spirit–body" dichotomy and asserts the presence of a sacred quality in natural objects – a "material spirituality" or "spiritualized materiality." Japan is a divine land not in the sense that God acts in history, but rather in the sense that its rivers, mountains, springs, and harvests are imbued with a numinous quality: they are *kami*, "sacred."

In today's world of commercialism and artificiality, Shintō has lost many of its adherents and much of its naturalistic appeal. Still, it is felt with a Japanese sense of uniqueness, safety and security of the home, and affirmation of natural instincts and impulses. Japanese idealize nature,[6] including human nature: unlike Buddhism, Shintō celebrates sexuality, the body, fecundity, and natural processes. In fact Shintō festivals contain an element of bacchanalian celebration with drinking, dancing and singing, the parading of immense phalluses, and an unusual license given to young men and women. Within Japanese culture as a whole, naturalism and spontaneity are valued as a counterbalancing force to communal social ethics, in the same way that Chinese balance Confucian ethical norms with Taoist-inspired individualism.

Though modern Shintō is a product of the late imperial period, it claims to have its roots in the fog of prehistory. Imagine a religion that sees gods or godlike qualities in water, tea, food, mountains, and streams. Imagine a religion that celebrates nature and human nature, including springtime, seeding and sprouting, birth, childhood and adolescence, sexuality and physical pleasures, drinking and carousing, and communal effervescence. Imagine a religion that celebrates the sacred quality of home, from the local landscape to the people that inhabit it, and feels the presence of the gods within the domestic sphere as well as in the temple or at the shrine. Such a religion is Shintō.

Notes

1   "Chinese characters" (*kanji*) can have two pronunciations in Japanese. The "on" (音) pronunciation approximates the original Chinese pronunciation of the kanji, and the "kun" (訓) pronunciation is the native Japanese pronunciation. *Shintō* and *kami-no-michi*, therefore, are the on and kun pronunciations of the same *kanji*.
2   The document can be found here: http://www.trinity.edu/rnadeau/Asian%20 Religions/Lecture%20Notes/Shinto%20and%20Zen/Shinto%20state.htm (accessed July 23, 2013).
3   "Mystic Rice Ritual by Emperor Fuels Japanese Outrage" (*Reuters*, November 23, 1990).

4 Shizuo Tsuji, *Japanese Cooking: A Simple Art* (New York: Kodansha USA, 25th anniversary edition 2007), p. 299; my italics.
5 See http://web-japan.org/trends00/honbun/tj990708.html, accessed 22 May 2012.
6 Japanese naturalism is highly idealized, masking a less than stellar record of environmentalist protection in the modern era. The Fukushima Nuclear disaster of March 2011 has inspired an anti-nuclear campaign allied with traditional environmentalist concerns.

28

Shrine Shintō
Dimensions of Sacred Time and Space in Japan

Religion – in whatever form and wherever found – divides experience into two kinds of reality: the sacred and the profane. Certain times – whether conceived of linearly, as the course of history, or cyclically, as day and night, as seasons, or as the calendar year – are demarcated as sacred times: times for worship or the remembrance of sacred events. These times are qualitatively different from the ordinary course of time: they are set aside and made "special." Similarly, certain places are demarcated as sacred places: they are places where the human and the divine meet, and one can pass from one to the other. Sacred places may be natural (a sacred mountain like Mt. Ararat or Mt. Fuji) or artificial (human constructions such as churches or temples). Mircea Eliade, in his book *The Sacred and the Profane: The Nature of Religion*, describes such times and places as "hierophanies of the sacred," where the sacred manifests itself in the material world.[1]

Shintō is an especially good example of the distinction between sacred time/space and profane time/space, though it differs significantly from the way this distinction is understood in the Abrahamic traditions (Judaism, Christianity, and Islam). In those religions the notion of a sacred time is grounded in history, in the unfolding of exceptional, unique, even extraordinary events: the founding of a nation, the appearance of God in dreams and visions or in human form, the revelations at Mt. Sinai, the crucifixion and resurrection of Christ, and so on. These sacred events are then commemorated daily, weekly, or annually, in the religious rites and holidays of the day, week, or year. Since the focus is on the founding event – the event that is remembered – the Abrahamic traditions emphasize a linear dimension of history over a recurring or cyclical one.

The acts of the *kami*, by contrast, are repeated and perennial, and the *kamis'* presence in the here and now is emphasized over their acts in prior times. The creation of the Japanese islands by the *ōmi-kami* Izanagi and Izanami is not said to have happened at any particular time, but rather in a prehistorical

Asian Religions: A Cultural Perspective, First Edition. Randall L. Nadeau.
© 2014 John Wiley & Sons, Ltd. Published 2014 by John Wiley & Sons, Ltd.

period, "before time." The great goddess Amaterasu acts on a daily basis, greeting the morning sun and guiding it across the sky with her magic mirror. In Japanese religion, morning is the sacred time of the day, and worshippers in the Gedatsu-kai (解脱會) sect, for example, recite prayers to Amaterasu and conduct daily meditations at dawn.[2]

The ritual calendar of a *Shintō* shrine is primarily seasonal, again emphasizing the cyclical and perennial qualities of time. For example, look at the detailed ritual calendar of one Shintō shrine – the Suwa Shrine (諏訪神社) in Nagasaki:

1/1	New Year celebrations
1/5	Chinka-sai (designed to control fires and to protect the local fire department)
1/15	Saiten-sai (coming-of-age rites at 20)
1/19	Kanae-sai (recitation of poems to the *kami*)
2/3	Setsubun (beans are thrown to drive away demons)
2/11	Kenkoku kinen-sai (commemoration of the mythical founding of the nation)
2/17	Kinen-sai (prayers for a bountiful harvest)
. . .	
10/7	Okunchi matsuri (Suwa Shrine festival)
11/15	Shichi-go-san (girls aged 3 and 7 and boys aged 5 dress in new clothes and pray for a safe and healthy future).[3]
. . .	

What is emphasized here is not the commemoration of the past, but rather the immediate presence of the *kami* in acts of sacred renewal through the course of the annual cycle.

Sacred Space

The notion of sacred space is especially emphasized in Shintō. The separation between the sacred and the profane is experienced as the separation between religious purity and religious pollution, which have opposing natures and characteristics:

Sacred	Profane
Clean	Unclean
Pure	Polluted
Secure	Threatening
Bright	Dark
Good	Evil

With such a powerful existential distinction, any transition between sacred space and profane space – and especially the movement or passage from the profane to the sacred – is potentially threatening. Two characteristics are always found where the sacred–profane distinction is felt: first, *boundaries* are emphasized, and physical or symbolic boundary markers demarcate the sacred space, ritually guarding its entrance; second, the movement from profane to sacred requires ritual acts of *purification*, to prevent ritual pollution from being carried into the sacred realm. Both boundary markers and purification rituals are readily found in Shrine Shintō.

In Shintō, the division between sacred space and profane space is relative, not absolute. Depending on one's frame of reference, the same place can be either sacred or profane: vis-à-vis the world as a whole, for example, all of Japan is sacred space – in contrast with foreign lands, which are dark and threatening. But, from another point of view, one's own community or village is sacralized by the presence of the *kami* of the local shrine, while places outside that community are profane, though they are still in Japan. The religious cosmos of Shintō, then, can be represented as a series of concentric circles, like in Figure 28.1.

For each dimension of the sacred–profane dichotomy, what is within any given circle is sacred and what is outside is profane. And, for each dimension, we can discover boundary markers that separate sacred space from profane space and rituals of purification for the passage from one into the other.

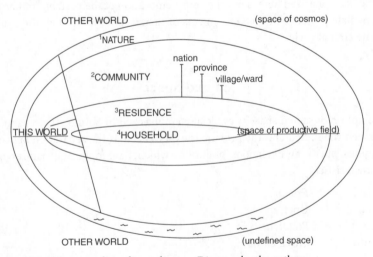

Figure 28.1   The centrality of sacred space. Diagram by the author.

The nation/natural world: kokoku *(故国, native land) – boundary: the sea*

The largest circle is the whole of Japan: this is regarded as sacred, the outside world as profane. As we saw in Chapter 27, in the eighteenth century and up until the twentieth, the emperor was the primary symbol of the nation in State Shintō, and his divine status represented the divinity of the nation as a whole. *Kami* associated with nature – with the natural landscape of Japan – are found in Japan and only in Japan, sacralizing the nation and its people. There are *kami* of winds, *kami* of storms, *kami* of constellations arching above the known (Japanese) world, *kami* of trees and forests, *kami* of streams and springs, *kami* of rice and rice paddies, *kami* of stones and mountains. These natural objects are felt to be especially sacred when they have some distinguishing or unusual characteristics; but in a broader sense all of the natural environment of Japan is imbued with sacred power.

Modern Shintō, arising in a period of Japanese isolationism (the Tokugawa shogunate, 1600–1868), emphasizes the sacred quality of Japan and the profane nature of the outside world, which is inherently dark, threatening, and impure. In its recent history, then, Japanese culture has shown characteristics of xenophobia – a fear of the foreign – and Shintō provided a religious justification for an isolationist tendency that survives to the present day. With the sea as a natural boundary between sacred and profane space, Japan was slow to develop maritime technologies, and this contributed to its humiliating defeats in the American and Russian naval battles of the late imperial period. In turn, these defeats led to the "catch-up" industrialization of the Meiji Period (1868–1912) and ultimately to the emergence of Japan as a formidable naval power in the early twentieth century.

A "fear of the foreign," partly inspired by the Shintō sacred–profane dichotomy, remains a Japanese predisposition in the modern era. A few years ago I was living in Japan during trade negotiations with the United States concerning the importation of Texas long-grain rice. When the tariffs were lifted and American rice came into the Japanese market in large volume, an unexpected development frustrated American exporters: shoppers refused to buy their rice. In my local grocery store, the 50-pound bags of Texas rice were piled from floor to ceiling, still sitting there long after the local rice had sold out. On television I was watching interviews with people in the street: one housewife remarked that American rice "tasted strange," and an elderly lady complained that it was dirty and polluted – at a time when local farmers regularly sprayed their paddies with noxious chemicals. This is not to say that Japanese "worship" their rice, but it is clear from this example that home-grown rice has special qualities, characteristic of sacred things: it is pure, clean, safe, right, and wholesome. Following the 2011 Great East Japan Earthquake and Tsunami (東日本大震災, *Higashi nihon daishin-sai*), the Japanese government was slow to accept foreign advisors and aid. Japan's self-reliance and reluctance to rely upon foreign assistance remain strong cultural values, bolstered by Shintō's emphasis on the purity of Japan and the pollution of the outside world.

The community/Shintō shrine: jingu 神宮 *(marked by the* torii 鳥居, *gate) – ritual demarcation: the* matsuri *(まつり) festival*

A second dimension of the spatial sacred–profane distinction is represented by the village or neighborhood community, as symbolized by the Shintō shrine. After the disestablishment of State Shintō in 1945, this was the most evident form of Shintō practice; and it remains so today. The Shintō shrine is a place where families come to pray when they have special needs and where community gatherings take place according to the festival calendar. The largest scale festival is the annual or semi-annual *matsuri* (まつり), a multi-day event featuring public performances of song and dance, displays of local handicrafts, and religious processions involving the whole community. Symbolizing the protection of the community by the local *kami* is a procession where dozens, even scores of residents carry a large palanquin or shrine chair representing the territorial inspection of the local god. The circular route of the procession defines the village or neighborhood as a sacred space.

Physically, the placement of Shintō shrines within the community also serves to demarcate the boundary between sacred space and profane space. Unlike the model of the European church or Chinese Taoist temple, which are situated at the town center, Shintō shrines are often on the outskirts of the community and, ideally, in places where natural forms meet – especially where a river basin meets a mountain. As one enters the shrine, one leaves the plain and ascends the mountain, and the various pathways and structures of the shrine complex carry one both upward and inward (into the sacred space). The innermost temple of the shrine is ritually inaccessible to all but the Shintō priest, who alone is permitted to enter it.

The shrine, as well as the various structures within it, is easily recognized by the *torii* (鳥居) – the gate at its entrance. The English word "gate" is deceptive, because there is no physical wall or fence to which the *torii* gives entrance, nor is there a hinge or clasp of the kind we normally associate with gates or doors. Nevertheless, the *torii* represents a symbolic gate, inviting passage from the profane space of the outside world into the sacred space of the shrine. The *torii* is the most ubiquitous and representative of all the sacred objects associated with Shrine Shintō. Passage through the gate, and the corresponding movement from sacred to profane, also require a ritual of purification, so that spiritual pollution may not be carried from the profane outside world into the *kami*-

Figure 28.2 Mizuya at the entrance to a Shintō shrine. Photo by the author.

blessed shrine space. Adjoining the *torii* is a basin of water, ideally fed by a bubbling spring that is set with ladles made of bamboo. Before entering the shrine, one rinses one's hands and sips the water, being careful not to allow any that has touched one's hands or mouth to re-enter the basin. This water is called *kuchi-susuru mizu* (口啜る水 [くちすするみず]), "water that purifies the mouth." Most prominent at Shintō shrines, a water basin (水屋 [みずや], *mizuya*, see Figure 28.2) of this kind can also be found at the entrance to homes and restaurants – a symbol of cleanliness, purity, and refreshment.

Some communities feature more than one shrine. For example, the mountain town of Toyakushi, in the "Japan Alps" of central Honshu, is marked by three Shintō shrines, which symbolically encircle the town and demarcate the whole of the village as a sacred space. The upper and middle shrines are located in elevated places, or at the boundary between the river basin and the surrounding hills, rising above the town below.

The enclosure/homestead – demarcation: the fence and torii

The third dimension of Shintō's spatially constructed sacred–profane distinction is the traditional farmstead, reflecting a dimension of Japanese culture – its pastoral or agricultural roots – that is now much more observable symbolically than it is in the actual lives of most Japanese. In some ways, Shintō represents the nostalgic reminder of an agrarian past, as well as the government's ongoing efforts – through subsidies and land use policies – to preserve domestic food production in a country that has for many years depended almost entirely upon manufacturing and financial services for its economic well-being.

The farmstead is marked as sacred space by the presence of walls and fences; it is an enclosure. Traditionally, farms consist of various buildings (barn, granary, stable, well, outhouse, and so on) along with the main house, and each of these buildings hosts a protective deity. The whole of the farm, therefore, is sacred space, in contrast to the profane space outside the fence. The entrance – which can be barred or bolted – is adjoined by a *torii*.

Though farmsteads of this kind are now rarely found in urbanized Japan, there are two symbolic remnants of Japan's agrarian past. First, Shintō shrines are modeled upon traditional farms, and the primary symbolism of the shrine is distinctively agricultural. For example, every shrine complex includes a "granary" as well as a storage building for rice wine (さけ, *sake*), and Shintō shrines are ritually connected to growth, harvesting, and plenty. Second, many Japanese homes, even in the most cramped urban neighborhoods, feature ornamental walls or fences, less for purposes of protection or security (crime rates have always been very low in Japan) and more for their aesthetic and religiously symbolic meaning. These enclosures are both an aesthetically pleasing architectural feature of Japanese domestic construction and a reminder of the sacred–profane dichotomy that differentiates between interior and exterior space in Japanese culture.

The home: ie *(家) – demarcation: the* genkan *(玄関)*

The fourth dimension of spatial concentricity in Japanese culture is represented by the home itself, ritually separated from the outside world by an entryway – *genkan* (玄関) – immediately inside the outer door and immediately outside the inner door. The *genkan* is a transitional space between the home's exterior and its interior, and it is physically distinct from the house itself; for one thing, the *genkan* floor is composed of dirt or concrete, as opposed to the wood or *tatami* (rice-straw) flooring of the home. The "ritual act" that one performs upon entering the *genkan* is to remove one's shoes – it is highly inappropriate to wear shoes in a Japanese home. Certainly shoes are dirty in a physical sense – one wouldn't want to carry the dirt into one's home any more than to put one's shoes on the bed or pillow – but they are also dirty in a symbolic sense, as they have been in direct and continuous contact with the profane space of the outside world. Though few Japanese would regard removing their shoes as a religious act, it is undeniable that this daily, even unconscious habit has Shintō roots.

There are *kami* associated with the home: *kami* of the bedroom, of the bath, of the kitchen stove, and so on. But the most important household *kami* are the *mitama* (み霊), the souls of the family dead; these are revered in a *kamidana* (神棚) or household shrine, where daily offerings are made. These *kami* mark the home as a sacred space, in contrast to the profane space of the outside world.

One cultural consequence of conceiving of the home as a "sacred space" is that Japanese do not customarily invite outsiders into the home. It is unusual, except in Westernized households, to "have people over" – that is, to invite guests into one's home; if one wishes to treat one's guests, one does so in an inn or restaurant. Japanese will often say that their homes are too small for entertaining, and in a highly urbanized island country this may indeed be true, but the reluctance to invite outsiders into the home is also a reflection of Japan's Shintō roots and of the traditional sacred–profane distinction.

The self (heart and belly): kokoro *(心) and* hara *(腹) – ritual purification: the* mizuya *(水屋) and the* omamori *(おまもり)*

The most personal dimension of the sacred–profane dichotomy is the inner–outer distinction as it applies to the human body. What is inside the body – especially the heart (the seat of thinking, what we would normally think of as "the mind") and the stomach – is sacred, and what is outside is profane. And so, Japanese are careful about what they express from the heart (they are culturally predisposed to speak briefly and to employ implicit or non-verbal forms of expression), and they are careful about what they bring into the body: food and drink should be clean, pure, and aesthetically pleasing. In fact the art of Japanese cooking is as much related to appearance as it is to taste, and it incorporates color and texture as key elements of food preparation and presentation. Sushi and raw vegetables and fruits, for example, must be pure and fresh, in order to be both tasty and healthy.

In addition to the cleansing fountain (*mizuya*), Shintō shrines have small shops where visitors can purchase amulets and charms (お守り, *omamori*; see Figure 28.3). *Omamori* protect their bearers from the polluting elements of disease, accidents, and obstacles. There are *omamori* for success in business or exams, for travel, for health, for marriage and childbirth, and so on.

From the outermost dimension – the nation as a whole – to the innermost dimension – the human body – the sacred–profane distinction is the predominant religious expression of Shintō. The sense that interior space is naturally clean and pure and should be protected from polluting influences from outside is a Japanese cultural trait.

Figure 28.3   *Omamori.* © Yasuko Takemoto / iStockphoto.

Notes

1   Mircea Eliade, *The Sacred and the Profane: The Nature of Religion* (New York: Harper Torchbooks, 1961), p. 11.
2   H. Byron Earhart, *Gedatsu-Kai and Religion in Contemporary Japan* (Bloomington: Indiana University Press, 1989).
3   John Nelson, *A Year in the Life of a Shintō Shrine* (Seattle: University of Washington Press, 1996), pp. 226–230.

29

Dimensions of Religion in Modern Japan

The modern-day legacy of Japanese religion can be found diffused throughout daily life, from moral values to aesthetic tastes and unreflective preferences and habits. Perhaps this is why, for many Westerners, Japan has been romanticized as a deeply spiritual culture. Japanese religion is expressed in diffused form from food and drink to sport and art. In this chapter we will look at two examples of Japanese artistic expression with Zen and Shintō roots: the tea ceremony (茶の湯, *chanoyu*) and *haiku* (俳句) poetry. And we will examine the new religions of the post-war period and perceptions of religion in contemporary Japan.

Religious Dimension of Japanese Aesthetics: Chanoyu and Haiku

Chanoyu was originally an "art of tea" that was associated with Zen concentration and with the Shintō sense of sacred space. It was practiced primarily in the samurai class, as an expression of *bushido* (武士道), the way of the warrior. Today it is a formal, aesthetic practice that is carried out in Zen gardens or in small, sparsely appointed rooms specifically set aside for this purpose.

The implements of the tea ceremony reflect Zen material culture, and yet, paradoxically, they are highly prized and can be appraised at astronomical values. Their form and appearance is often extraordinarily simple, even crude, and yet they are aesthetically pleasing – a ritualized expression of appreciation for the tea jars and bowls is in fact built into the ceremony itself. The tea bowls are made by pressing and molding, not on a potter's wheel, and they are fired with subtle glazes. They are given individual names and are registered with families or with schools of tea practice. Japanese green tea, which must be

Asian Religions: A Cultural Perspective, First Edition. Randall L. Nadeau.
© 2014 John Wiley & Sons, Ltd. Published 2014 by John Wiley & Sons, Ltd.

Figure 29.1   Japanese tea whisk. © Radu Razvan / Shutterstock.

beaten with a whisk to infuse the water, is prized not merely for its flavor, but also for its careful preparation and its vivid color.

A model of Zen simplicity, the whisk itself (Figure 29.1) is made from a single three- to five-inch length of bamboo, cut on two sides of equal length from the joint. Dozens of straight cuts are made from one end to the joint, giving the whisk its whiskers, secured with thread woven into the delicate filaments. *Chanoyu* whisk makers have practiced their traditional, non-mechanized trade for as many as 20 generations.

The setting for the tea ceremony is a simple room of six to eight *tatami* mats, ideally within a natural setting. The great tea master Takuan (澤庵, 1573–1645) described the ideal tea room in this way:

> Let us then construct a small room in a bamboo grove or under trees, arrange streams and rocks and plant trees and bushes, while [inside the room] let us pile up charcoal, set a kettle, arrange flowers, and arrange in order the necessary tea utensils. And let all this be carried out in accordance with the idea that in this room we can enjoy the streams and rocks as we do the rivers and mountains in Nature, and appreciate the various moods and sentiments suggested by the snow, the moon, and the trees and flowers, as they go through the transformation of seasons, appearing and disappearing, blooming and withering. As visitors are greeted here with due reverence, we listen quietly to the boiling water in the kettle, which sounds like a breeze passing through the pine needles, and become oblivious of all worldly woes and worries; we then pour out a dipperful of water

Figure 29.2   *Tokonoma* with hanging scroll and *ikebana*. Tenryū-ji (天龍寺), Kyoto.
© B.S.P.I. / Corbis.

from the kettle, reminding us of the mountain stream, and thereby our mental
dust is wiped off. This is truly a world of recluses, saints on earth.[1]

When guests enter the tea room, they are often required to stoop and to
slide forward in a sitting position, as the entry door is only three to four
feet high. Having entered the room, their eyes are drawn immediately to an
alcove or *tokonoma* (床の間) facing them (see Figure 29.2); it displays a
hanging scroll depicting a Zen sentiment (an empty circle; a single character
meaning "quietude," "tranquility," "well," or the like; a simple portrait of the
patriarch Bodhidharma or a Zen monk), as well as a bowl containing an
arrangement of flowers that represents the Japanese art of flower arranging
(生け花, *ikebana*) – another of the Zen-inspired aesthetic practices now taught
in schools, in community centers, and in Buddhist monasteries.

The tea ceremony itself is slow and deliberate; it requires steady concentration on the part of both the host and his or her guests. The tea master Rikyū
(利休, 1522–1591), said to have been one of the "founders" of *chanoyu*, emphasized this deliberative effort in his "seven rules":

1   Make a delicious bowl of tea.
2   Lay the charcoal so that it heats the water.
3   Arrange the flowers as they are in the field.
4   In summer suggest coolness; in winter, warmth.

5   Do everything ahead of time.
6   Prepare for rain.
7   Give those with whom you find yourself every consideration.

Looking at these rules cynically, we might think, "What could be more obvious than 'placing the coals so that they heat the water?'" or, even more simply, "'preparing a delicious bowl of tea?'" – but, to do so, one must be careful and attentive; and "mastery of the obvious" is a Zen spiritual practice that the greatest masters have taught as the highest form of Zen. How often do we carry out seemingly simple tasks in unconscious, inattentive, unaware, careless, wasteful ways? In fact it requires the greatest concentration to do simple things right. This is the abiding principle of *chanoyu*, *ikebana*, and other Zen-inspired practices. No wonder popular instruction manuals on hobbies ranging from food preparation to golf swings draw from the well of Zen! As the Tokugawa Prince Hideyoshi (秀吉, 1536–1598) wrote in a poem dedicated to the tea ceremony:

> When tea is made with water drawn from the depths of Mind
> Whose bottom is beyond measure
> We truly have what is called *chanoyu*.[2]

Haiku is short-form poetry that expresses both Shintō naturalness and Zen sensibility. Traditionally it is nature poetry describing natural scenes that are temporary, short-lived, transient. It expresses the aesthetic principle of the "floating world" (浮世, *ukiyo*), the sense that beauty and happiness are "here and gone" in the blink of an eye. If you do not focus upon them, if you do not concentrate, they are gone before you know it. R. H. Blythe described *haiku* as the poetic evocation of the experience of *satori*[3] – an experience of awakening that comes swiftly, unexpectedly, and intuitively and is both momentary and transient.

Here is a list of thematic elements of Haiku:

- meditative function: the reader is invited to practice contemplation of every line;
- ephemeral naturalism: beauty is fleeting and temporary;
- anti-subjectivism (and yet evocative of mood);
- anti-romanticism (and yet suggestive of feeling);
- unity with concrete things.

Most, though not all, *haiku* are 17 syllables in length, with a "pause" at the end of the first line of five syllables or the second line of seven. The pause is sometimes marked by the "cutting" syllable (切れ字, *kireji*), *ya* (や):

古池や 蛙飛込む 水の音
furuike ya   old pond
kawazu tobikomu   frog flying –
mizu no oto   the sound of the water

Basho (芭蕉, 1644–1694)

しづかさや 湖水の底の雲のみね
shizukasa ya   so still –
kosui no soko no / kumo no mine summit of clouds of the deep of the lake

Kobayashi Issa (小林 一茶, 1762–1867)

Here are some characteristics of *haiku*, with representative examples:

1 *Haiku* describe ephemeral (short-lived) phenomena in nature:

釣鐘に とまりて眠る 胡てふ哉
tsuri-gane ni   on the one-ton temple bell
tomarite nemuru   a moon-moth
kochô kana   folded in sleep

Yosa Buson (與謝蕪村, 1716–1783)

2 *Haiku* display the strength of nature over man-made things, which are also
   short-lived:

焼けし野の 所々や すみれ草
yakeshi no no   violets have grown
tokorodokoro ya   among the ruins
sumiregusa   of my burned house

Nagamatsu Shūkyū-ni (永松諸九尼, 1714–1781)

3 *Haiku* emphasize direct experience over rational thought or intellectual
   ideas:

御佛に 尻むけ居れば 月涼し
mihotoke ni   I turn my back
shirimuke oreba   on Buddha
tsuki suzushi   and face the cool moon

Masaoka Shiki (正岡 子規, 1867–1902)

ちる花に 仏とも法とも しらぬ哉

chiru hana ni	in scattering blossoms
butsu tomo nori tomo	Buddha and Buddhism
shiranu kana	unknown

Issa (一茶)

4   *Haiku* evoke surprise, usually with an unexpected twist or revelation in the
    third line:

朝顔に 釣瓶取られて 貰い水

asagao ni	since morning glories
tsurube torarete	hold my well-bucket hostage
morai mizu	I beg for water

Fukuda Chiyo-ni (福田 千代尼, 1701–1775)

5   *Haiku* suggest a mood of melancholy, loneliness, or nostalgia:

さびしさの うれしくもあり 秋の暮れ

sabishisa no	an autumn eve
ureshiku mo ari	there is joy too
aki no kure	in loneliness

Buson (蕪村)

「今帰る」 妻から返信 「まだいいよ」

Imakaeru	"Going home now"
Tsumakaruenshin	(text) reply from the wife
"Mada – iiyo"	"No need to come home yet"

A contemporary haiku: 2nd place prize winner in
Daichi Life Insurance Company Haiku Writing
Competition 2010

Religion in Japanese Culture

In this book we have surveyed two dimensions of religious expression in Japan,
as represented by Zen Buddhism and Shintō. Though Zen was introduced to
Japan from China and Korea while Shintō is the indigenous or autochthonous
religion of Japan, the two traditions have been synthesized in various forms of
hybridity. One of the most evident forms of Zen–Shintō syncretism is the dual
naming of Shintō gods and Buddhist *mahāsattvas* (buddhas and *bodhisattvas*),

known in Japanese as *shinbutsu-shūgō* (神佛習合, the syncretism of *kami* and buddhas). Most Shintō shrines have images of buddhas and *bodhisattvas* (described as both *butsu* and *kami*), and many Buddhist temples host small shrines to local gods and goddesses.

Similarly, most Japanese are religiously inclusivistic. They marry in a Shintō shrine, bury their loved ones at a Buddhist temple, and make daily offerings at both the *kami* shrine (*kamidana*, 神棚) and Buddha shrine (*butsudan*, 佛壇) in the home. In social surveys Japanese often respond to questions of religious identity by checking every available box: Shintō, Buddhist, and even "non-religious" (無宗教, *mu-shūkyō*). Most Japanese participate in local religious festivals, make regular offerings to shrine *kami*, and register their households at prestigious Buddhist temples; and yet they see these as "non-religious" activities.

Why? In their understanding of what it is to be "religious," *exclusivity* is a defining characteristic and is associated with the voluntary and deliberative religious choice of a Christian proselytizer or an ordained Buddhist monk or nun. In his book *Why are the Japanese Non-Religious* (日本人はなぜ無宗教なのか, *Nihonjin wa naze mushūkyō nano ka*), Ama Toshimaro (阿満利麿) notes that, for most Japanese, it is only very "troubled" or "strange" people who identify themselves as "religious." And so they wish to avoid the designation in order to "fit into" the broader society and to manifest a cheerful, uncomplicated, approachable persona.[4]

In the post-war period religion took a unique turn in Japan with the establishment of a number of new religions (*shin shūkyō*, 新宗教) that have drawn thousands of followers. Among the most popular are Sōka Gakkai (創價學會), Gedatsu Kai (解脱會), Risshō Kōsei Kai (立正佼成會), and Kurozumi-kyō (黒住教).[5] The most notorious of the new religions was Aum Shinrikyō (オウム真理教), a "doomsday cult" that came to an apocalyptic end with a series of murders and with the 1995 sarin gas attacks on the Tokyo subway. It was only in June 2012 that the last of the conspirators – a key figure in the subway poisonings – was apprehended in a manga café in central Tokyo, after 17 years of being on the run. Though Aum is a unique case, many of the new religions suffered negative publicity in the wake of the tragedy.[6]

Some Japanese social critics have argued that the "decline" of traditional family structures, ethical values, and religious practices has created a sense of meaninglessness and purposelessness in contemporary society. Possibly the new religions offer benefits that are no longer found in traditional religious practices and institutions:

- a sense of belonging and of higher purpose among like-minded believers;
- a solution to modern problems of social alienation, loneliness, urbanization, and breakdown of the family;

- a belief in the basic goodness and purity of one's heart;
- total dependence upon benevolent buddhas and *kami*;
- a spirit of resilience and perseverance;
- a spirit of compassion, cheerfulness, charity, and giving, through volunteer efforts in disaster areas and on behalf of the elderly and indigent.

At the height of popularity of new religions in Japan, membership extended to as much as one third of the population,[7] but in contemporary Japan "non-religious" identity is the chosen designation of three quarters of Japanese.[8]

Behaviors that are not readily identifiable as "religious" – choosing Japanese over imported rice, attending a sumo (wrestling) tournament, removing one's shoes before entering a home, composing poetry or drinking tea – have religious roots in Shintō or Zen. We know from historical and sociological analysis that these everyday acts are stems and branches of Shintō and Buddhist tradition. That is to say, "religion" is not limited to particular beliefs or institutional forms, but includes cultural forms and practices that, for most Japanese, are not related to *shūkyō* (religion) at all. We can conclude from this that religion in its explicit manifestations involves a self-conscious commitment to a distinctly religious institution or prescribed set of practices, but its implicit aspects embrace a wide range of everyday beliefs and norms. Just as Confucianism is the "cultural DNA" of East Asia as a whole, at a pre-reflective level Shintō and Buddhism are formative of Japanese values and self-understanding.

Notes

1 Quoted in D.T. Suzuki, *Zen and Japanese Culture* (Princeton, NJ: Princeton University Press, 1959), pp. 275–276.

2 D. T. Suzuki, *Zen and Japanese Culture* (Princeton, NJ: Princeton University Press, 1959), p. 280.

3 R. H. Blythe, *A History of Haiku in two volumes*, vol. 1: *From the Beginnings up to Issa*; vol. 2: *From Issa up to the Present* (Tokyo: Hokuseido Press, 1963).

4 Ama Toshimaro, *Why are the Japanese Non-Religious? Japanese Spirituality: Being Non-Religious in a Religious Culture* (Lanham, MD: University Press of America, 2004).

5 For detailed treatments of these movements, see Daniel Métraux, *The History and Theology of Sōka Gakkai: A Japanese New Religion* (Lewiston, NY: Edwin Mellen Press, 1988); Byron Earhart, *Gedatsu-Kai and Religion in Contemporary Japan: Returning to the Center* (Bloomington: Indiana University Press, 1989); Stewart Guthrie, *A Japanese New Religion: Risshō Kōsei-kai in a Mountain Hamlet* (Ann Arbor, MI: Center for Japanese Studies, 1988); Helen Hardacre, *Kurozumikyo and the New Religions of Japan* (Princeton, NJ: Princeton University Press, 1988).

6 Ian Reader, *Religious Violence in Contemporary Japan: The Case of Aum Shinrikyo* (Honolulu: Curzon Press, 2000).

7 The 1991 *Shūkyō Nenkan* (= *Religion Yearbook*, 宗教年鑑, published in Tokyo), reported some 40 new religious movements that claimed over 46 million adherents out of a total population of 123 million at the time. It should be noted, however, that the membership rolls were self-reported by each group and were not based on general population surveys; they are likely to have been exaggerated. The Aum incident and the growth of "non-religious" identity have reduced these numbers considerably.

8 "According to a 2000 survey by the Yomiuri Shimbun, 76.6 percent of the Japanese polled said they do not believe in a specific religion" (Hiroshi Matsubara, "Western Eyes Blind to Spirituality in Japan," *The Japan Times Online*, January 1, 2002, at http://www.japantimes.co.jp/text/nn20020101b2.html#.UAmLzbVST0c, accessed 20 July 2012). For a critique of the designations "religious" and "non-religious" as applied to Japan, see Ian Reader, *Religion in Contemporary Japan* (London: Palgrave Macmillan, 1991), pp. 1–22.

Part VIII

Conclusions

30

"Religion" and the Religions

While we have tried to employ a religiously neutral definition of religion for this book, most people have an intuitive sense of what religion is – regardless of whether they "approve" or "disapprove" of it, and regardless of whether they think it has had a "positive" or a "negative" impact on the world. One thing that all people can agree upon, however, is that religion has multiple manifestations. That is, there are many religions and many forms of religious expression. Of course this has always been true, but it is only in the last generation that awareness of this fact has become nearly universal.[1] Due to advances in communication and transportation, people are aware that *their* religion is not the *only* religion in the world, but exists in relation to (and sometimes in conflict with) many others.

Each semester I survey my students about their attitudes to the multiplicity of religions and ethical systems in the world. Here is the survey. For each of the 20 statements below, simply "agree" or "disagree." The statements are divided into four groups, A, B, C, and D, each with five statements. Create a label of one or two words for each of the four groups.

A. _____

1. There can only be one true religion; all others worship false gods.
2. All religions essentially worship the same God, though they call it by different names.
3. All religions are true for those who follow them, but there is no absolute truth.
4. All religions have elements worth integrating into a personal worldview.

Asian Religions: A Cultural Perspective, First Edition. Randall L. Nadeau.
© 2014 John Wiley & Sons, Ltd. Published 2014 by John Wiley & Sons, Ltd.

5. All religions are true for those who follow them, and all should be tolerated and appreciated.

B. _____

1. (The practice of) homosexuality is a sin.
2. All persons are essentially bisexual, though they are socialized to be "straight" or "gay."
3. I am heterosexual (or homosexual) but believe people are what they are and it is wrong to judge them.
4. I am bisexual.
5. There are in fact many sexual orientations, not just two.

C. _____

1. There are objective standards of beauty or aesthetic value (in art, music, dance, writing, etc.)
2. Though cultures appear to have different standards of beauty, they all conform to one, higher standard.
3. "Beauty is in the eye of the beholder."
4. Everyone has a sense of beauty that is derived from exposure to a diverse set of experiences.
5. Though cultures have different aesthetic standards, all should be tolerated and appreciated.

D. _____

1. Goodness is absolute; some things are right, some things are wrong.
2. There is one standard of goodness for the world, but no one person, culture, or religion knows "perfectly" what it is.
3. Every person should determine what is "good" for him or herself.
4. There are many standards of "goodness," and we can learn from all of them.
5. Though "goodness" exists, it is wrong to judge others for not conforming to an abstract idea of the good.

The labeling of these statements is fairly straightforward. Perhaps you chose "A = Religion," "B = Sexual Orientation," "C = Aesthetic Appreciation," and "D = Morality," or a similar set of terms.

More interesting still is the second task I assign the students, and that is to label the statements across categories. What do all the 1s have in common, all the 2s, all the 3s and so on? I encourage the students to describe the statements, not to place value judgments on them (for example, students often describe a person who agrees with the 1s as "closed-minded," not realizing that a "closed-minded" attitude could accompany any of the statements, depending on how strongly – or how inflexibly – they were held). If we look at them in this way, we might label the cross-referenced sets of statements as follows:

1 Exclusivism
   A. There can only be one true religion; all others worship false gods.
   B. (The practice of) homosexuality is a sin.
   C. There are objective standards of beauty or aesthetic value (in art, music, dance, writing, etc.)
   D. Goodness is absolute; some things are right, some things are wrong.
2 Inclusivism (sometimes termed "universalism")
   A. All religions essentially worship the same God, though they call it by different names.
   B. All persons are essentially bisexual, though they are socialized to be "straight" or "gay."
   C. Though cultures appear to have different standards of beauty, they all conform to one higher standard.
   D. There is one standard of goodness for the world, but no one person, culture, or religion knows "perfectly" what it is.
3 Relativism
   A. All religions are true for those who follow them, but there is no absolute truth.
   B. I am heterosexual (or homosexual) but believe people are what they are and it is wrong to judge them.
   C. "Beauty is in the eye of the beholder."
   D. Every person should determine what is "good" for him- or herself.
4 Syncretism
   A. All religions have elements worth integrating into a personal worldview.
   B. I am bisexual.
   C. Everyone has a sense of beauty that is derived from exposure to a diverse set of experiences.
   D. There are many standards of "goodness," and we can learn from all of them.
5 Complementary pluralism
   A. All religions are true for those who follow them, and all should be tolerated and appreciated.
   B. There are in fact many sexual orientations, not just two.
   C. Though cultures have different aesthetic standards, all should be tolerated and appreciated.
   D. Though "goodness" exists, it is wrong to judge others for not conforming to an abstract idea of the good.

These labels are important, because they characterize how people view the pluralistic nature of the modern world – the fact that there are many cultures, religions, and value systems in the world (not to mention one's own society) – and how receptive or adaptable they are to the existence of many religions.

Having examined examples of each orientation, let us create definitions as they apply specifically to religion:

- *Exclusivism*   The religious exclusivist insists that one's own tradition is the "right" or "orthodox" way, while other religions are "heterodox" or "superstitious." Exclusivism states that there is only one true religion, often only one true God, while other religions worship "false gods."
- *Inclusivism*   The religious inclusivist (or "universalist") believes that there is only one truth (often expressed as monotheism, the belief in one God), but that the truth/God is "known by many names." The inclusivist sees no significant difference between one religion and another.
- *Relativism*   A relativist recognizes that there are many standards of truth, beauty, and goodness, but sees no way of resolving the differences. All religions are "true" in their own way to their own adherents, and there is little need for interaction between them.
- *Syncretism*   The religious syncretist takes what is "best" from various traditions to form a creative unity out of the diversity. Syncretistic religions tend to be highly individualistic or to attract a small following (such groups are often identified as "cults" or "sects" by more mainstream believers).
- *Complementary pluralism*   The religious pluralist recognizes real differences between religions, but sees those differences as complementary. The world is a "mosaic" of religious and cultural traditions existing, ideally, in a harmonious relationship.

As a student of religion, I consider myself a "pluralist" in the ideological sense of the term – that is, I believe that the religions of the world can, and should, exist in a complementary relationship vis-à-vis one another. But I take the other orientations seriously, and to slight them is unwise and short-sighted. For my students' generation and their children's generation, what is more pressing than conflicts between Catholics and Protestants, or between Hindus and Muslims, or between Confucians and Taoists, are conflicts between pluralists and exclusivists, or between inclusivists (who are often deeply religious) and relativists (who are often "irreligious") – these are the conflicts that will shape cultural interaction in the coming decades, and they may well determine the healthy evolution of societies and the very survival of the human race. Non-exclusivistic Jews and Muslims can get along well (and already do); what needs to be addressed is how to resolve differences between exclusivists and non-exclusivists across all religious traditions, not by wishing that one or the other would "go away," but by engaging in meaningful, constructive dialogue based on empathy and understanding of one another's deepest commitments, hopes, and fears.

Final Thoughts

The survey on religious pluralism consists of statements and assertions, opinions and beliefs: it is interesting to reflect upon religious differences in the expression of belief both within and among religious traditions. But religion, as we have repeated time and again, is not limited to beliefs and assertions; nor is it limited to explicitly religious norms and behaviors. If it were, then we would be content with a bullet-point list of gods, beliefs, and rites across cultures. Certainly the comparative study of beliefs and rites is important, and scholars are still engaged in this kind of research, both historically and ethnographically. But this approach cannot give us an understanding of the cultural dimensions of religion. Rather, our focus has been on cultural traditions, values, subconscious desires and motivations, views of personal identity (often formed in contrast to those of "foreigners" or cultural "outsiders"), interpersonal relationships, artistic expression, personal hopes and expectations, and the sense of meaning and purpose in life. Whether or not these elements are explicitly religious today – and many times they are not – they all have roots in religion and are tied to religious traditions both socially and historically. We have encountered in this book a number of examples of such culturally imbedded conceptions and behaviors, all having their origins in traditional religious teachings and practices:

- an Indian professor who remarked: "I am not any better than you; I simply started sooner";
- Chinese immigrant students who are expected to score "perfect 800s" on the SAT (Scholastic Aptitude Test) and to attain admission to top universities;
- a Japanese public bath that turned away a healthy foreign guest by raising fears of AIDS;
- American yoga classes that teach the "centering" of the body and mind;
- charitable work after the Great East Japan Earthquake and tsunami of May 2011;
- non-competitive Chinese "sports," from shadow boxing to deep breathing exercises;
- Chinese dumplings prepared for the New Year;
- Mahatma Gandhi's non-violent resistance to British rule – a resistance based on his devotional reading of an ancient war epic;
- nationalist movements in India, China, and Japan;
- a public apology made by a Taiwanese pop star for kicking a taxi driver – an apology directed not to the driver, but to the pop star's mother;
- a middle-aged Japanese man who continues to address his third-grade teacher as *sensei*, "revered teacher or master";
- Chinese landscape painting;

- views of animals and meat-consumption in Tibet and Japan;
- Aung San Suu Kyi's calls for democracy in Burma;
- the architecture of I. M. Pei;
- *sumo* wrestling;
- ideals of sexual harmony based on diminishing "passion";
- the veneration of teachers;
- a traditional wedding after the sudden death of a young fiancée.

These are customs, practices, preferences, social and political movements, personal habits, hopes and dreams . . . many of which we might not think of as being "religious" at all, and yet all having roots in religious traditions that have existed in India, China, and Japan for two millennia or more. Many of them seem quite foreign to the outsider, and indeed, without reference to religion, they would remain inexplicable.

I often tease my students that they will receive an "incomplete" in my course on Asian religions until they travel to and (ideally) live in Asia for an extensive period of time. In the study of religion and culture, there is no substitute for personal encounter and personal experience. Moreover, for there to be any possibility of real dialogue, we must (especially in North America) develop our aptitude for learning foreign languages and for practicing intercultural communication as both "givers" and "receivers." This is impossible if we refuse to learn the languages in which the social, cultural, and religious histories of the world's great civilizations are expressed.

The decline of institutional religion is a phenomenon that is inevitable in an increasingly pluralistic world, in spite of virulent pockets of resistance to this trend. The beliefs and rites of traditional religion have been undermined or abandoned in every country. But this is hardly the "end of religion" or of the impact of religious conceptions and norms through generations of tradition and acculturation. While the explicit, visible forms of religion are practiced less and less, the implicit, subconscious or liminal aspects of religious thought and action remain formative and meaningful. They go to the heart of cultural identity, as close to one's conscious and unconscious mind as the very words we use for speaking and thinking. In this sense the forces of pluralism, syncretism, secularization, and modernity have not changed the fundamentally religious nature of humankind.

Survey 6   "Religion" and the Religions

The Pluralism Survey reproduced above can be found online. After completing it, you will be able to see how others have responded to statements that reflect exclusivistic, inclusivistic, relativistic, syncretistic, and pluralistic orientations. The survey weblink is http://goo.gl/ehqtnJ.

Note

1 For example, the existence of Asian religions as distinct traditions (as opposed to their being simply labeled as "heathen" or "pagan") was recognized in the West only in very recent times. In *The Meaning and End of Religion* (New York: Fortress Press, 1962, 2nd edition 1991), Wilfred Cantwell Smith found the earliest English usage of the traditions we have examined in this book: Boudhism: 1801; Hindooism: 1829; Taouism: 1839; Confucianism: 1862; Shintoism: 1894.

Appendix
Suggestions for Further Reading

Academic studies of Asian religious traditions are too numerous and special-ized to discuss in a book of this kind – though this book could not have been written without them. While the first generation of Western scholars focused on the religious thought of India, China, and Japan primarily by means of the study of scripture and other texts produced by educated elites, contemporary scholarship focuses more on action (ritual, institutional organization, and social behavior) and on religion from the ground up, that is, community- or locality-based religious practice. In this book I have tried to present both of these dimensions of Asian religions: the idealized textual tradition as well as the religious self-understanding of individuals in community, in a living cul-tural context.

Many Asian religions courses have their students read foundational texts in translation, most of which have now been re-translated over three or more schol-arly generations. Today's translations are eminently readable, in more modern idioms with full annotation. In particular I would recommend the following:

- For Chinese Religions: The *Daodejing* translated by Robert Henricks;[1] *The Book of Zhuangzi* translated by A.C. Graham;[2] *The Analects of Confucius* translated by Roger Ames and Henry Rosemont;[3]
- Hindu Scriptures translated by Dominic Graham;[4]
- Buddhist Scriptures translated by Donald Lopez;[5]
- Zen koans translated by Kazue Yamada;[6]
- Shintō scriptures translated by William Theodore de Bary, Donald Keene, George Tanabe, Paul Varley.[7]

Asian Religions: A Cultural Perspective, First Edition. Randall L. Nadeau.
© 2014 John Wiley & Sons, Ltd. Published 2014 by John Wiley & Sons, Ltd.

But there are good reasons not to begin with these texts, and in my introductory courses on Asian religions I use scriptures and foundational texts sparingly. Why?

First, religious texts in these traditions are not employed in the same way as religious texts are employed in the West. They are used primarily in ritual contexts: often they are invoked simply by title; or portions are chanted or recited, but in a classical or foreign parlance that is all but incomprehensible to the reciter; or they are not read at all but are treated as sacred objects (displayed, encased, aired or fanned, transmitted from teacher to student, stamped, inscribed, hidden, buried, burned as offerings). Only rarely, if ever, are they simply "read." I have never met anyone, religious or not, who has ever read a religious scripture from cover to cover in order to be informed of its content – with the rare exception of some scholar of religion trained in the West!

Second, religious texts are often incomprehensible to the Western reader. This is because they are not simply discursive but reflect the circumstances of their composition – they are often comprised of multiple accretions, which can be either repetitive or contradictory: prose and poetry, straight description, narrative, assorted lists, institutional records, incomplete or abbreviated shorthand, allusions to other texts and traditions, often difficult to recognize or identify – not to mention the inherent problems of translation involving texts written in languages that are no longer spoken or in languages in their classical form. No wonder that students generally find them boring. Modern, heavily annotated translations are strongly recommended if these texts are to be used in the classroom.[8]

As a result of all these factors, religious texts *as texts* – as words expressing meaning – cannot do the job that texts are "supposed" to do (to give information) and in fact can be deceptive and counterproductive as tools for instruction. Of course they are important as foundational materials, and they can give us insight into values and attitudes that are perennial and long-lived, but only with the benefit of interpretive work and contextualization. In this book I have quoted scriptural materials as *illustrative* of beliefs, values, and practices, not as their definitive expression.

A better substitute – if our goal is to understand religions as living traditions – is to read biographies, local histories, personal essays and autobiographies, and fiction. In my undergraduate courses I have found that novels and films are the most effective means for conveying the lived experience of religious life. They inspire the "sympathetic imagination" that is at the heart of cross-cultural understanding, and they are more readily comprehensible, more evocative, and more fun to read or watch. I employ a mix of "highbrow" and "low-brow" works, so this is not a critically sophisticated list; the following books and movies are especially useful for seeing religion as it is actually lived and practiced in Asian cultures.

Shusaku Endo, *Deep River*, and John Dalton, *Heaven Lake*

Most of my students are Bible-belt Americans who were raised in theologically and socially conservative Catholic or Protestant households. I recommend two novels about Christians in Asia. A classic is *Deep River*[9] by the Japanese Catholic writer Shusaku Endo (遠藤 周作, 1923–1996), a story about four Japanese travelers to India, all struggling in various ways with questions of faith and loss. Osamu seeks to pacify the spirit of his wife, who has recently died of cancer; Kiguchi wishes to arrange a penitentiary rite for comrades he lost in Burma during the war; Numada visits a bird sanctuary, believing that his pet bird died so that he could live; and Mitsuko searches for her lover Otsu, who has dedicated himself to the Catholic priesthood though he himself is overwhelmed by spiritual doubt. The novel also portrays Hindu practices sympathetically and the "magic" of India, as well as its poverty and hardships, from a Japanese perspective.

John Dalton's *Heaven Lake*[10] – a prize-winning first novel published in 2005 – takes his young American protagonist from a small town in Taiwan, where he has been posted as an evangelical missionary, to the western reaches of northwest China, on an odyssey that is both spiritual and physical – in fact, both for Taiwan and for the People's Republic, it serves as an entertaining Chinese travelogue. Torn between the demands of faith and the yearnings of adolescent love, Dalton's characters evoke traditional depictions of "Americans abroad" in a way that does justice to the complex meeting of the familiar and the foreign. Dalton's four years as an English teacher in Taiwan and his extensive travels through China give the descriptive passages detail and authenticity. Though the book does not deal with Chinese religions per se, its themes of spiritual doubt and intercultural conflict are provocative and expertly drawn. This is a very good novel.

Though Endo's novel begins with doubt and ends with faith and Dalton's protagonist moves in the opposite direction, both books are complex explorations of personal encounters between Christians (both Asian and Western) and non-Christian Asians.

Michio Takeyama, *Harp of Burma*, and R. K. Narayan, *The Guide*

Christian missionaries play a minor but significant role in *Harp of Burma* by Michio Takeyama (竹山 道雄, 1903–1984).[11] Set in Burma in the last days of the Pacific War, the novel describes the physical and spiritual odyssey of a Japanese soldier who disguises himself as a Buddhist monk in order to carry out a final mission to rescue a band of soldiers from a final, fruitless battle. It is when he sees a funeral rite carried out by Anglican missionaries that he commits himself fully to Buddhist renunciation, vowing to bury the Japanese dead scattered across the Burmese countryside before he returns home. Corporal Mizushima, faced with the Sisyphean task of pacifying the souls of thousands of abandoned corpses, exemplifies an ideal of self-sacrifice that his fellow soldiers can barely understand. The novel creates probing contrasts between the simplicity and pacifism of the Burmese on the one hand and the aggressive militarism of industrial modernization on the other. Takeyama demonstrates that patriotism is often most heroic when contrasted with colonialism and militarism. Regarding Mizushima's transformation from military scout to wandering monk, the novel depicts a profound story of religious conversion, in which the hero authentically becomes what he had first only pretended to be.

The theme of the "pretender" is explored by the Indian writer R. K. Narayan (1906 – 2001) as well, in his satirical novel of a reluctant holy man: *The Guide*.[12] *The Guide* takes an obvious con man, who provides advice and solace to a village beset by poverty and drought as an itinerant guru, and suggests that, in spite of his undeniably selfish nature, he "becomes what he pretended to be." Whether or not Raju undergoes a genuine transformation is left to the reader's interpretation (and relates well to Hindu ideas of ignorance and enlightenment) – but in the eyes of the villagers he is a savior. Far from making the villagers appear ignorant or gullible, Narayan gives them a profound dignity of their own, overcoming the manipulative cynicism of their charlatan priest. One of the virtues of the novel as a teaching aid is that it takes us through the four *ashramas* (Hindu stages of life) of the main character, from student to householder and ultimately to holy renunciant, in a way that is both humorous parody and creative reinterpretation.

Set side by side, *Harp of Burma* and *The Guide* are effective introductions to the theme of renunciation as well as to that of appearance versus reality in the Buddhist and Hindu traditions, through the eyes of complex, provocative characters in Corporal Mizushima and the "holy" Raju. In addition, both novels explore the meaning and value of religion at both a personal and a social level, respectfully yet unsentimentally. They are superb novels.

As for feature films related to modern India, two contemporary women directors are recommended for their lush and provocative films: Mira Nair (b. 1957) and Deepa Mehta (b. 1950), especially the latter's *Elements Trilogy*: *Fire, Earth,* and *Water.*

Wes Anderson's film *The Darjeeling Limited* is a thoughtful, funny tribute to the Western search for spiritual awakening set in India. Vikram Gandhi's documentary film *Kumaré*, about a young Indian American pretending to be a spiritual guide in the southwest United States, addresses the same themes with humor and pathos. Both films would make for an effective topic of comparative conversation with *The Guide.*

Hermann Hesse, *Siddhartha*

Siddhartha is one of the best known Western novels treating Asian religious themes, and it is a standard "source" for introductory courses in Buddhism.[13] Once a high school text for "world literature" classes, *Siddhartha* tells the story of the spiritual journey and awakening of a solitary seeker who experiences every dimension of life in its totality, rebelling against both parental and religious authority. Alternately immersing himself in wealth, sexuality, ascetic renunciation, and holistic oneness with nature and the cosmos, Siddhartha finds awakening in the fullness of personal experience. Critics argue that the protagonist is little more than a doppelgänger of the author, Hermann Hesse (1877–1962), relating a romanticist fantasy of self-exploration in an oriental world. Despite misgivings, however, I use it in my Asian religions classroom. Aided by a symposium printed in *Education about Asia* in 1997,[14] I challenge students to critique the novel in relation to what they have learned about the Hindu and Buddhist traditions. For example:

- Why does Hesse have two separate characters, Siddhartha and Gotama the Buddha? What prompts Siddhartha to leave the Buddha?
- What is the significance of Siddhartha's being a "Brahmin's son"? What are the Brahminical values, as portrayed by Hesse? For what reasons did Hesse *not* create his protagonist as a Ksatriya's son?
- What are the major steps in Siddhartha's path of self-discovery? What are the important lessons he learns along the way? What is the thematic significance of the reversal of order in Siddhartha's experience (from asceticism to hedonism) from that of the historical Buddha (from hedonism to asceticism), and how does this impact the spiritual teaching of the novel in relation to the spiritual teachings of the Buddhist tradition?
- What are the main "religious" or "spiritual" messages of *Siddhartha*? Are these messages in accord with the teachings of the Buddhist tradition? Do the spiritual lessons of the novel more closely parallel Theravāda Buddhism or Mahāyāna Buddhism?
- What are the potential problems with using this novel to introduce Buddhism to Western students?

Films of Bae Yong-kyun (b. 1951) and Kim Ki-duk (b. 1960)

A complete course on Asian religions would include independent treatment of religion in Korea. It is missing from my course, and from this book. Though they cannot compensate, two of the best new films on Buddhist themes are by the Korean directors Bae Yong-kyun and Kim Ki-duk. Poignant, beautifully filmed, with story lines that capture the draw of Zen (Korean Son) Buddhism to the modern generation of urbanites and global citizens, either film complements the study of Buddhism in Asia:

- Bae Yong-kyun, "Why has Bodhi-dharma Left for the East?" (달마가 동쪽으로 간 까닭은, *Dharmaga tongjoguro kan kkadalgun*) (1989);
- Kim Ki-duk, "Spring, Summer, Fall, Winter . . . and Spring" (봄 여름 가을 겨울 그리고 봄, *Bom yeoreum gaeul gyeoul geurigo bom*) (2003).

Wu Cheng'en, *Journey to the West* and Robert van Gulik, *The Haunted Monastery*

It is difficult to find Chinese novels that are explicitly religious, reflecting the fact that religion is conceptually indistinct from other elements of Chinese culture. But two novels work well in the Asian religions classroom.

For a classic novel that brings the magical mythology of Chinese religions to life, there is no substitute for the sixteenth-century *Monkey* or *Journey to the West* (西遊記, *Xiyou ji*), translated in full by Anthony Yu, or by Arthur Waley in a very serviceable abbreviated version in one volume.[15] Ostensibly retelling the tale of the retrieval of the Buddhist canon from India and its transmission to China by the monk Xuanzang (玄奘, "Tripitaka," c. 602–664 CE), the novel is an imagistic and energetic introduction to the fantastic visions and supernatural powers of Chinese religious heroes, from Sun Wukong (孫悟空), the Monkey King, to his companions Zhu Bajie (猪八戒, "Pig of the Eight Prohibitions") and Sha Wujing (沙悟浄), the Sand Monk. Historically, *Journey to the West* is among the first non-European novels in the modern sense of the term (one of the "four great novels" of the Ming Dynasty), but it illustrates the universal and timeless lesson that the "journey of the heart" is more arduous and rewarding than any physical journey, no matter how perilous it might be.

An accessible companion to *Monkey* is Ang Lee's Oscar-winning film *Crouching Tiger Hidden Dragon* (2000), a tribute to the rousing martial arts novels of the director's youth. With its evocative imagery, the interplay of human resolve and supernatural power, and themes of Confucian righteousness and Taoist magic, *Crouching Tiger* is a marvelous cinematic treatment of the myths and legends that inspire the stories of the gods. For the imagery and feel of Chinese religion, it is more immediate than scholarly anthropological studies of Chinese temples and their gods.[16]

Robert van Gulik (1910–1967) was a Dutch customs officer who devoted his retirement to academic research and creative reconstructions of Chinese historical sources. He was especially enamored of the "arts of the bedchamber" and compiled an illustrated history of Chinese sexuality in the late imperial period, with a separate book of print reproductions.[17] He also wrote a series of novels depicting a Tang Dynasty magistrate named "Judge Dee" – novels based on Chinese operas and plays composed in the Yuan Dynasty about the same semi-legendary figure. Van Gulik's novels are entertaining, if a bit simplistic in their narrative form, and students love them. My favorite is *The Haunted Monastery*,[18] where Judge Dee solves a string of kidnappings and murders that he encounters at a Taoist abbey in which he (along with his three wives) has taken refuge during a storm. Using his deductive reasoning and thoroughly materialist skepticism regarding the ghosts and spirits said to haunt the monastery, Judge Dee exhibits his Confucian biases in defeating the evil Taoist abbot and thwarting his nefarious plans. The novel plays upon traditions of Taoist sexual rites and puts Confucianism and Taoism in creative opposition; Dee is a model Confucian gentleman, and his discomfort with Taoist ritual, sexual, and dietary practices is both informative and amusing.

Yasunari Kawabata, *Thousand Cranes*, and Haruki Murakami, *1Q84*

I recommend two novels that focus on very different aspects of Japanese religions: Zen and contemporary new religious movements.

Thousand Cranes is a brilliant novel about the psychological costs of cultural decline, and especially about the impact of modernity on traditional norms and practices, by the Nobel Prize winning writer Yasunari Kawabata (川端 康成, 1899–1972).[19] As the tea ceremony loses its traditional meaning and significance and becomes merely an occasion for interpersonal manipulation, the possibility of healing and redemption – as represented by the "girl with the thousand crane handkerchief" (and symbolized by the traditional belief that any illness could be healed by folding a thousand origami cranes) – is irretrievably lost. Exploring themes of the inheritance of wrong ("the sins of the fathers . . ."), male sexuality, purity and pollution, the novel is written in the spare style of traditional Japanese poetic expression. It is a commentary on the loss of religious meaning in the modern world, and on the clash between tradition and modernity, against the backdrop of the Pacific War and Japan's post-war search for meaning.

An excellent complement to *Thousand Cranes* is a film by Jūzō Itami (伊丹 十三, 1933–1997), *The Funeral*. The movie begins with the death of the elderly father of a fashionable television actress who, with her philandering husband in tow, attempts to carry out the seven-day rites of a traditional Buddhist funeral. With scenes of the family watching a "how-to" video on funeral etiquette, children's impatience with the seemingly endless rites of sitting and chanting, the interference of numerous aunts and uncles in varying degrees of inebriation, the sudden arrival of the husband's hysterical mistress, and the widow's tender expressions of thanks for the family's presence, the film takes us on a journey from modern self-indulgence to traditional dignity and repose. A hilarious and touching film, it treats the same issues of religious disengagement seen in *Thousand Cranes* in a completely different style.

With *1Q84*, the contemporary novelist Haruki Murakami (村上 春樹, b. 1949) returned to writing in his native language after a series of novels written in English. *1Q84* (in Japanese pronounced the same as the numbers 1-9-8-4, and thus a play on themes in George Orwell's novel) is a work of magical realism against the backdrop of Japan's "new religions."[20] Murakami himself wrote a journalistic work of non-fiction about Aum Shinrikyo and the sarin gas attacks of 1995,[21] and *1Q84* evokes the same intrigue (with murders and kidnappings parallel to those of the Aum extremists), but in a way that is strangely sympathetic to a magical view of life that supersedes all worldly judgments. Epic in length, wonderfully descriptive, haunting in its imagery and psychological depth, *1Q84* creates unforgettable characters struggling with questions about the meaning of life in an increasingly secularized and materialistic world.

Notes

1 Robert G. Henricks, *Lao Tzu's Tao Te Ching* (New York: Columbia University Press, 2000).

2 A.C. Graham, trans., *Chuang-tzu: The Inner Chapters, and Other Writings from the Book "Chuang-tzu"* (London: Allen and Unwin, 1981).

3 Roger Ames and Henry Rosemont, *The Analects of Confucius: A Philosophical Translation* (New York: Ballantine Books, 1999).

4 Dominic Graham, *Hindu Scriptures* (Berkeley: University of California Press, 1996).

5 Donald S. Lopez, *Buddhist Scriptures* (London: Penguin Books, 2004).

6 Kazue Yamada, *The Gateless Gate: The Classic Book of Zen Koans* (Somerville, MA: Wisdom Publications, 2004).

7 William Theodore de Bary, Donald Keene, George Tanabe, and Paul Varley, *Sources of Japanese Tradition: From Earliest Times to 1600* (New York: Columbia University Press, 2002).

8 To give just one example, I have found it best to supplement readings from Hindu scriptures with a guidebook: Barbara Powell, *Windows into the Infinite: A Guide to the Hindu Scriptures* (Fremont, CA: Jain Publishing Company, 1996).

9 Shusako Endo, *Deep River* (深い河, *Fukai kawa*), trans. Van C. Gessel (New York: New Directions, 1994).

10 John Dalton, *Heaven Lake* (New York: Scribner, 2005).

11 Michio Takeyama, *Harp of Burma* (ビルマの竪琴, *Biruma no tategoto*) [1946], trans. Howard Hibbett (Clarendon, VT: Charles Tuttle, 1966).

12 R. K. Narayan, *The Guide* (New York: Viking Press, 1958).

13 Hermann Hesse, *Siddhartha* [1922], trans. Hilda Rosner (New York: New Directions, 1951).

14 The symposium can be accessed at http://www.asian-studies.org/eaa/Siddhartha .htm. See in particular the essays by Robert Mossman ("*Siddhartha* still works") and Catherine Benton ("Teaching Indian Buddhism with *Siddhartha* – or Not?").

15 Anthony C. Yu, ed., and trans., *The Journey to the West* [1983)], rev. edn. (Chicago, IL: University of Chicago Press, 2012). Wu Ch'eng-en, *Monkey: Folk Novel of China*, trans. Arthur Waley [1943] (New York: Grove Press, 1970).

16 An effective introduction to modern Chinese culture can be found in another set of Ang Lee's films. For a vivid sense of conflicts between Confucian family values and the impact of both modernization and globalization on relationships between parents and children, Ang Lee's Confucian fatherhood trilogy is as poignant, touching, and well crafted as any of the films in Lee's brilliant directing career. These are modern films without explicitly religious themes, but they are a great introduction to Confucianism as a cultural practice. The films are *Pushing Hands* (推手, 1992), *The Wedding Banquet* (喜宴, 1993), and *Eat Drink Man Woman* (飲食男女, 1994).

17 Robert van Gulik, *Erotic Colour Prints of the Ming Period* (Privately printed, Tokyo, 1951); *Sexual Life in Ancient China: A Preliminary Survey of Chinese Sex and Society from ca. 1500 B.C. till 1644 A.D.* (Kuala Lumpur, 1961; Leiden: Brill, 1974).

18 Robert van Gulik, *The Haunted Monastery: A Judge Dee Mystery* (Chicago, IL: University of Chicago Press, 2010; first published in 1961).

19 Yasunari Kawabata (川端 康成, 1899–1972), *Thousand Cranes* (千羽鶴, *Zenbazuru*), trans. Edward G. Seidensticker (New York: Alfred Knopf, 1958; repr. New York: Vintage Books, 1996).

20 Haruki Murakami, *1Q84* (いちきゅうはちよん, *Ichi-Kyū-Hachi-Yon*) (Tokyo: Shinchosha, 2009–2010), trans. Jay Rubin (New York: Harville Secker, 2011).

21 *Underground* (アンダーグラウンド, *Andāguraundo*) (Tokyo: Kodansha, 1997–1998), trans. Alfred Birnbaum and Philip Gabriel as *Underground: The Tokyo Gas Attack and the Japanese Psyche* (New York: Vintage Press, 2000).

Glossary

Amitābha (Chn. *Omituofo*, Jpn. *Amida-butsu* 阿彌陀佛) – Buddha of the Pure Land: an illustration of the Buddha as *sambhoga-kāya*, "celestial" or "bliss" body in the Mahāyāna Buddhist tradition

anatta (*anātman*) – non-self: the Buddhist teaching that no permanent, unchanging self (*Ātman* in the Hindu tradition) is discovered in the process of meditation

anicca – impermanence: one of the three marks of existence, together with *anatta* and *duḥkha*; in his final sermon the Buddha stated that "impermanence is the nature of all things"

ashrama (*āśrama*) – stage of life: student, householder, retiree, *sannyasin*; in the Hindu conception of *dharma* (ethical responsibility), the practice of *varna-ashrama-dharma* – that is, ethical responsibility according to one's caste and stage of life – is conducive to karmic benefits

aśubha – "revulsion," the Theravāda monastic attitude toward the pleasures and desires of lay life

Ātman – self in the Hindu sense: as a permanent, unchanging core underlying the changeable, impermanent self/ego that is subject to innumerable rebirths; in the experience of *moksha* (liberation), one realizes the identity between the "true" self (*Ātman*) and limitless spiritual oneness (Brahman)

Avalokiteśvara (Chn. *Guanyin*, Jpn. *Kannon* 觀音) – the *bodhisattva* of compassion: an illustration of the Buddha as *sambhoga-kāya* in the Mahāyāna Buddhist tradition

bodhi – literally "to wake up": wisdom, enlightenment; the root of "Buddhism"

Bodhidharma – legendary first patriarch of Zen, the "wall-gazing barbarian from the East"

bodhisattva – enlightened being who vows to remain within the world of suffering (*samsāra*) until all sentient beings can be enlightened as well; a savior with supernatural powers of "skillful means" (*upāya*)

bodhisattva-yana – the linear 10-stage *bodhisattva* path incorporating lay, monastic, and *bodhisattva* attainments

Brahman – Ultimate Reality in the Hindu tradition of *advaita-vedānta*, the non-dualism of self (*Ātman*) and the "over-soul" (Brahman)

Asian Religions: A Cultural Perspective, First Edition. Randall L. Nadeau.
© 2014 John Wiley & Sons, Ltd. Published 2014 by John Wiley & Sons, Ltd.

Buddha – "the awakened one"

cakravartin – "wheel-turner"; noting the "32 major marks and 80 minor marks" of the infant Buddha, seers prognosticated that the Śākyamuni Prince would become either the greatest conqueror the world had ever known or the greatest renunciant; as *cakravartin*, Śākyamuni Buddha became both, though he is a spiritual conqueror rather than a military one

chanoyu (茶の湯) – tea ceremony

dao (道) – the "Way": both in the sense of "the Confucian Way" (= the way of virtue) and in the sense of "the Taoist Way" (= the way of nature or of the cosmos)

dharma – duty (especially in the Hindu tradition); teaching, truth (in both the Hindu and the Buddhist tradition)

Dharmacakra pravartana sūtra [= *The Sūtra Setting in Motion the Wheel of the Dharma*] – scripture (*sūtra*) recounting the first sermon of the Buddha, in a deer park near Benares: the declaration of the Four Noble Truths

dharma-kāya – *dharma* body: third of the "three bodies" (*trikāya*) of the Mahāyāna; abstract conception of the Buddha

duḥkha – suffering; characteristic of life in general (*saṃsāra*), according to the first sermon of the Buddha

Eightfold Path – the path of Buddhist traditional practice, composed of three major categories: *prajñā* (wisdom), *śīla* (ethical conduct), *samādhi* (meditative concentration)

Eka-ksara prajñā-pāramitā sūtra [= *The Sūtra of Perfect Wisdom in One Letter*]: this is the letter "a" in Sanskrit, meaning "non-," "un-," "im-," void, emptiness; this *sūtra* is an illustration of the Mahāyāna doctrine of emptiness (*śūnyatā*)

fengshui (風水) – geomancy: felicitous placement of human habitations, both for the living and for the dead; designed to secure future blessing for oneself and one's family

five constants (*wuchang*, 五常) – fixed relationships in the Confucian tradition: ordered as parent–child, husband–wife, sibling–sibling or friend–friend, teacher–student, ruler–subject

Flower Sermon of the Buddha – the "sermon" in which, according to Zen tradition, the Buddha held up a flower instead of speaking; the "first Zen patriarch," Kasyapa, attained enlightenment upon "hearing" this "wordless teaching"

Four Noble Truths – taught in the *Dharmacakra-pravartana sūtra* or "first sermon" of the Buddha: the fourfold teaching that life is characterized by suffering (*saṃsāra*); that the cause of suffering is attachment and desire (*tanhā*); that the end of suffering is *nirvāṇa*; and the way to the end of suffering is the Holy Eightfold Path

Four Passing Sights – the encounters of the Śākyamuni Prince (the future Buddha), in four excursions from his father's palace: an old man, a sick man, a corpse, and a renunciant

Great Going Forth (*pravrajya*) – the departure of the Śākyamuni Prince from his father's palace into homelessness; a phrase also used to describe the initiation of a young monk or nun

haiku (俳句) – a poetic form inspired by Zen, consisting of a fixed metric scheme and alluding to Buddhist teachings of impermanence and awakening; according to R. H. Blythe, the "poetic transposition of *satori*"

hua (化) – transformation, transmutability, as described by the Taoist philosopher Zhuangzi and realized in Taoist alchemical traditions of the cultivation of immortality

Huineng (慧能) – Sixth Patriarch of Chinese Chan (Zen), the "illiterate woodcutter" and master of the "wordless teaching"

hun (魂) – *yang* souls of mind, heart, and seminal energy, in complementary relationship with *po* (*yin* souls); after death, the *hun* souls depart the body and ascend to the heavens (ancient Chinese mortuary rituals included "calling the *hun* souls" to restore life to the dead)

hundun (混沌) – the "Cosmic Egg": name given to the primordial sea in Chinese cosmogony, as recounted in *Huainanzi* (Han Dynasty period)

ikebana (生花) – flower arranging: a Zen art of "one-pointed" concentration

Jātaka Tales – stories recounting prior lifetimes of the Buddha; often used as morality tales in children's education

jiva – individual ego: in contrast to *Ātman*, the shared spirit or Brahman as universal soul; *jiva* is the aspect of soul that is subject to rebirth in the spinning wheel of *samsāra*

junzi (君子) – gentleman, in the Confucian sense; attained through self-effort and the cultivation of knowledge and virtue

karma – action; law of consequence

karunā – compassion: a principal value in Mahāyāna Buddhism

kōan (公案) – "public case": employed as a meditation device in the Zen Buddhist tradition; *kōans* include "unanswerable questions" and "question–answer" (*mondō*) pairs that are surprising or illogical

Kongfuzi (孔夫子) – Confucius, "first sage"

Krishna (Kṛṣṇa) – the "blue god," representative of the Hindu *bhakti* (devotional) tradition

Kṣitigarbha (Jpn. *Jizō*, 地藏) – *bodhisattva* of the underworld; protector of children who have died prematurely, of aborted fetuses, and of persons whose wrong-doing would condemn them to one of the Buddhist hells; an example of the Buddha as *sambhoga-kāya* in the Mahāyāna Buddhist tradition

li (禮) – rites, propriety: the model of Confucian individual and social cultivation

līlā – play, sport; the nature of the cosmos from the perspective of Brahman; the creative energy/force/spirit of the universe

liṅgam – male mark; symbol of the god Shiva

Lunyu (論語) – *The Analects*: sayings and conversations attributed to Confucius

mahāsattvas – great beings: they include innumerable Buddhas and *bodhisattvas* of the Mahāyāna tradition

Maitreya Buddha (Chn. *Milefo*, 彌勒佛) – Buddha of Future Blessing

māyā – illusion, ignorance; the world of *samsāra* as seen from the enlightened perspective of Hindu liberation

moksha (*mokṣa*) – liberation; realization of the unity of *Ātman* and Brahman in the Hindu *advaita-vedanta* (non-dual) tradition

mondō (問答) – question and answer in which the answer is illogical or unexpected; a type of *kōan*

mu (無) – "no," "non," "emptiness," "*woof*" (the "solution" to the *mu kōan*, "Does a dog have Buddha-nature?")

Nirguṇa Brahman – aniconic (that is, symbolic or non-representational) forms of Brahman

nirmāna-kāya – transformation body; first of the "three bodies" (*trikāya*) of Buddha in the Mahāyāna tradition

nirvāṇa – cessation; annihilation of the individuated ego and of false conceptions of an independent, unchanging self; expression of Buddhist enlightenment

Parable of the Burning House – story from *The Lotus* sūtra recounting how the "children" of the world, caught up in their imaginary play, are brought to salvation by *upāya* (skillful means)

pārājika – "failure": name given to four violations of the Buddhist monastic code, all of which result in expulsion from the monastery

pari-nirvāṇa – "complete annihilation": physical death of the Buddha

philosophical Taoism – Taoist teachings about spontaneity and freedom from convention, as represented in books attributed to Zhuangzi (*The Book of Zhuangzi*, 莊子) and to Laozi (老子) (*The Dao de jing*, 道德經)

po (魄) – *yin* souls associated with the internal organs of the body and with the "seven emotions" (joy, anger, pleasure, sorrow, like, dislike, desire); after death, the *po* souls adhere to the bones; in Chinese, they are the "white souls" and are venerated at graveside rituals

pratītya-samutpāda – co-dependent origination: a key teaching in Mahāyāna Buddhism

pu (樸) – uncarved block; image of the individual who has not been "bent" or corrupted by societal influences, as taught in the Taoist philosophical tradition

puruṣārtha – want, preoccupation: name given to *kāma* (pleasure), *artha* (wealth), *dharma* (duty), and *moksha* (liberation); loosely associated with the *varnas* (castes) and with spiritual progression through lives

qi (氣) – breath, vapor, energy, power; the primary "stuff" of the universe, as taught in the *Huainanzi* and other ancient Chinese compendia

religious Taoism – spatio-temporal dimensions of *yin–yang* cosmology, emphasizing temple-based cults dedicated to local gods

ren (仁) – co-humanity, kindness, benevolence: a primary Confucian virtue

Rinzai (臨済) (Chn. Linji) – Japanese school of Zen emphasizing the "wordless teaching" of the "stick and shout"

rōoshi (老師) – Zen master who assigns a *kōan* to the student for meditation

Rujiao (儒 教) – Confucian school, "school of the scholars"

Saguṇa Brahman – anthropomorphic representations of Brahman, especially in the *bhakti* tradition

sambhoga-kāya – "celestial" or "bliss" body of Buddha: one of the "three bodies" (*trikāya*); represented by *mahāsattvas*

samsāra – wheel; world cycle; seen ultimately as painful, limiting, and unsatisfying in Hindu and Buddhist traditions

sanskara – mark of learning in the progression of the *jiva* through life (*samsāra*)

sangha (*saṅgha*) – religious community where Buddha and *dharma* are, together, one of the "three jewels" of the Buddhist tradition; monks and nuns

Sanskrit – classical language of India

sanzen (参禅) – consultation with a Japanese Zen master regarding a *kōan* assigned to a student

sat-chit-ānanda – perfect being, consciousness, bliss; the Hindu experience of *moksha* and the ultimate nature of the soul (*Ātman* or Brahman)

satori (悟り) – enlightenment in Japanese Zen

Shiva (Śiva) – the Destroyer: one of the Hindu Trimūrti (three forms of Brahman)

shu (恕) – reciprocity, treating others as one wishes to be treated, and assuming the "like-heartedness" of all persons: a primary Confucian virtue

Siddhārtha Gautama – Śākyamuni Buddha (the enlightened prince of the Śākya clan)

skandhas – five aggregates: the five components of personal identity (form, sensation, perception, mental formation, consciousness), all characterized by suffering (*duḥkha*), change (*anicca*), and impermanence (*anatta*)

Sukhāvatī – Pure Land or "Western Paradise," ruled by the Buddha Amitābha (a *mahāsattva* in the Mahāyāna tradition)

śūnyatā – emptiness, the absence of "own-being" or independent existence, as described in the Mahāyāna tradition

tanhā – thirst, craving: attachment to things and ideas one already has, and desire for things and ideas one lacks; according to the Buddha, the cause of suffering (*duḥkha*)

Tianming (天命) – the Mandate of Heaven, the "divine right to rule" in ancient China

trikāya – the "three bodies" of Buddha in the Mahāyāna tradition: *nirmana-kāya* (transformation body), *sambhoga-kāya* (celestial or bliss body) and *dharma-kāya* (formless body of emptiness)

trimūrti – the three "forms" or manifestations of Brahman in the Hindu *bhakti* tradition: Brahma (the Creator), Vishnu (the Preserver), Shiva (the Destroyer)

upāya – efficient means; a *bodhisattva*'s self-transformational power, designed to bring all beings to salvation in the Mahāyāna tradition

varna – social class according to Hindu dharma (law of the cosmos): Brahmin (priestly), Kshatriya (governing), Vaishya (merchant), Shudra (labor)

Vinaya – the first of the "three baskets" of the Buddhist canon: the Vinaya (monastic code), *sūtras* (teachings of the Buddha), and Abhidharma (commentaries)

wuwei (無為) – non-action in the Taoist sense: non-interfering, reactive, yielding, natural, non-aggressive

wuxing (五行) – the "five elements" in their active senses: the hardening of metal, the moistening of water, the burning of fire, the covering of earth, and the growing of plants

wuyong zhi yong (無用之用) – the usefulness of uselessness, as taught by Zhuangzi and in the Taoist philosophical tradition

xiao (孝) – filial piety: a primary Confucian virtue

yin (陰)/*yang* (陽) – principle of receptivity / principle of aggression in Taoist cosmology

yoga – "discipline": it includes *jñāna-yoga* (discipline of mind), *bhakti-yoga* (discipline of emotion), *karma-yoga* (discipline of action), *rāja-yoga* (discipline of psychophysical exercise) in the Hindu tradition

yoni – female mark; symbol of the female aspect of Shiva; Shakti, the Goddess

Zen (禅) (Jpn.) – Chan (Chn.): school of Buddhist practice originating in China and developing in Japan (as Zen), Korea (as Seon), and Vietnam (as Thiền)

ziran (自然) – nature, spontaneity, as taught by the Taoist philosophical tradition

Index

Asian Religions: A Cultural Perspective, First Edition. Randall L. Nadeau.
© 2014 John Wiley & Sons, Ltd. Published 2014 by John Wiley & Sons, Ltd.